A GUIDE TO **urban studies**

contours: studies of the environment

Series Editor
William A. Andrews
Professor of Science Education
The Faculty of Education
University of Toronto

A Guide to the Study of ENVIRONMENTAL POLLUTION
A Guide to the Study of FRESHWATER ECOLOGY
A Guide to the Study of SOIL ECOLOGY
A Guide to the Study of TERRESTRIAL ECOLOGY
A Guide to URBAN STUDIES

A GUIDE TO
urban studies

Contributing Authors:
John K. Wallace
Mary E. Carroll
Rosemary E. Clark
Bruce W. Clark
Janet L. Seabrook

Editor:
William A. Andrews

Prentice-Hall of Canada, Ltd., Scarborough, Ontario

Canadian Shared Cataloguing in Publication Data
Main entry under title:
  A Guide to urban studies
  (Contours: studies of the environment)
ISBN 0-13-939280-7 pa.
  1. Cities and towns.   I. Andrews,
William A   1930-   II. Wallace,
John K
HT151.G77   301.3'6

The S I units and symbols used in this text have
been reviewed by the Canadian Government
Specifications Board and are found to be in accor-
dance with the requirements of the two National
Standards of Canada—the International System of
Units, Can-3-001-01-73 and the Metric Practice
Guide, Can-3-001-02-73.

A Guide to
URBAN STUDIES
© 1976 by W. A. Andrews
Published by Prentice-Hall of Canada, Ltd.
Scarborough, Ontario
All rights reserved.
No part of this book may
be reproduced in any form
or by any means without
permission in writing
from the publisher.
Printed in Canada
ISBN 0-13-939280-7   2 3 4 5 JD 79 78 77

Prentice-Hall, Inc., *Englewood Cliffs, New Jersey*
Prentice-Hall International, Inc., *London*
Prentice-Hall of Australia, Pty., Ltd., *Sydney*
Prentice-Hall of India, Pvt., Ltd., *New Delhi*
Prentice-Hall of Japan, Inc., *Tokyo*
Prentice-Hall of Southeast Asia (PTE.) Ltd.,
Singapore

Design by Jerrold J. Stefl and Julian Cleva,
cover illustration by Tom Daly,
text illustrations by James Loates

PREFACE

Ecology is the study of the relationships between living things and their environment. Quite literally, it is the "study of home". Urban ecology, then, deals with the relationship between man and his most common home, the urban environment. This book on urban studies was written to help you investigate that relationship.

Why do we choose to live in an urban environment? Why do we locate urban places where they are? Why do some communities grow while others die? Why are stores, factories, and houses located where they are? Why are the downtown areas of many large cities dying while others are flourishing? What effects do automobiles have on the urban environment? Is living in a high-density urban area hazardous to human health? Are we running out of land to expand our cities? Are expressways the answer to urban traffic congestion? These are typical of the questions that you should be able to answer after you have studied the material in this book. The pursuit of answers to such questions should provide you with an exciting few weeks, both in the classroom and in the field. Wherever you live there is an urban community near you. Use it to discover your relationship with the urban environment.

But this book will not have attained its main objective if you only learn how to answer such questions. Ultimately, you should understand the basic principles of urban ecology well enough to start asking questions. If man creates the urban environment for himself, why does he not make it a better place to live? Why are we letting expressways destroy the cores of our cities? Why are some people moving from the centers of cities to the suburbs while others are moving from the suburbs into the cities? Why do we tear down good buildings in the name of urban renewal? Why do we use the best farmland around our cities for building residential suburbs? Why do we subsidize the use of the automobile by building expensive roads and not subsidize public transportation systems to the same extent? What will the urban environment be like 5, 10, or 20 years from now? Is this the kind of environment in which we want to live? What can the individual do to affect the future course of urban development? When you start asking questions like these, you will have become the type of citizen that is desperately needed in urban communities today.

ACKNOWLEDGMENTS

The Contours program in Environmental Studies was initiated at the Faculty of Education, University of Toronto, and developed in the schools in which the authors teach. The authors and the editor thank their respective students and colleagues for the many ways in which they assisted in the development of this book in the Contours series.

The authors wish to acknowledge the competent professional help received from the editorial and production staff of the Publisher. In particular, we extend our thanks to Rob Greenaway for his assistance in the planning and development of this book. His constant enthusiasm and interest were a real inspiration to the team.

The authors are particularly appreciative of the attractive, imaginative, and accurate art work of Jim Loates. Jim has been a valued member of our team since its inception. We are equally appreciative of the work of Lois Andrews who has prepared the manuscript with great care and dedication.

W.A.A.

DIAGRAM CREDITS

Fig. 2-16, 2-17, and 4-8—after illustrations in C. D. Harris and E. L. Ullman, "The Nature of Cities", *Annals of the American Academy of Political and Social Science,* Vol. 242 (1945).

Fig. 3-7—after H. L. Green, "Hinterland Boundaries of New York City and Boston in Southern New England", *Economic Geography,* Vol. 31, pp 283-300, Fig. 3-9.

Fig. 4-13—adapted from B. J. L. Berry, *Commercial Structure and Commercial Blight,* University of Chicago Press, 1963, Table 2.

Table 17 and Fig. 9-3—adapted from Table 1 and Fig. 2 of J. F. Rooney, Jr., "The Urban Snow Hazard in the United States", *Geographical Review,* October 1967, pp 538-59.

Fig. 5-8—adapted from R. A. Murdie, "Factorial Ecology of Metropolitan Toronto, 1951-1961", Research Paper No. 116, Department of Geography, University of Chicago, 1969, p 9.

Photograph on title page courtesy Northway Survey Corporation Limited.

CONTENTS

7

RESEARCH TOPICS 222

8

CASE STUDIES 260

The Urban Ecosystem

1

1.1 WHAT IS AN URBAN ENVIRONMENT?

Do you live in an urban environment? The chances are that you do. More than seven out of ten North Americans did by 1975. Every year more and more people are moving to urban places from rural parts of the country. The proportion of urban dwellers is increasing in both Canada and the United States. This *urbanization* is expected to continue (Fig. 1-1). So, even if you do not live in an urban community now, there is a good chance that you may some day. Do you know what an urban environment is?

    Urban is one of those words that you are sure you can define until you have to do it. Before continuing, think for a moment about what you imagine an urban place to be. Look at Figure 1-2. An urban place is a community of people living together. But, are all communities urban? Webster's dictionary defines an urban place as a town or city. Villages, then, would not be considered urban. Webster's definition causes some problems. It implies that a town is larger than a village. How large is a community before it becomes a town? We have legal definitions of town size, but they vary from country to country. Find out what the minimum size of a town is where you live. Do you think it is right to say that, because one community attains that minimum size by having fifty more people than another community, it is urban and the other is rural? The reason that we make such a distinction between communities in the first place is that ways of life are supposed to be very different. What might some of these differences in ways of life be? But obvi-

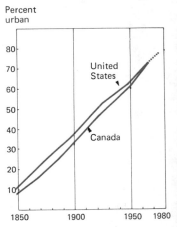

Fig. 1-1
The trend of urbanization: the urban population expressed as a percentage of the total population (1970 to 1980 projected on past trends). Sources: H.U.D. Statistical Yearbook, 1967 and 1970, U.S. Government Printing Office, and Canada Census, 1961 and 1971, Information Canada.

2

Fig. 1-2
What are the main differences between an urban and a rural environment?

ous differences exist only when we compare very large communities to very small communities. Between the two extreme sizes of communities, changes in life style vary so gradually that they are hardly noticeable. There is no magic population size that automatically transforms a rural community into an urban one. Thus, for the sake of statistics, census bureaus in every country are forced to make an arbitrary size definition. It may not even have any relation to the legal definitions of towns or cities. In Canada, all communities larger than 1 000 are classified as urban. In the United States, a population of 2 500 is necessary before a place is considered urban. Because Canada is a country with a much lower population density than the United States we might expect it to be less urbanized. Yet Figure 1-1 shows little difference. Why is this so?

Do you know yet whether you are an urban or a rural dweller? There may be a few of you who still cannot decide. You may live just outside the community boundary in a new subdivision. You may live in the country but not on a farm. New definitions of urban have been made to include "urbanized" territories adjacent to but not within an urban place. This has become necessary because of the great suburbanization that has taken place around urban areas since 1945. *Suburbanization* is the process whereby large numbers of people have chosen to live in low-density areas originally outside the political boundaries of a city. The common dwelling is the single-family home on a large lot. Lacking the urban characteristics of high-density areas and community government, such areas were called *suburban,* or "less than urban". The dwellers in these single-family homes on the edges of communities are as much a part of the urban community as are inner-city dwellers. They are separated from it only legally for tax purposes. Figure 1-3 shows the growing importance of these suburbanites. The extent of these urbanized territories, however, is again decided arbitrarily on the basis of residential population densities. If you are in doubt whether or not you are an urbanite, consult the census for your community to find out how it was classified.

So You Are In the Rural Minority. This does not mean that studying the urban environment is of no use to you. There is a strong chance that some day you may move to an urban environment. Furthermore, this environment is essential to your rural existence. Think of the number of ways that the rural dweller is related to the urban environment. As a farmer, he produces food and other necessities for the urbanite. The urban community is his marketplace. Unlike his pioneering ancestors, the modern farmer is dependent on the urban community for machinery, fertilizers, pesticides, clothing, electricity, and transportation. Many rural dwellers work in the urban community for extra money. Perhaps the least obvious relationship is the many ways in which the urban environment can modify the character of the rural environment. For better or worse, air pollution produced by a large city can increase rainfall in rural areas downwind from it. Severe air pollution has, in some cases, destroyed vegetation for 80 km around a city. Urban development using septic tanks may contaminate ground water used by neighboring farms. If you are a rural dweller you can probably think of many other ways that link you to the urban environment. The concerns of the urban dweller are your concerns.

Man's Role in the Urban Environment. Unlike a lake or a forest, the urban environment is largely man-made. Man therefore takes a more prominent position in the development of the environment. Not only does man react to it as an animal, but he has the power to control it. Because it is our creation, we have an even

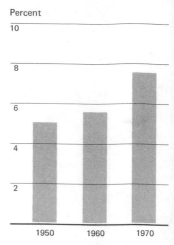

Fig. 1-3
Population of non-incorporated urban territories expressed as a percentage of the total population of the United States. Source: H.U.D. Statistical Yearbook, U.S. Government Printing Office, 1967, 1970.

greater need to understand our relationship with it. Understanding how and why we are affected by the environment will surely make us better able to achieve the kind of environment we want.

Are you satisfied with the urban environment you live in? What can you do about it if you are not? Looking at your relationships with this environment can provide you with some of the answers. When you decide to go downtown by car, how does your decision affect the kind of urban environment you will have? When stores in the downtown area go out of business and are replaced by parking lots and office buildings, how does this affect you? Does it make any difference to the environment if you go downtown to shop or if you shop in a suburban shopping center?

The key to answering these and similar questions is an understanding of the relationships between man and the environment in which he lives. There is nothing you do that is not in some way affecting or affected by the urban environment. Similarly what we create is not independent of the natural environment that existed before. How do hills, rivers, swamps, and shorelines influence the shape of communities? How do prevailing winds affect where industries and houses should be located? Are temperatures in the urban area different from those in the surrounding countryside? These are some of the relationships that this book explores. But before you start exploring, you need to understand some basic principles of ecology, and of urban ecology in particular.

For Thought and Research

1 a) Define the terms ''urban'', ''suburban'', and ''rural''.
   b) List at least five differences between an urban place and a rural place.
   c) Could some people who live in areas outside the city have, in fact, the same characteristics as urban dwellers? Explain.
2 a) What is the statistical minimum size for a town in your country?
   b) Why does the legal definition of a town differ from country to country?
   c) Why are new definitions of the term ''urban'' constantly being created? (In Canada, for example, the definition of urban was changed after World War II.)
3 In Section 1.1 urban and rural residents of a country are said to be dependent upon one another. Give three examples of this dependence that are not given in this text.

1.2   THE ECOSYSTEM CONCEPT

A system is a whole, made up of interacting parts. The automobile is a good example. Each part of the car acts with the other parts to make the car operate. The engine, transmission, wheels, and frame each have a particular function. The failure of one part can prevent the automobile from running. But the car is not complete in itself. It requires gasoline to power it. Byproducts of the combustion of gasoline—heat, water, carbon dioxide, and carbon monoxide—are released into the atmosphere. Because of this importing and exporting of energy and materials, the automobile is called an *open* system. Most systems are open. Like most systems, the automobile is a system within a larger system and is itself composed of subsystems. It is part of a transportation system and has within it heating and electrical systems.

An *ecosystem* (ecological system) has many of the characteristics of the automobile system. Plants, animals, land, and climate take the place of engines and transmissions as the components of the earth ecosystem or *biosphere*. Can you imagine what the earth would be like without any one of these components? What would be the effect on the other components if there were a major cooling of the earth's climate? On what does the earth depend for its heat? Can you think of anything on earth that is not included in the components already mentioned? If not, then the entire system has been defined. If there is something missing, then it must be added to the components listed.

The earth ecosystem, like the automobile, must import energy. In what ways does the sun's energy affect the components of the ecosystem? The earth shares this relationship with other planets in the solar system. In turn we can recognize sub-ecosystems on the face of the earth. Different groups of organisms inhabit different kinds of environments, establishing their own particular ecosystem. Whether we look at a pond, a woodlot, or an urban community, we are dealing with an ecosystem, open to import and export of energy and materials, and functioning within the global ecosystem. Unlike that of the pond or woodlot, however, the environment of the urban ecosystem is largely man-made. Man therefore takes a more prominent place in the environment's development. Man-made structures become a component that must be added to the ecosystem. Although the urban ecosystem depends on other elements of the global ecosystem for its existence, once created it exerts influences of its own. The high-rise apartment building may obstruct and channel winds, increasing the wind speed at street level. Concrete prevents rainwater from soaking in, thereby increasing runoff.

Think for a moment about the various parts of the urban ecosystem in which we have an integral role. We rely on plants both directly and indirectly. Not only do we eat them, but they are also food for animals which, in turn, make up a large portion of our diet. Trees provide wood for our houses and furniture and shade on a hot day. Horses and other animals provide transportation in some societies. We locate our communities where we have access to the plants

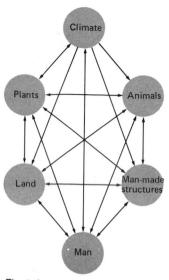

Fig. 1-4
The ecosystem concept, including man-made structures characteristic of the urban environment.

and animals that we require to survive. Temperature, precipitation, topography, and soil determine our existence through the quantity and quality of plants available. More important for us as urban dwellers, these factors affect the kinds of shelters we need and where they are placed.

Figure 1-4 illustrates the important relationships in the urban ecosystem. Consider each component individually and ask yourself how it is affected by any of the components with arrows pointing to them. Discuss your conclusions with others.

The most important thing about an urban ecosystem is the interdependency of the components. What are the effects of buildings? How does the urbanization of the rural environment affect animals native to it? What is the importance of each species of plant or animal in the ecosystem?

Each individual species has a role or *niche* in the ecosystem. Some, like green plants, produce food. Some consume plants. These consumers are called *herbivores*. Some consume animals and are called *carnivores*. Life forms in an ecosystem are linked together through predator-prey relationships in a *food chain*.

Producer ♦ Herbivore ♦ Carnivore ♦ Higher-Order Carnivore

Grass (a producer) is eaten by a rabbit (herbivore). The rabbit is eaten by a fox (carnivore). The fox is eaten by an eagle (higher-order carnivore). If a link in the chain is broken by the extinction of a species, those who depend on that species for food must convert to another food source or face extinction. The animal that eats more than one species of plant or animal is obviously more adaptable to changes in the food chain. Man has a very varied diet, but he is still very much dependent on the other species in his food chain. As he modifies the environment he must take care not to break the chain.

Man is more than a simple predator in an environmental food chain. He has the power to control and change the environment for his own benefit. If the climate is not comfortable, an artificial climate can be created within man-made structures. If water is insufficient to support people where they want to live, it can be piped in from distant places. If trees are in the path of a needed road, they can be removed. If more land is needed, it can be reclaimed from the sea. If pigeons and squirrels are a nuisance in the urban environment, they can be exterminated. If there is a drought, the clouds can be seeded to induce rainfall. If solid wastes are a problem, we can dump them in gravel pits or burn them. In the man-made environment man assumes the role of producer, consumer, and waste disposer. In order to carry out his varied activities he builds houses, factories, stores, roads, and reservoirs, among other things. When these are concentrated in one place, such as an urban community, they form a man-made environment. The following example shows the relationships that exist within a simple urban community. In particular, it emphasizes the relationships of the man-made environment to the rest of the components of the ecosystem and the effects of particular man-made structures.

An Example of a Simple Urban Community. A group of men decided that it was in their best interests to live together at the mouth of a river along a sea coast. There they tied up their boats in a protected inlet close to a good fishing area. Working together they could catch more fish than if they worked as individuals. In a flat area near the river, they cleared a site for their homes, using the lumber to build their houses and as fuel to warm their homes in cold weather. Drinking water was obtained from a stream which flowed to the river. A row of houses was built along this stream. A path was worn from the houses to the place where they tied their boats. Eventually they built a dock to make tying up their boats easier.

A simple urban environment has been set up at the mouth of this river (Fig. 1-5). Man has modified the natural environment by cutting the trees and displacing the animals that had previously lived in the area. He has concentrated his environmental demands for water, food, and waste disposal in a small area. He releases smoke into the atmosphere and waste into the river. His home is an artificial environment protecting him from wind, rain, and cold.

We can see that the natural environment and the man-made environment (composed of houses, a path, and a dock) are mutually dependent. The trees are essential for building and heating homes. Proximity to fish and the availability of a protected harbor for boats determined the location of the community. Proximity to a source of water determined where the houses were built. But by using the trees, man altered the environment. Cleared of trees, the land no longer acted as a natural sponge in times of heavy rain. Rainwater quickly ran off the land, carrying soil with it into the river. The river became more turbid. Fish, adapted to clean, clear water, were affected by the muddy waters. Fish catches became smaller. The fishermen were forced to fish farther and farther away from home or catch species that were less desirable. Hunting for deer was a popular means of supplementing the daily diet. But, as the woods were cleared around the community, the deer moved farther and farther from the community. The stream water became noticeably less clean. The outhouses near its bank might have contributed to this. Occasionally the smoke from the chimneys would linger for several days over the village. But this fluke of wind occurred only occasionally and, with the small number of homes in the area, it was no real problem. At least once a year the river flooded, threatening a few of the homes nearest the river. As more and more land was cleared upstream for other settlements, flooding became more serious.

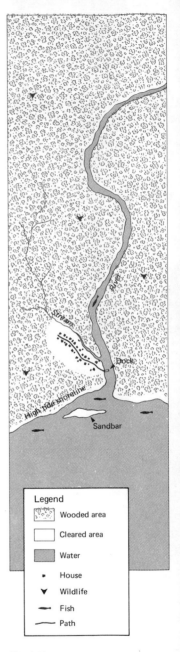

Fig. 1-5
Representation of the original settlement.

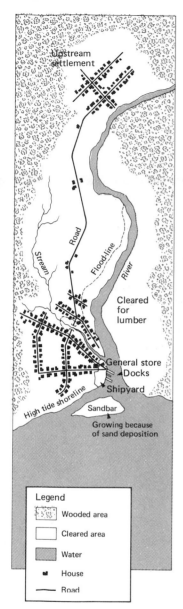

Fig. 1-6
Representation of the growing community.

Legend

- Wooded area
- Cleared area
- Water
- House
- Road

Even with these minor environmental setbacks, the community grew swiftly. A local entrepreneur decided that the fishermen needed bigger boats so that they could fish farther out to sea and thereby catch more fish. Some fishermen became workers in his shipyard. Others sold lumber from nearby woods for his boats. Business was good. Ships sold fast. The availability of jobs and money soon attracted large numbers of men and their families to the community. It doubled in size. Another entrepreneur opened a general store to provide goods for the factory workers who no longer supplied their own food by fishing or hunting.

Many changes accompanied the rapid growth of the community. Perhaps most significant was the realization that the old dock was obsolete. Bigger ships required a larger dock in deeper water. Ships from other countries were now unloading supplies there for the store and for communities upstream. A problem arose. Who would pay for the new dock? The harbor was also becoming shallower from the deposits of eroded materials. It required dredging. Who would pay for this? By this time lumbering had cleared much more of the land around the community. Erosion increased. Flash floods wiped out half of the homes one year. Deer were no longer found anywhere in the lower river valley area. Over-cutting and over-hunting had taken their toll. Garbage piles were attracting rats. Outhouses polluting the drinking water caused health problems. Traffic had increased so much within the community that the main street needed widening. When the smoke from the fireplaces lingered over the community, breathing was difficult. Homes on the edge of the community, away from the evils of town life, became more popular (Fig. 1-6). Many of the problems were now beyond the control of individuals.

Eventually civic-minded members of the community got together to attack their problems. A government was established. Better roads and a new dock were built. New homebuilders were encouraged not to build in the flood plain. Outhouses were prohibited within 15 m of the stream to lessen pollution. To pay for these improvements, a tax on citizens' property was imposed. In the long run it was hoped that new industries and businesses, attracted to the community because of its docking and transportation facilities, would pay for the improvements. Some wealthier citizens who resented the tax moved out of the community. Still, they traveled into the town daily for work.

You should be able to see by now how complex the interrelationships between the man-made and natural environments are. Everything man does causes a chain of actions and reactions in the environment. What problems can you foresee for this community in the future? Do you see evidence of similar occurrences in your own urban environment?

This example is a simple case. Most urban environments are far more complex. But, by using the ecosystem approach, that is, by examining relationships among the components, you can unravel the complexities and understand them. With such an understanding we can foresee the consequences of our actions in the urban environment and do what is best for us and the environment. What is best for the environment is, in the long run, best for us.

For Thought and Research

1   a) Define the term "system".
  b) Give an example of a system not mentioned in the text, identify its components, and show how its components are interrelated.
  c) What is meant by an open system? Is the system you described in b) an open system? Explain.
2   a) Define the term "ecosystem" and identify its components.
  b) Explain how the components of an ecosystem are interrelated.
3   The earth has been compared to a spaceship, with the suggestion that both are closed systems in which all materials must be recycled to ensure the survival of the inhabitants. Discuss the validity of this idea.
4   a) A simplified version of an ecosystem with an urban or man-made component is shown in Figure 1-7. Explain the relationship indicated by each arrow in the diagram.

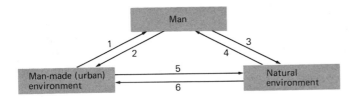

Fig. 1-7
An ecosystem with an urban component.

  b) List five main components of an urban ecosystem and explain how they interact with one another.
5   Answer the following questions after you have read the story in this section about the development of an urban place.
  a) Why did the people choose to live together in a community?
  b) What were the considerations taken into account in selecting a site for their community?
  c) How did the construction of their community modify the natural environment of the site?
  d) How did the environmental changes affect the residents of the area?
  e) Why did the community grow in spite of these changes?
  f) What changes accompanied the new growth of the community?
  g) How did the residents attack their urban problems?
  h) Will the community continue to grow? Explain your answer.
6   "What is best for the environment is, in the long run, best for us." Do you agree or disagree with this statement? Justify your answer.
7   a) List five food chains in which man is the last link.
  b) How else does man depend on plants and animals?

c) In what ways does the man-made urban environment affect the plants and animals on which man depends?

8   Explain how clearing trees from a watershed to create a site for a community can lead to the river flooding and the harbor silting up.

9   Investigate the history of your community. Why did your community develop in the first place? Why was it located where it was? How has the physical environment of the area affected its development? How was the physical environment modified by the man-made environment?

1.3   WHY URBANIZATION?

Why are more and more people choosing to live in an urban environment? Why did urban communities develop in the first place? An understanding of the urban community today can be gained by answering these questions. Read again the example in the preceding section. This time look particularly for the reasons that contributed to the community's development and growth. Why did the fishermen decide to live together? Why did they build the community where they did? Why did the community double in size? How does growth lead to more growth? In what ways does the way of life of the community change with growth?

The first settlers of North America were mainly farmers. They settled on their own individual pieces of land. Their isolation forced them to be self-sufficient. Food, clothing, furniture, and tools, among other things, could not be bought in stores then. The farmer had to produce his own food and supplies Transportation was poor. But, as the population of North America grew and transportation improved, it became more efficient to provide services communally. Grist mills, blacksmith shops, schools, and general stores were built to service the rural community. The people who worked in these specialized occupations tended to live near their businesses rather than on scattered farms. Businesses located near each other for the convenience of their customers and also because they often depended on each other for supplies. These communities, in turn, attracted other specialists—carpenters, doctors, merchants, barbers, and ministers. Each new settler in the area provided business for everyone. The farmer's response to these developments was to become less self-sufficient. He, too, could be more efficient if he devoted his time to farming rather than being a jack-of-all-trades. The efficiency of specialization, then, plays a large part in the development of communities. With each member of the community performing his own special task, the community can produce more than it could if each individual performed all these tasks for himself. In addition, the quality of the product is usually better. A man who specialized in blacksmithing could do a better job of shoe-ing a horse than the man who only did it once in a while. The black-smith could also afford to invest in the best tools of his trade because he used them so often.

Each community develops and grows for its own unique reasons, but the trend to urbanization is rooted in the advantages of specialization and concentration. Working together, men can produce more than they can separately. No small consideration, ei-ther, is the richness of urban life—its diversity of experience and its increased human contact. However, we may be reaching the point of diminishing returns in quality of life with the super-cities of today.

The next units examine in more detail why communities locate where they do and why some grow and others die. Keep in mind as you read these units the relationships between the urban en-vironment and man that affect development and growth.

For Thought and Research

1 a) List what you feel are the five main advantages of urbanization.
    b) List what you feel are the five main disadvantages of urbanization.
2   Table 1 gives population information for three countries.

TABLE 1

		Total population	Urban population
Country X			
	1960	5 689 000	2 431 000
	1970	8 534 000	3 846 000
Country Y			
	1960	200 189 000	180 560 000
	1970	221 860 000	199 835 000
Country Z			
	1960	12 987 000	10 110 000
	1970	19 496 000	16 389 000

a) Which countries are undergoing the process of urbanization? (*Hint*: Urbanization is considered to be occurring when the percentage of a country's urban population is in-creasing. You should therefore calculate the percentage of the population that is urban in each year for each country.)

b) Of the countries that are urbanizing, which is urbanizing at the faster rate? (*Hint*: Rates can be easily compared if you plot graphs of percentage of urban population versus time.)

c) Which country has undergone the largest absolute increase in the number of urban residents?

d) Can a country have urban growth (that is, increased numbers of urban residents) without undergoing urbanization? Prove your answer.

e) Is the proportion of urban residents in a country likely to reach 100%? Explain.

f) What would happen to the rate of urbanization as it approaches 100%? Explain.

3   Some experts say that today's super-cities may be reaching the point of diminishing returns in the quality of life provided for their residents. What is meant by this statement? Do you agree or disagree with it? Why?

Recommended Readings

1   Consult companion volumes to this book in the Contours series for further information on the ecosystem concept and basic ecological principles.

2   *Urban Geography* by J. Johnson, Pergamon Press, 1967. Consult the chapter on "Factors of Urban Growth".

3   *Cities,* a special issue of *Scientific American,* September 1965. Read particularly the articles by K. Davis and G. Sjoberg.

4   *The American City* by R. E. Murphy, McGraw-Hill, 1974. Read in particular Chapters 1, 2, and 3 which introduce the concept of urbanization and provide many basic definitions.

5   *The North American City* by M. H. Yeates and B. J. Garner, Harper and Row, 1971. See Chapters 1 and 2 and Appendix A for the definition and development of urban form.

6   *A Geography of Mankind* by J. O. M. Broeck and J. W. Webb, McGraw-Hill, 1968. Read Part IV, "Settlements".

7   *The New City* edited by D. Canty, Praeger, 1969. See the sections on "The Process of Urbanization—a Photographic Essay" and "The Concept of Urbanization".

Types, Location and Distribution of Urban Communities

2

Do you live in a large metropolitan city, in a small town, on a farm? Wherever you live you are part of an urban pattern that covers most of the globe and an urban tradition that extends back more than 6 000 years. Why are urban communities located where they are? Are they there simply because of chance, or are there reasons for their location? Is there a pattern to the distribution of urban communities around the globe, just as there is a pattern to the distribution of natural communities?

We can define the soil, temperature, and moisture conditions necessary for the growth of most species of plants. Can we, in like manner, define the requirements for the development of a city? The answer, whether yes or no, is likely to be very complex because here we are dealing with a creation of man rather than nature. Nature obeys certain known laws, but does man?

Urban geographers and other students of the urban scene have asked and attempted to answer a number of questions about the hows and whys of urban distribution. Many of these questions may have occurred to you. For instance, what kind of land has usually been covered by the buildings and roads of a city, good farmland or wasteland? Why must you travel only a short distance to buy a loaf of bread, a longer distance to buy a television set and, perhaps, several hundred kilometres to buy an expensive foreign sports car? Why is Pittsburgh called the Steel City when only a small percentage of that city's population is employed in the iron and steel industry?

For the answers to many of these questions we may have to go back to the origins of man's desire to live together in communities. Some answers may reveal that man's requirements for his cities have changed over time, along with his needs and his ability to supply those needs. Most of the answers can be discovered by a careful look at the environment the city is found in, and a study of the historical influences in which the city developed. But before you attempt this, you are probably wondering, why bother?

Knowing why communities are located where they are has a greater purpose than just to satisfy academic curiosity. Once we know why a community is located where it is, we can do a better job of locating new communities. This is particularly important in an age in which new communities do not simply develop gradually, with time for changes when mistakes are made. Today, complete new communities are being planned by our governments to solve the growing need for housing and the decentralization of people away from established urban centers. We cannot afford to place such communities in poor locations.

The basic question, then, is what makes a location good or bad for a community. When you have found the answers to this question you may also wish to ask yourself if a location can be *too good* and, as a result, attract *too many people* or *too many communities* to a small area. Pollution has become a major problem in areas like the Eastern Seaboard of the United States due, in large part, to the concentration of numerous large cities there. Why did so many large cities locate in this area? Why are there not more large cities in the vast area of the Great Plains? Is there or should there be some regularity in the spacing of communities? Can we use any of this information to plan a better distribution of communities in the future?

This unit explores the various factors responsible for the location and types of urban communities so that you can better answer questions like those asked in these introductory paragraphs.

2.1   ENVIRONMENTAL FACTORS

Before any urban center is established, its founders choose the location they think is best for the intended function of the center. This is equally true of the carefully chosen location of Brasilia and of the seemingly random choice of the position of Regina, Saskatchewan. When Brasilia, the new capital of Brazil, was being designed, the planners had in mind specific requirements for its location. They considered the architecture and building technology to be used, existing and future transportation systems, and, most important, the desire to stimulate growth in an economically undeveloped part of

the country. Regina (Fig. 2-1), on the other hand, was established as a patrol base by an expedition of the North West Mounted Police. It was a frontier post in virtually unknown territory. It was established with less regard for its function since, in contrast to Brasilia, the locational requirements were slight. Beyond being located near the center of the area to be patrolled and having an adequate supply of water and grass for the Mounties' horses, any location would have been equally suitable. However, the difference in the locational processes for Regina and Brasilia is simply one of degree not nature.

Fig. 2-1
Regina's founding was essentially a historical accident. (Courtesy of Canadian Government Travel Bureau.)

SITE AND SITUATION

Geographers have traditionally used two related terms in discussing the location of towns and cities. *Site* is usually defined as the natural features of the landscape on which the town or city is built and onto which it expands. *Situation* is not as easily defined. It is usually considered to be the characteristics of the land surrounding the settlement. It relates the location of one place to that of others and includes consideration of such things as physiography, distance, direction, and transportation capability. Thus it includes a much larger area than does the site. Study Figure 2-2 to help clarify the difference between site and situation. The characteristics of urban sites are revealed in the following problem.

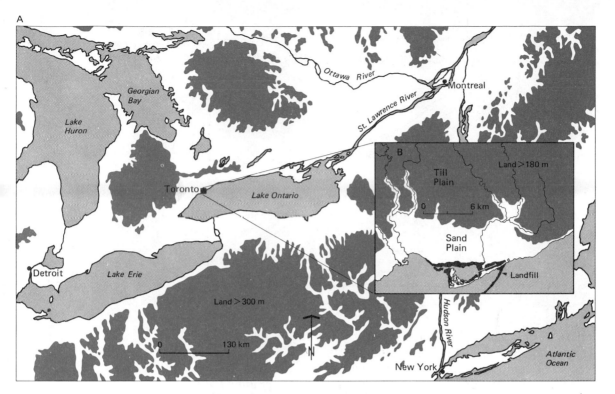

Fig. 2-2
The different scales of situation (A) and site (B) can be easily seen using Toronto as an example.

Site Selection. Examine Figure 2-3. It represents the setting of a future town in the new territory of Westerland. This is how the area appeared to a group of pioneers who decided to locate a town in this area. Is there *one* best site for the town? Probably not, since the value of a site is closely related to the function the town is to fulfil. In fact, a good site is regarded as the best place to do whatever it is that has to be done. Accordingly, to choose the best town site in the area, you must examine the main functions of the town.

Beyond some common basic needs such as an ample supply of fresh water and access to such things as a food supply and building materials, different towns and different town functions involve different optimum site characteristics. A harbor city, for example, must be located next to a deep basin with ready access to the ocean and yet protected from storms. A fortress city, on the other hand, must occupy a position that is naturally defensible. Such specific site requirements can be established for most urban functions.

Suppose that Westerland was being settled around the year 1800. Which sites are best suited to various urban functions? If the new town is to be a fortress designed to control travel on the river, then either *The Heights* or *Point-of-the-Island* would be chosen. Each is easily defensible and in a position to dominate the river with the weapons available. *North Shore*, in comparison, is badly suited for defence since it is a low, exposed location with limited military

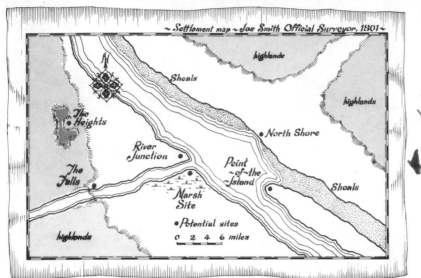

Fig. 2-3
Possible town sites in the territory of Westerland.

Know

potential. However, if the new town is to be the commercial and transportation center for Westerland, *North Shore* is an excellent choice. It combines access to the navigable river with the possibility of overland transport to the north, east, and west. *River Junction* is also well suited for this function, although overland transportation would be more difficult because of the surrounding highlands and the tributary river which would have to be bridged. In spite of its excellent location, *Marsh Site* is not likely to be chosen since the swampy terrain would make construction difficult, present a health hazard, and, in general, make life unpleasant for the town's residents.

The final site, *The Falls*, has very different characteristics and, therefore, a different optimal use. Its location adjacent to the power source of the waterfalls on the tributary river would enable it to be developed as a mill or manufacturing town. For such a town, transportation capability to markets and raw materials is also important. Does this site have that capability?

Remember that all desirable site characteristics rarely, if ever, combine to form a perfect site. For example, if Westerland was being developed as a commercial and transportation center, a choice would have to be made between the power advantages of the tributary river and the transportation potential of the main river. If The Heights was chosen because of its easily defensible position, the founders would have to accept its poor transportation capability. The founders of any town must, consciously or unconsciously, make choices and compromises on the basis of what they foresee as the new town's chief function.

A Modern View of Site. You have seen how the idea of site is useful in helping to determine why a town or city is located in a given place. However, this idea must be used carefully in order to avoid misinterpretations. When examining an existing town or city remember that either the site or the site requirements may have changed since the founding of the settlement. Since most North American cities are over 75 years old, the technological changes between their founding and the present are great—from the steam age, or earlier, to the nuclear era.

The most common conditions leading to a conflict between a city's site and its function occur where a town's original site has been outgrown by a rapidly expanding metropolitan city. The best example of this is New York City. New York (or New Amsterdam as it was originally called) was established in 1615 as a commercial center at the southern tip of Manhattan Island (Fig. 2-4). The choice of this site was an admirable one for a trading center based on sailing ships. The Hudson and East rivers are both wide and easily navigable at this point. Also, their shorelines are suitable for docking and warehousing facilities.

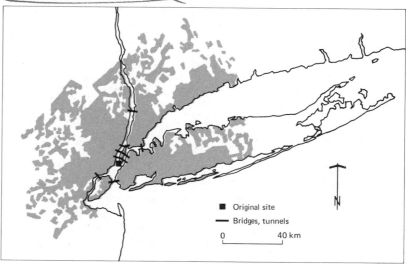

Fig. 2-4
The urbanized area of Greater New York. Note the size of the original site and the present need for bridges and tunnels in the city.

■ Original site
— Bridges, tunnels
0   40 km

A combination of ambitious businessmen, a good overall location, and other factors resulted in the phenomenal growth of the city. As Figure 2-4 shows, it now completely covers Manhattan Island as well as large areas of the surrounding mainland and islands. New York's site, which provided the original stimulus for its location, has become a liability. Manhattan Island has become greatly congested and massive expenditures have been necessary for bridges and tunnels to connect the various parts of the city.

A conflict between a city's site and its functions also occurs when the balance of the city's functions changes after the founding of the community. This is partially the case with New York. Its main function has changed from commerce to a diverse base, including large elements of administration, manufacturing, and retail and wholesale trade. It is even more true for Quebec City which was originally built as a walled, fortified city on an inaccessible height of land above the St. Lawrence River (Fig. 2-5). Since that time, however, the city's defence function has become obsolete. It has expanded markedly both above and below the heights, making the development of transportation awkward. In the case of both New York and Quebec City, the site conditions responsible for the city's founding now hinder its future development.

Year	Type of human occupance
1500	Pre-European
1800	Pre-industrial
1975	Modern

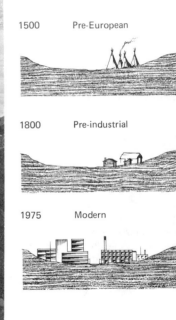

Fig. 2-5
The old town of Quebec City. Note the transportation difficulties imposed by the terrain. (Courtesy of Canadian Government Office of Tourism.)

THE FUTURE: SITE MODIFICATION AND SITE PRODUCTION

Modern-day urban development has been freed from many of the limitations imposed by natural features of the site. With today's construction equipment, large-scale modification of the existing site is possible. In fact, engineers can actually produce many of the site features that planners consider desirable. To date such developments have been relatively limited in scope. They have resulted from very specific economic and human needs. But they point the way to larger and more diverse forms of site production in the future. Table 2 summarizes some examples of site modifications that were and are being made to meet certain economic and human needs.

TABLE 2

Site deficiency	Types of solutions	Examples
Susceptibility to flooding	Dikes, levees, bypass canals, channel straightening	New Orleans Winnipeg
Shortage of recreational land	Erosion control, landscaping	Miami Beach Toronto
Shortage of fresh water	Aqueducts, reservoirs	Los Angeles San Diego
Poor quality (or quantity) of port facilities	Dredging, canals, breakwaters, artificial harbors	Houston Vancouver
Shortage of land in accessible areas	Landfill (extension of mainland, artificial islands)	Montreal San Francisco

When flooding occurs

Damage   Casualties

none   none

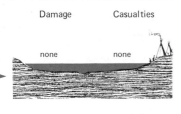

$ $ †

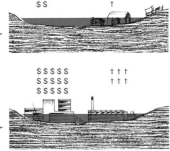

$ $ $ $ $ † † †
$ $ $ $ $ † † †
$ $ $ $ $

Fig. 2-6
The changing effects of floods on the residents of a flood plain through history. As man's technology (and settlement pattern) becomes more complicated, it also becomes less flexible.

Flood Control. Perhaps the most common type of site modification has been for flood-control purposes. Many large cities originated as small settlements on the flood plains of rivers. These sites had initial advantages such as easy transportation and an ample water supply. As a result they flourished. Subsequent technological and social changes eliminated these early advantages, leaving only the hazard of large loss of life and massive damage in the event of a flood taking its natural course and spilling onto the flood plain (Fig. 2-6). As a result, governments in many countries have greatly modified the original sites of numerous urban communities in an attempt to reduce flood losses. These site modifications range from the simple installation of dikes to the complete rerouting of large rivers (Fig. 2-7).

Fig. 2-7
Flood control channels are an expensive but important form of site modification.

Recreational Land. The shortage of recreational land in cities is seldom considered to be as serious a problem as flood hazards. Solutions to this problem have not, therefore, been as drastic. Yet many cities do provide for additional recreational land through site modification. For example, many of the coastal resorts of Florida were developed by stabilizing the shifting sands of the offshore banks. Once the constant erosion of these areas was held in check, towns and recreational areas could be developed on them.

Recreational lands have sometimes been developed in conjunction with flood-control projects. Following a disastrous flood in 1954, the river valley lands in Toronto, which had previously been residential or vacant, were developed for public recreation (Fig. 2-8). Without the stimulus of the flood, this development would have been, at best, piecemeal.

Water Shortage. While no North American city has experienced a water shortage serious enough to threaten its existence, some of the large cities of Southern California have faced water problems serious enough to curtail growth. These problems have made it necessary to spend hundreds of millions of dollars to transport water from the mountains to the east. In the case of Los Angeles this involves an aqueduct from Owens Valley, 400 km to the north. While much of this water is used to irrigate agricultural land, a great deal is needed for the city.

Fig. 2-8
Site modification may take many forms. What modifications do you see here?

Port Facilities. Certain harbor characteristics such as an adequate depth of water and a protected berthing area are essential for a port city. In many instances a harbor that was suitable for the ships of an earlier age cannot handle the larger and deeper commercial vessels of today. Also, some harbors have filled with silt. Common solutions to the problems of inadequate harbors include continual dredging and building breakwaters to protect port facilities and maintain maximum depth. In some instances port facilities have been developed where none existed before. Houston lies 80 km from the sea behind the sandbars and shallow lagoons bordering the Gulf of Mexico. It was only with costly dredging and cutting that the Houston Ship Canal was constructed, allowing Houston to become the largest port on the Gulf of Mexico.

Land Shortage. Land in the harbor sections of large cities is generally quite accessible and hence of great value. Accordingly, in many parts of the United States and Canada, coastal areas have been filled with debris from construction sites and incinerators to extend the mainland or to build islands. The land produced is generally used for such things as heavy industry, docks, airports, or recreational facilities.

These and other forms of site modification foretell a time when the site of a new city or town will be made to order.

For Thought and Research

1 a) Explain what is meant by a town's site.

b) What is a site deficiency?

c) How could site quality change from year to year? Could a site become a liability in time? Explain.

2 Describe the site characteristics that are most suitable for the following types of urban communities: military, port, commercial, and manufacturing.

3 a) Explain the meaning of the term "situation".

b) Using your own town (or one near you) as an example, explain clearly the difference between site and situation.

4 a) Consult your local historical board or municipal hall to discover why your town or city was built where it is.

b) What was the original function of your community?

c) What advantages and disadvantages did the site present for the community's founders?

5 a) Has the major function of your town or city changed since its founding?

b) If it has changed, how well-suited is the site to the demands of the new function(s)?

6 Consult Figure 2-6 as you answer the following questions about flood-control site modifications.

a) What technological and social changes eliminated the water supply and transportation advantages of riverside locations?

b) Floods would have occurred in flood plains when towns were first built there. Why would they not appear to be as great a problem then as now?

7 a) Has your town ever been threatened or damaged by floods?

b) If it has, what site modifications have been attempted to protect the community?

c) What desirable and undesirable side effects have these modifications had?

8 Make a list of at least six other different site modifications in your community. For each indicate the problem which existed, the solution, and the good and bad features of the modification.

Recommended Readings

1 *The Challenge of Megalopolis* by Wolf Von Eckardt, Macmillan, 1964. This book is very readable and contains a discussion of the sites and situations of the cities of the American Northeast.

2 *Urban Prospects* by John Wolforth and Roger Leigh, McClelland and Stewart, 1971. See pp. 14-38 for the growth of Canadian cities.

3 *The Geography of Towns* by Arthur E. Smailes, Hutchinson University Library, 1966. See pp. 40-52 for a good account of the sites of towns and cities.

4 *First Lessons in Human Geography* by G. H. C. Walters, Longmans, 1968. The chapter on "Settlements" discusses why towns developed where they did.

5 *The Canadian City* by J. N. Jackson, McGraw-Hill Ryerson, 1973. Chapter 3, "The Historical Components of Urban Analysis", looks at site and situation factors.

6 "City Location and Growth" in *High School Geography Project*, Unit 1, Macmillan, 1969. See student resources, pp. 1-5.

2.2 ECONOMIC FACTORS

Obviously site quality alone cannot explain the location of the urban places dotted across the map of North America. People gather in urban settlements to make a living. Thus each community has an economic reason, or, more commonly, a number of such reasons, for its existence. These economic reasons for urban location are of two types. This leads to towns and cities with two main types of functions—central place and specialized.

Central-place or *service* functions involve the provision of goods and services for the surrounding countryside. This includes such things as grocery stores, newspapers, doctors, and farm-implement dealers.

Specialized-function towns, in contrast to service centers, owe their existence to the presence of a specific resource or combination of resources in an area. The type of resource can vary greatly, from the rich deposits of nickel responsible for Sudbury, Ontario, to the favorable climate, pleasant beaches, and warm ocean waters responsible for Daytona Beach, Florida. The distribution of specialized and central-place centers is discussed in more detail in Section 2.4.

Situation and Economic-Location Factors. You will remember from Section 2.1 that situation is the physical character of the land surrounding the site of an urban place. The economic-location factors are, of course, very closely related to the situation of a town. A town would not develop as a service center if the surrounding area completely lacked any resources that would cause people to live in the region. Similarly, before a town develops as a ski resort, the area must have a favorable combination of climate and physical factors.

You must keep in mind that site and especially situation are *dynamic* or changing concepts. As you have seen previously, a site characteristic can be both an advantage and a disadvantage at different times in a town's history as circumstances change. The way men think about or perceive a town's situation changes even more quickly and completely. For example, before 1849 the town of San Francisco was a sleepy trading and shipping center supplying the needs of the people of a large area of central and northern California. It apparently had limited economic potential. However, the chance discovery of gold in the interior completely altered the *perception* of the situation of the city and quickly pushed the city toward its present position of prominence. How would the discovery of gold 160 km away stimulate the growth of San Francisco?

The locational characteristics of the town's economic activities, as indicated by the town's situation, together with site characteristics, are the main determinants of the actual location of many communities.

For Thought and Research

1 Distinguish between a central-place and a specialized-function town.

2 What were the major economic activities of your community when it was founded? After your class has listed what it believes were the main economic activities, a committee should visit the municipal library and consult such publications as local histories to check the list.

3 Does your town or city have a nickname? Is it related to its function? Detroit, for example, is called the Motor City. Give as many more examples as you can.

4 Give an example of each of the following: a mining town, a resort town, a forestry town, an educational town, a petroleum-refining town, a steel-making town, and a service center for an agricultural area.

5 Describe what is meant by the perception of a town's situation. How is this different from the actual situation?

Recommended Readings

1 *The Geography of Towns* by A. E. Smailes, Hutchinson University Press, 1966. See pp. 52-64 for an extensive discussion of situation.

2 "Cities with Specialized Functions" in *High School Geography Project,* Unit 1, Macmillan, 1969. See student resources pp. 65-84.

3 *Urban Prospects* by J. Wolforth and R. Leigh, McClelland and Stewart, 1971. See "What Cities are For", pp. 39-55.

2.3 SOCIAL AND POLITICAL FACTORS

The previous two sections may have left you with the impression that the choice of a town's location is always the result of a logical, systematic evaluation of the economic and physical factors involved. In the real world, however, other factors are involved. In fact, quite often a town's location is determined by such a complex combination of factors that it is impossible to isolate any factor as the main one.

Perhaps human nature is the most important factor which results in the less than perfect selection of town locations. In the past, urban communities were rarely established after conscious deliberation over the relative merits of various potential sites and situations. More often a town grew haphazardly around a farmstead that had gradually developed into a store, or around a mill or mine site. Planning for the future town or city was non-existent since it was not apparent that there was going to be a town at all.

The careful planning and location of urban communities is a relatively new thing and even today it is not very common. Our knowledge and technology are just becoming sophisticated enough to allow accurate measurement and evaluation of many of the factors of urban location. Thus, for the first time, new urban settlements are being situated rationally in approximately the best location.

What other factors, besides site and situation, affect where cities are placed? Obviously non-economic and non-physical considerations enter into the decision. Perhaps the chief ones are political. Ottawa's position as the capital of Canada was almost entirely a political decision made by Queen Victoria in 1857. Following the burning of former capitals at Niagara-on-the-Lake and York (Toronto) by American forces during the War of 1812, it became apparent to the British Government that a new capital was needed at a safer distance from the American border. As shown in Figure 2-9, a number of sites were considered. In the end, Bytown, a small lumbering settlement on the Ottawa River, was selected and renamed Ottawa. Its location between Upper and Lower Canada (now Ontario and Quebec) was the main factor influencing the final choice. Considering that the decision was made at a great distance (in London, England) with limited information, an attractive and practical location was selected (Fig. 2-10).

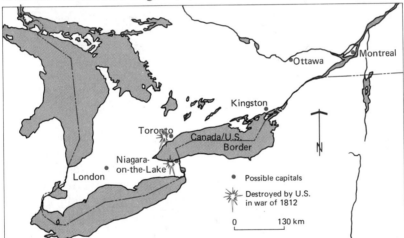

Fig. 2-9
The choice of Ottawa as the new capital of Canada was a political one, made out of fear of American attack.

Pure chance can also be an important element in the location of some towns. The establishment of a town to exploit a randomly located resource is the result of a chance factor. This is especially true of a resource such as gold which is located in widely separated points and was, in the past, usually found by chance. The discovery of gold in such areas as north central California, the interior of British Columbia, and the Klondike resulted in gold rushes and the haphazard establishment of towns such as Dawson City in the Yukon Territory. These towns reached populations of tens of thousands in less than five years. They later became small villages or even ghost towns as the gold output declined. The lives of towns that owe their existence to one resource are limited by the amount of the resource and by the demand for it.

Fig. 2-10
Ottawa, the capital of Canada.
(Courtesy of Canadian Government Travel Bureau.)

In a typical town with a number of important activities, it is often difficult to isolate the importance of various locational factors. Nevertheless it is useful to try to analyze the location of towns and cities in terms of the environmental, economic, and human factors involved. By so doing, some order may be brought to the seemingly haphazard scattering of urban places on the map.

For Thought and Research

1 Consult a book on local history to discover why the capital of your state or province was located where it is.

2 Discuss the relative importance of physical, economic, and other factors in the location of your community.

3 Describe why each of the following must be well-advanced before there can be complete planning of cities:
a) theory of urban planning;
b) building technology;
c) government control.

4 Consult an atlas to discover the location of San Francisco and Dawson City. Both of these cities owe their existence to a gold rush that ended many years ago. San Francisco has prospered and become one of the United States' great cities while Dawson City now has only a few hundred residents. Why have these two cities with similar origins had different subsequent histories?

Recommended Readings

You will find that the following sources are helpful in elaborating some of the ideas presented in this section.

1 "Why Planners Fail" by John H. Stanford, *Landscape,* Winter 1963-64. (Reprinted in *A Geography of Urban Places* edited by Putnam et al., Methuen, 1970.)

2 "A Geography of Cities" in *High School Geography Project,* Unit 1, Macmillan, 1969. See student resources book for readings such as "Frontier Lawyer" which deal with town location in America's early days.

3 *Urban Geography* by J. H. Johnson, Pergamon Press, 1967. See pp. 79-80.

2.4 THE DISTRIBUTION OF URBAN COMMUNITIES

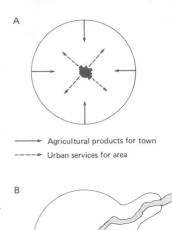

How can the location and patterns of urban settlements be explained by the basic economic activities carried out there? What patterns of urban communities result from the various types of urban functions? How are these patterns related to the basic activities? These and other questions are considered in this section.

If you look at a map of your state or province, the pattern of towns and cities appears to be without order. In actual fact, however, there are a number of factors that tend to cause order in the apparent disorder. Different types of cities are found in different urban patterns. Service centers exhibit one pattern and different types of specialized centers have other patterns. Since many types of cities are found in one area, the pattern you see on a map combines elements of the individual patterns.

Urban Patterns: Service Centers. Much research has been done on the theoretical location pattern of *service centers* or *central places*. Von Thünen, a German farmer writing in 1826 about the area in which he lived, suggested that a town will locate at the center of a productive agricultural area, both to be supplied by the farms in the area and to act as a service center for them. Barring any physiographic obstacles or pathways, these service areas will be circular (Fig. 2-11). Why will this be so?

If we introduce successively more towns on the agricultural plain of Figure 2-11, competition for service areas will develop where zones of influence come into contact. Circular service areas placed tangentially do not completely cover the land surface (Fig. 2-12A). On the other hand, overlapping circular areas cover the entire area, but do not define clear service areas (Fig. 2-12B). Obviously a different geometric figure is needed to indicate the shape of urban service areas. The figure most closely approximating the circle but covering the entire surface without overlap is the regular hexagon (Fig. 2-13). Accordingly hexagonal service areas are used in theoretical considerations of central places.

> → Agricultural products for town
> ----→ Urban services for area

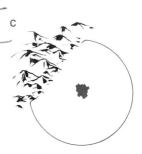

Fig. 2-11
Shapes of service areas surrounding a town: A, on a plain; B, with a physiographic pathway (a navigable river); C, with a physiographic obstacle (a mountain range).

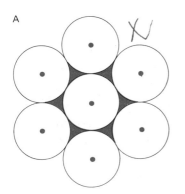

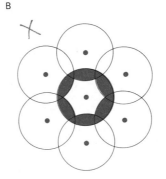

Fig. 2-12
A, tangentially placed circular service areas leave some areas unserved; B, overlapping circular service areas do not indicate clearly the areas served by each town.

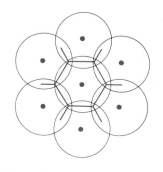

Fig. 2-13
Hexagons most closely approximate circles, yet cover the entire area without overlap.

So far we have assumed that the service centers are of equal size and influence. Obviously this is not the case in actual practice. It might be possible for a farmer to buy a loaf of bread or a kilogram of nails at the general store in a nearby hamlet. However, he would have to go to a more distant town to buy a new automobile and, perhaps, to a large city many kilometres away to attend a symphony concert. This relationship between urban size and sophistication of available goods and services points to the existence of *urban hierarchies.*

Hierarchies exist because larger service areas are needed for more specialized goods and services. For a town to provide a product or service there must be a large enough potential for sales in the area to cover operating costs and provide a satisfactory profit for the businessman concerned. Once this level has been reached in an area a new *threshold* is said to have been met and the service can be provided. For instance, in a town of 15 000 people, the demand for

Fig. 2-14
Size-threshold relationship for urban places.

	Low order good (bread)	Middle order good (auto repair)	High order good (art gallery)	
Increasing urban size	□	□	□	City
	□	□		Town
	□			Village
	Increasing threshold			

groceries, a low-order good, might be large enough for five supermarkets to survive profitably. The demand for appliances, a medium-order good, might only be sufficient for one appliance store. The demand for a high-order good, such as specialized technical books, might not be great enough for even one such bookstore to exist. A person who wants to purchase such books would have to go to a nearby town or city where the threshold is met by the demand from the city and its service area. In this example it can be assumed that the threshold for supermarkets is about 3 000 people and for appliance stores about 15 000. The threshold for a specialized bookstore is in excess of 15 000. Clearly a city meets more thresholds than a town, and a town meets more thresholds than a village (Fig. 2-14).

Walter Christaller, writing of southern Germany in 1935, combined the ideas of hexagonal service areas and differing thresholds in his *central-place theory.* The major characteristic of his theory is that the small service areas around villages are nested in the larger service areas of towns. These, in turn, are nested in the still larger service areas of cities (Fig. 2-15). The result is that, in an area lacking in specialized towns, cities and towns of different sizes are distributed evenly across the landscape.

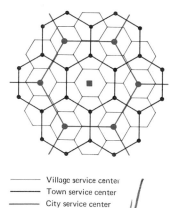

—— Village service center
—— Town service center
—— City service center
• Village
● Town
■ City

Fig. 2-15
Central place theory suggests that urban centers will be spread evenly across the landscape, with service areas proportional to the population of the centers.

Urban Patterns: Specialized Centers. Theoretical considerations helped us to explain the distribution of service centers. No such explanations are possible for specialized-function centers. We can only say that such towns and cities are found where their supporting resources occur.

Most resources occur in a relatively small, distinct area. Thus there is a concentration of towns and cities there. The majority of mineral and fuel towns follow this pattern, as do lumbering centers. The very large mining-industrial complex of the Ruhr Basin of West Germany is an example of this type of development. The coal-mining areas of West Virginia and Pennsylvania and the hard-rock mining areas of northeastern Ontario are other areas where resource-based towns dominate the urban landscape.

Some resources are linear rather than clustered. The most typical of these are recreational resources. The resort cities of Florida are located along a narrow belt on either side of the fringing coastal lagoon. Similar urban distributions are found among the fishing towns of New England, the Maritime Provinces, the Great Lakes, and the Pacific Coast.

Urban Patterns: Transportation Centers. Urban settlements specializing in transportation are a special case of urban location. Their only resource is their location. Their distribution combines elements of the patterns of both specialized-function towns and service centers. Transportation centers are related to their supporting resource but, like service centers, they are located at an efficient distance from one another.

Transportation towns are of two types. The first type occurs along transportation routes and acts as a service depot, supplying labor, fuel, and other needs for the transportation system. The most common town of this type is the railway town. Chicago, Winnipeg, and St. Louis all owe much of their stimulus for growth to early railroad concentrations. Many other towns, especially in the central part of the continent, owe their existence to the railway.

The second and less common type of transportation center is found at a *break-of-bulk* point. Break-of-bulk occurs where a change in the nature of transport is necessary. The most obvious example of a break-of-bulk point is a port city where goods are transferred from ships to railroads and highways and vice versa. A break-of-bulk point may also be an entrepôt (storage and distribution center). In the case of a port city, goods may be kept in storage prior to their distribution by rail and highway. Break-of-bulk also occurs where rail lines end, at the entrance to mountain passes where loads may have to be reduced, and, in fact, at any railroad, highway, or maritime transhipment point. Where are the break-of-bulk facilities in your area?

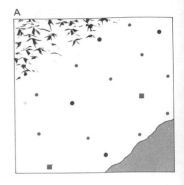

Fig. 2-16
Four theoretical urban patterns combine to produce the real-world urban landscape: A) service centers pattern; B) clustered resource-based centers pattern; C) linear resource-based centers pattern; D) transportation-based centers pattern.

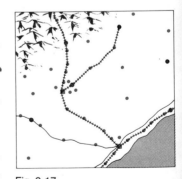

Fig. 2-17
The urban landscape combines elements of the four patterns of Fig. 2-16.

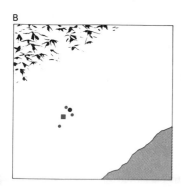

B

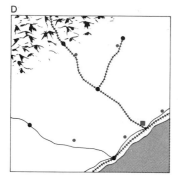

D

Urban Patterns: Composite. We have examined a number of different types of urban centers and the patterns in which they occur. How do these patterns combine to produce the urban landscape? Obviously the resulting landscape will reflect the influences that each individual pattern has on the others (Fig. 2-16). Where two or more patterns tend to reinforce one another a larger urban complex than expected will develop. Conversely the need for a town of one type in an area may be eliminated by a nearby town.

Examine Figure 2-17. It represents a composite view of the theoretical urban patterns of Figure 2-16. Which elements of the resource-based patterns can you spot in the composite? What changes have been made in the service-center pattern and the transportation pattern? Why?

Obviously the location of a resource such as in the mining areas of Figure 2-16B cannot be changed, while the locations of service and transportation centers are somewhat more flexible. Accordingly, if we assume that these mining towns were established early in the area's history, they would completely alter the urban structure of the area. The largest mining center becomes a more diversified center with a large service and transportation function. The regular pattern of service centers is greatly disrupted by the need for large-scale urban development of a location on a major transportation route.

Urban location is an immensely difficult problem. We have attempted to outline some of the environmental, economic, and human factors that determine the shape of the large-scale urban environment covering North America. While we have not examined every factor, you should by now have sufficient background to enable you to examine the history of the location of your own community and to determine where it fits into the larger urban landscape.

For Thought and Research

1 a) What is a service center?

b) What is an urban hierarchy? Give an example of such a hierarchy from your region.

c) What is meant by the term "threshold"?

d) Explain the central-place theory.

2 a) What is a specialized center?

b) Why do some specialized centers occur in clusters whereas others are in a linear arrangement?

3 a) What are the two types of transportation centers?

b) What is a break-of-bulk point?

4 Consult an atlas of North America and find two examples of each of the following:

a) a railway town;

b) a break-of-bulk point;

c) an agricultural service center;

d) a resort center.

5 a) What physiographic barriers or pathways influence the shape of your community's service areas?

b) Do any non-physiographic barriers or pathways (political, economic, etc.) have an influence on your community's service areas?

6 Why did Christaller use hexagons for denoting service areas rather than triangles, squares, or some other geometric shape? (*Hint*: Use graph paper to draw the patterns you are considering.)

7 How far does your family have to travel to hear a symphony concert, buy groceries, or see a doctor? Which of these is a high-order good (service)? medium-order? low-order? List ten other goods and services used by your family and the families of your classmates. What is the lowest-order good or service purchased and the highest?

8 Explain the relationship between service-area sizes and thresholds when changes occur in the following:

a) cost of the good or service;

b) average income of the residents of an area;

c) population density;

d) a change in consumer preference;

e) advertising by a business.

9 Consult Figure 2-15. Using a table like Table 3 describe the shopping patterns of people living at 1, 2, and 3.

TABLE 3

Person living at	Goods shopped for		
	Low-order	Middle-order	High-order
1			
2			
3			

10 Consult Figures 2-16 and 2-17. What elements of the patterns in Figure 2-16 can you locate in Figure 2-17?

Recommended Readings

1 *Urban Geography* by J. H. Johnson, Pergamon Press, 1967. See pp. 80-102 for an examination of theoretical and real aspects of urban spacing.

2 *Towns and Cities* by E. Jones, Oxford, 1966. See pp. 85-92.

3 *The American City* by R. E. Murphy, McGraw-Hill, 1974. See pp. 72-97.

4 *A Geography of Urban Places* by R. Putnam, F. Taylor, and P. Kettle, Methuen, 1970. Read the articles "The Nature of Cities", "Christaller's Central Place Theory", and "External Relations of Cities: City-Hinterland".

5   ''Sizes and Spacing of Cities'' in *High School Geography Project,* Unit 1, Macmillan, 1969. See student resources, pp. 47-64.

6   *The Canadian City* by J. N. Jackson, McGraw-Hill Ryerson, 1973. See pp. 184-92 for central-place theory and recent work in Canada.

The Growth of Urban Communities

3

Why do some cities grow while others die? While North America has undergone a generally rapid urbanization, Figure 3-1 shows clearly that the pattern of growth has varied greatly from place to place. Similarly, a comparison of two maps of your county made 100 years apart would probably show that some settlements have grown much more than others, and that some of the smallest have disappeared. The maps would show differences in total *amount* of growth.

Towns and cities also have different *rates* of growth. To illustrate the difference between amount and rate of growth, imagine two towns of population 1 000 and 10 000 respectively. They each put in a new subdivision and each population grows by 500. You can see that their amount of growth is equal, but their rates of growth are 50% and 5% respectively. Similarly, in Figure 3-1, New York's rate of growth has decreased over time due to the large population involved, in spite of the thousands moving into the area annually. In metropolitan centers, much of the new growth occurs on the outskirts, as in the area of rapid change shown in Figure 3-2.

What causes growth? In reality, it is the result of many decisions made by the people who live and work in our urban places—decisions to move the family; decisions to seek a new and better job or a more interesting social life; decisions to relocate or expand businesses; decisions at all governmental levels. In this study of general urban growth we cannot look at each individual decision that helps a town or city grow. We can, however, look for *patterns* among urban communities from an overall perspective or macroview. Many questions can be asked. Do some towns have a natural advantage that makes them prosper or is it the local businessmen who make or break the town? How important is a head start? Does the physical environment have any effect on growth? How can politicians influence the prospects and prosperity of competing towns? Clearly, economic, environmental, political, and social factors affect growth. Let us examine each of these factors in turn.

Fig. 3-1
Percentage growth of six Eastern Seaboard communities, 1790-1970.

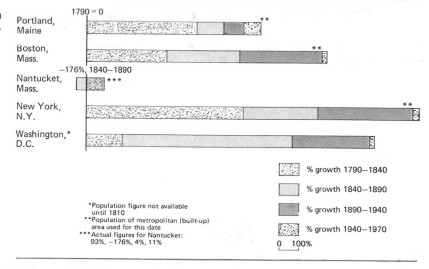

*Population figure not available
 until 1810
**Population of metropolitan (built-up)
 area used for this date
***Actual figures for Nantucket:
 93%, −176%, 4%, 11%

% growth 1790–1840
% growth 1840–1890
% growth 1890–1940
% growth 1940–1970
0   100%

Fig. 3-2
A large metropolis expanding outward. The two pictures of this area were taken approximately ten years apart. (Original photos supplied by the National Air Photo Library, Department of Energy, Mines and Resources.)

3.1 ECONOMIC FACTORS

The major factors influencing the rapid urban growth of the past century have been economic. These can be divided into three groups: the general technology and sophistication of the national economy; the town's accessibility to main types of transportation; the town's economic functions (its industries and services). The first factor will affect most urban places in a country, while the other two factors will give some towns a local advantage over nearby centers.

Technology. Historically this has been a very important factor in urban growth. For example, a country must possess a certain level of sophistication in agriculture to produce a surplus to feed its city dwellers. We read of the cities of past civilizations in both the Old and New Worlds—Egyptian, Greek, Roman, Mayan and Aztec—but the agricultural achievements that made these cities possible are rarely recognized. Agricultural efficiency in ancient times varied from a ratio of 50-90 farmers per urban dweller in the ancient Middle East to one or two farmers supporting each Mayan city dweller. Over the centuries improvements in farm implements, crop strains, agricultural techniques, and the transportation of produce to market have made possible both the surplus of food and the surplus of workers needed for large-scale urbanization.

Many other technological innovations have also facilitated urban growth, beginning with the steam engine and other inventions during the Industrial Revolution. Try making a list of inventions and improvements we now may take for granted that make our cities more efficient, healthy, and attractive. Consult your friends. You will find that your completed list is surprisingly long and includes almost every aspect of urban life.

Accessibility and Transportation. Accessibility is closely related to the transportation systems available. Since many towns function as a center of exchange for a certain service area, changes in the ease and cost of access to these towns can greatly affect growth. If two neighboring towns are competing for a local market and one of them improves its rail or highway links with other places, it is more likely to experience greater growth.

Transportation links between a city and its service area can take many forms—water, rail, road, or air. These types are not of equal importance to every urban place, however, and a dominant form of transport can strongly influence a city's character. For instance, Chicago is famous as a railway town, Los Angeles as a city of expressways, and Halifax as a port. An improvement in accessibility thus involves growth in a different type of transportation for each of these three cities.

The various types of transportation have also differed in importance historically. Many authors have described the effects of changing trends in transportation on urban growth in North America. Innovations in long-distance transportation such as the steamboat, the railroad, and the internal combustion engine have allowed many new towns to grow. Also, innovations in intra-urban (within the city) transport such as the electric streetcar and the automobile have allowed existing centers to spread outward to low-density areas. All these historical trends in transportation technology that have influenced the growth and form of North America cities are summarized in Table 4.

TABLE 4   TRANSPORTATION AND URBAN GROWTH IN NORTH AMERICA

	Year		
	1790-1850	**1850-1920**	**1920 to present**
Dominant types of long-distance transportation	Water (canals, rivers) Steamboats important after 1830 Roads (carriages and wagons)	Railroad-building era Water transport declines in importance	Automobile era (cars, trucks and, later, aircraft) Continual increase in size of ships; decline of canals
Dominant types of intra-urban transportation	Pedestrian Horse-drawn carriages and railways	Horse-drawn vehicles in smaller centers Electric streetcars in most large cities by 1890	Automobiles and trucks Expressways Rapid transit (buses, subways, commuter trains)
Implications for urban growth	Cities limited in size and density Port cities most important Water power River cities boomed after 1830	Growth of iron and steel industry New railway towns Westward expansion Suburbanization began Growth of manufacturing	Urban sprawl Concentration of population in large metropolises Growth of car and oil industries N. American society becomes 70-80% urban
Some cities of greatest growth	New York Philadelphia Montreal New Orleans	Chicago Winnipeg St. Louis Pittsburgh	Detroit Los Angeles Miami Calgary

Economic Functions. The economic functions of an urban center can also influence its growth. An increased demand for any one of a city's hundreds of products or services can help to stimulate growth. There are, however, certain key functions that are vital to the continued growth of a town or city. What are these key functions?

Basic or town-forming functions can be defined as those activities that bring revenue to a city by serving an external market. For example, Detroit is known as the Motor City and Ottawa as a government center. In each case, the basic industry is vital to that city's existence, although it sells its products mainly to areas outside the city. *Non-basic* or town-serving activities, on the other hand, involve the provision of those goods and services that a town's own population needs. As suggested by the terms town-*serving* and town-*forming*, the non-basic element of a town's economic structure exists only as a support for the basic activities the town performs which are responsible for the town's continued existence and growth (see Fig. 3-3).

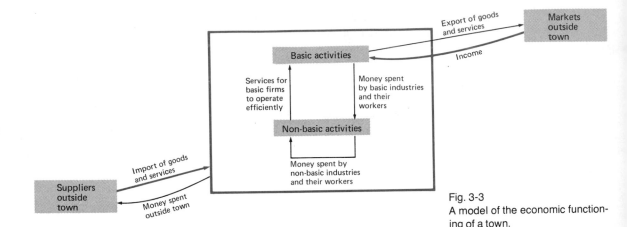

Fig. 3-3
A model of the economic functioning of a town.

The basic/non-basic concept can be confusing. Perhaps it can better be understood if we use an example. Let us follow $1.00 as it enters a town as part of the wages of one person employed in a basic activity. Figure 3-4 is a simplification of what happens millions of times each day in North America. We begin with an iron-ore miner who earns $1.00 which is paid (indirectly) by an automaker in Detroit. The miner spends his dollar to pay for his daughter's piano lesson. The music teacher spends 40¢ for a loaf of bread which is baked in another town. Therefore this is lost from Irontown. The music teacher spends 60¢ of the original dollar on a haircut. You can follow the rest of the expenditures yourself.

Now add together all the money spent in the town and all the money spent outside the town. You will see that, with $1.00 coming into the town originally, $2.39 was spent within the town and $1.00 went out of the town. More important, notice that, without basic activities (in this case without the miner's dollar), this town could not exist.

For urban growth to take place, the basic industries must expand. Expansion of the basic segment brings more income and new population to the city, thereby increasing the demand for local services. The non-basic service industries therefore also expand, further increasing the population, purchasing power, and demand. This process is called the *multiplier effect*. The multiplier effect is measured using the ratio of the number of employees in basic industries to the number of non-basic employees (B/N ratio). For example, consider a town where the B/N ratio is 1:3. If 1 000 new employees are hired in a basic industry, they will create enough new business, construction, demand for education, and so on to support 3 000 more employees in the non-basic sector. Thus the total increase becomes 4 000.

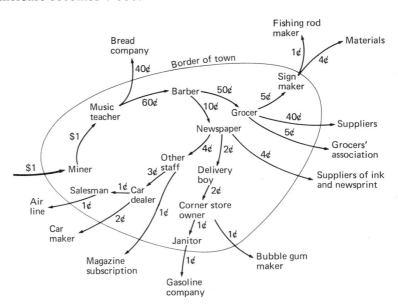

Fig. 3-4
Income from basic activities is essential to a town's economy.

In the large modern metropolis, however, development of the basic industries has become less important to growth. People and industries are now concentrating in these very large cities because of the wider range of services they are able to offer. This reflects the general rise in the importance of the tertiary or service sector of national employment as our standard of living rises and our economy becomes more complex. In Canada, service industries employed 27% of the labor force in 1900, and 62% in 1970.

The expansion of service industries has been a widespread factor in urban growth. However, more localized growth can also result from one rapidly expanding industry. For example, the aerospace industry has contributed to the growth of Los Angeles,

Seattle, and Houston. The thriving cities of St. Petersburg, Atlantic City, and Niagara Falls reflect the boom in tourism (a special case of the growth in the service sector). The petroleum industry has helped build Calgary and Corpus Christi. In all these cases one economic *function* has been the main cause of urban growth.

For Thought and Research

1 Briefly describe the three major factors influencing urban growth.

2 Which of the three economic factors has the most influence on urban growth? Justify your choice.

3 a) Define "the multiplier effect" and draw a diagram to show how it works.

b) What is the tertiary sector? Give three examples of this type of activity.

4 Explain the connection between urban growth and each of the following inventions:

a) the plow;

b) the automobile;

c) the elevator;

d) corn (the Mayan staple food).

5 a) Match the correct city from the right-hand column with the new development that was a major factor in its growth.

1.	automobile	A.	Calgary and Houston
2.	steamboat	B.	Chicago and Winnipeg
3.	iron and steel	C.	Miami Beach
4.	canal	D.	Detroit and Windsor (Ont.)
5.	expressways	E.	Pittsburgh and Hamilton (Ont.)
6.	railroads	F.	Los Angeles
7.	petroleum	G.	New York
8.	tourism	H.	New Orleans

b) Classify each development in a) as a factor of either technology, accessibility, or basic economic function.

6 a) What was the period of greatest growth in your town or city's history? (*Hint*: A visit or telephone call to your municipal offices may be necessary.)

b) What part did transportation developments play in this growth (see Table 4)?

7 a) Write down what you feel is the basic/non-basic ratio for your community's industry.

b) Interview your classmates and make a list of their parents' occupations. Classify these occupations into basic and non-basic industries.

c) Calculate a B/N ratio for your sample.

d) Average your B/N ratio with the ratios calculated by three other classmates to obtain a figure for the basic/non-basic ratio of your community.

e) Compare the two estimates (parts a and d). How close was your initial guess to your calculated ratio?

Recommended Readings

1 *The North American City* by M. H. Yeates and B. J. Garner, Harper and Row, 1971. This upper-high-school university-level book includes a clear, well-illustrated presentation of economic factors in the evolution of the urban pattern. Transportation is especially well-handled.

2 *An Urban Planet?* by B. Ward, Girard Bank, 1971. The first chapter is a brief and easy-to-read description of the economic and social changes that have made us into an urban planet.

3 *Towns and Cities* by E. Jones, Oxford University Press, 1966. This book is a good introduction to urban studies in general. It also includes some useful facts on the process of urbanization, both in our Western cities and in pre-industrial cities.

4 *Modern American Cities* edited by R. Ginger, Quadrangle Books, 1969. A collection of *New York Times* articles on the growth and characteristics of various US cities.

5 "Geography of Cities" in *High School Geography Project,* Unit 1, Macmillan, 1969. The student resource book contains several excellent readings on urban growth which illustrate economic and other factors at work.

3.2   ENVIRONMENTAL FACTORS

Each town is built in a given site and situation. If the surrounding terrain is mountainous, a town's accessibility and, therefore, much of its potential for growth is limited. Most of our large cities have grown on fairly flat land. Here they have ready accessibility as well as the important advantage of the low cost of developing and servicing flat land. Thus topographic differences between towns, affecting accessibility and cost, can help some communities grow at the expense of others.

Nevertheless, landforms are more often important in determining *how* (that is, in what shape) towns and cities grow than *why* they grow (see Section 4.3). For example, Amsterdam, a city virtually built on water, and San Francisco, which is built on steep hills and surrounded on three sides by water, continue to grow and prosper. Each of these has developed a unique character, partly because of its physical setting. In the early days of town building, when sites were chosen for defence (for example, the island location of Montreal), the landforms limited the towns' outward growth. Although these original limitations have ceased to affect any but the downtown areas, some modern communities must still adapt to their sites. The outports of western Newfoundland, which are limited to a narrow strip of land between the mountains and the ocean, provide one picturesque example.

It has often been observed by conservationists that cities such as Vancouver, Toronto, and Los Angeles have grown at the expense of some of our best farmland. This phenomenon does not mean, however, that good soils are a prerequisite for urban growth. Many of these cities were originally agricultural market towns and grew because farming prospered. Only when transportation improvements enabled long-distance shipping of food could the city afford to "bite off the land that feeds it". The ease and low cost of building on flat land were also significant factors. *to city growth.*

An example of this conflict between urban and agricultural land uses is found in the Niagara Peninsula fruit belt of Ontario. This district has both sandy, well-drained soils and a moderate climate suited for tender-fruit growing, a very rare combination in Canada. However, the soils and climate, combined with its proximity to the Toronto-Hamilton urban industrial complex, make this region ideal for urban growth. As a result, some of the most valuable and irreplaceable farmland in Southern Ontario has been taken out of production and built on.

A pleasant climate has played a significant role in the growth of some towns and cities. Many Florida cities have prospered because of an almost year-round tourist trade. Arizona's warm dry winters attract many people, often with respiratory diseases, to Tucson, Phoenix, and other urban centers. The famous climate of Southern California has been one of the major factors in its rapid urbanization and general population growth. Much of the California boom was also due to the fact that the film and airplane industries located there to take advantage of the sunshine and warm winters. Thus some urban growth can best be explained by environmental factors.

For Thought and Research

1 a) Describe an ideal environment for maximum urban growth. Draw sketch maps or diagrams to illustrate your ideal.

b) How does your community differ from this ideal setting? In what ways have these differences affected its growth?

2 The following urban places are all located in difficult environments. Choose one from the list, look it up in an atlas and/or encyclopedia, and write a short description of that town or city's physical setting and explain how it has affected growth.

Amsterdam, The Netherlands
Venice, Italy
Aklavik, Canada
Timbuktu, Mali
Quito, Ecuador

Calcutta, India
Yakutsk, USSR
Las Vegas, USA
Hong Kong

3 Because of the population explosion, many people are saying that we should use the polar and desert regions of the world to ease population pressure in the East. From the findings of your class as you answered question 2, do you think that cities are possible in these regions? If so, is this massive relocation likely to happen in the next 50 years? Why or why not?

4 a) Do Case Study 9.9, "A Second Airport for Toronto?"

b) Explain how the statistics in this case study illustrate the influence of the physical environment on growth and also the influence of urban growth on the surrounding physical environment.

5 It has been suggested in Ontario that the remaining farmland in the Niagara Peninsula fruit belt should be preserved by limiting growth in nearby cities like Toronto, Hamilton, and St. Catharines. Discuss the pros and cons of this suggestion.

Recommended Readings

Although no books specifically discuss environmental factors in growth, the following high-school-level books do include sections on certain aspects of the topic, such as site features and technological achievements that have overcome environmental problems.

1 *Urban Problems, A Canadian Reader* edited by R. Krueger and R. C. Bryfogle, Holt, Rinehart and Winston, 1975.
2 *The World Cities* by P. Hall, McGraw-Hill, 1966.
3 ''Cuidad Guayana: A New City'' by L. Rodurn, *Scientific American,* September 1965.
4 Your local town or county history should include a description of the original environment, which can give clues about its importance as an influence on growth.
5 Further references are found in Research Topic 8.2, ''The Urban Impact on Agricultural Land''.

3.3 SOCIAL AND POLITICAL FACTORS

City dwellers may seem hard to understand. More and more people are moving to cities, but once they live there they long for country life. Why does this happen? Both parts of this apparent contradiction can be explained by understanding the social advantages and disadvantages of city life.

Social and Cultural Advantages. As our standard of living has risen, we have gained more leisure time and, consequently, seek more recreation of all types. Young people, especially, are attracted to places where they can choose from a long list of activities—sports, theaters, restaurants, taverns, nightclubs, orchestras, ballet, art galleries, museums, and university programs. Since the amount of choice generally increases with the size of the city, the large metropolises continue to grow faster than other centers.

As well as its cultural attractions, the large city usually offers more job opportunities. There are also greater possibilities of upward mobility for one's children. They can often obtain a better education, job, and social position than they can in many rural areas or small towns. New immigrants settle almost exclusively in the largest cities where they can find others of their culture. This helps them to gradually make the transition to North American life. Many disadvantaged people also see city life as a sort of insurance. Often they cannot find work or a home in a small community. However, financial aid, subsidized housing, and a good education are usually available in the big city. The advantages of metropolitan welfare programs have been obvious for over 30 years. One-time New York City mayor, Fiorello LaGuardia, pointed out that cities that enacted more social reforms were only penalized by increased immigration of poor and uneducated people. These factors—educational opportunities, cultural affiliation, and welfare programs—have all contributed to the increasing concentration of people in a few metropolitan centers.

Cities of all sizes have benefitted from the fact that physical amenities are generally available to all urban dwellers. Shopping facilities are close by, sewage and garbage are disposed of, water supply and electricity are taken for granted. Thus it is easy to see that instead of asking ourselves "Why do we live in cities?" we should perhaps be asking "Why not live in cities?"

Social Disadvantages. Many people have answered this latter question by pointing out the social evils of cities. Poverty, crowding, anonymity, alienation, and pollution are just some of the arguments against city life. In an attempt to strike a compromise between the efficiency of economic and cultural urban life and the ideal of the green tranquil countryside, our cities have grown outward, suburbanizing huge areas of land. The most disaffected urban dwellers are taking even more extreme measures. They have become part of the rapidly growing category of rural non-farm residents commuting daily to the city. This recent movement away from big city life has revived many stagnating small towns and villages. Further, it indicates a new trend in growth of satellite towns, whether newly planned communities or revitalized older settlements. Thus the social advantages and disadvantages of cities can both be responsible for growth, the first for the growing population of the city, and the second for its spreading area.

Political and Business Factors. Social factors in urban growth work over a long period of time. Political and business decisions have a more immediate effect. This was shown in the example given in Section 1.2, where one business's decision to start a ship-building factory was a major cause of the town's growth. This factor is called *entrepreneurship*. An entrepreneur is a businessman who is willing to take risks to earn large profits. To a certain extent, the economic situation of a trading center becomes what its businessmen make it. Many Eastern Seaboard towns of the early nineteenth century commanded potential access routes to the developing interior. However, New York's businessmen were the most aggressive. In 1825 they opened the first canal to the continent's interior, the Erie Canal, which brought goods from as far inland as Lake Michigan. New York maintained the head start that this gave it and, with the greater available capital in the 1850s, became the leader in railway transport as well (Fig. 3-5). A similar pattern of success can be found in Kansas City, where community leaders built the first bridge over the Missouri River and thus gained a commanding position on major railway routes.

As governments at all levels increase their powers, political decisions become more important in influencing urban growth.

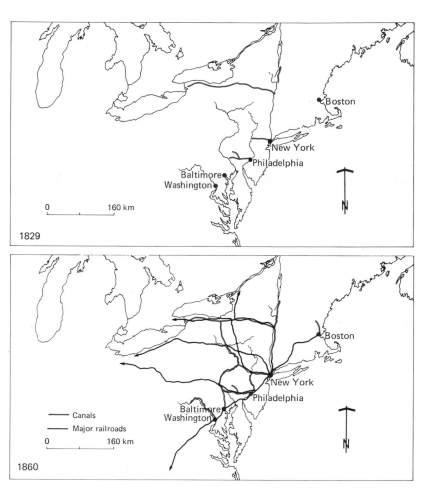

Fig. 3-5
New York keeps its lead over other eastern seaports during two different transportation eras.

1829

1860

- Canals
- Major railroads

There are many ways in which governments can encourage growth in a certain community—by locating new public offices or agencies there or expanding old ones; by improving transportation facilities such as highways to the town; and by granting tax concessions and low interest rate loans. Although the effects of government policies on urban development may be increasing, they are not new. In the 1890s Hamilton City Council offered long-term tax exemptions, free land, and a large cash bonus to an iron and steel company. This attracted the plant which later became the headquarters of the Steel Company of Canada (Stelco) and gave Hamilton the nickname of the Steel City of Canada.

For Thought and Research

1 a) What features of a city attract new residents?
   b) List what you feel are the five main social evils of cities.
   c) How do business decisions affect a town's growth?

2   Explain each of the following terms and describe how it affects the quality of life in a city:

    a) poverty;

    b) crowding;

    c) anonymity;

    d) alienation;

    e) pollution.

3   Examine a map of the northeastern United States. Find the Erie Canal. Explain how the construction of this canal enabled New York to grow at the expense of Boston and Philadelphia.

4   What is the relationship between the growth of large cities and a) spare time; b) the lure of the countryside?

5   Use the information given in the two maps of Figure 3-5 to explain the different rates of growth of Boston, New York, and Washington in the time periods 1790-1840 and 1840-1890 (see Fig. 3-1).

6   Telephone the chamber of commerce or the municipal offices of your community and ask what they are doing to encourage industry and business to locate and develop there. Compare their answers with the methods implied in this section. Account for any differences.

7   In 1935 the government of the USSR decided that the growth of Moscow should be limited to natural increase alone. In this way its population would not exceed 5 million by 1950. However, the population overshot this figure and today the Moscow region has over 9 million inhabitants. Where did the Soviet planners miscalculate? Do you think it possible for any government to control urban growth? Why?

8   Recently many city residents, having viewed the problems of large and rapidly growing cities with alarm, have elected anti-growth politicians. Should a city have the right to refuse new developments and thus prevent any more people from moving into the city? How else can growth be controlled?

9   a) Many people have left the problems of the downtown area to live in dormitory communities in the suburbs. What is meant by a "dormitory" community?

    b) What are the social and economic advantages and disadvantages of the dormitory suburb? Consider the residents, the local government, and the city to which the residents commute.

    c) Suburbs create many city problems. What alternatives for future growth are available to urban planners?

Recommended Readings

1   "The Modern Metropolis" by H. Blumenfeld, *Scientific American,* September 1965. This article discusses the end product of the evolution of cities. Both social and economic forces are described.

2   *The Challenge of Megalopolis* by W. von Eckardt, Macmillan, 1964. This is an easy-to-read, profusely illustrated description of the origin, development, and characteristics of the continuous city on the US Eastern Seaboard. The chapter on "Why Cities Grow and Suburbs Scatter" describes social changes.

3   *The Rise of Urban America* by C. M. Green, Harper and Row, 1965. This historical description covers four centuries of urban growth. A wealth of facts about numerous cities is presented in a conversational tone. The book contains many social and political insights.

4 *Problems in the Bosnywash Megalopolis* by L. A. Swatridge, McGraw-Hill, 1972. This book deals with the urbanized Eastern Seaboard region and its problems.
5 *The Making of Urban America* by B. Habenstreit, Julian Mesmer Division of Simon and Schuster, 1970. Especially good on social factors influencing the movement of blacks to northern cities and the middle-class flight to suburbia.

3.4   INTERACTIONS BETWEEN URBAN COMMUNITIES

In Unit 1 it was noted that an urban ecosystem is made up of a complex system of interactions. In this unit we have looked at the interaction of economic, environmental, and social factors, which has led to the growth of individual towns. We will now look at how these same factors have led to the development of a much larger urban ecosystem made up of the general pattern of urban places in North America.

All towns and cities belong to larger regional and national groupings. They may interact by competing, complementing, or merely co-existing with one another. Each of these types of interaction has a parallel in the food webs of a natural ecosystem. Can you give an example of each type from a natural ecosystem, for instance? Just as ecologists can measure interaction in a natural ecosystem, urban geographers have developed many ways of measuring the interactions between cities and of mapping the patterns resulting from urban growth and interaction.

The City and its Region. One of the basic types of interaction experienced by a city is with the surrounding region it serves. The extent of these *service areas* can be measured in many ways: the distance people will commute to work in the city; the trading area of its largest department stores; the listening area of its radio stations; and the greatest distance regional retailers will travel to buy from the wholesale outlets in the city. Perhaps the most common method of determining service-area size, and the one most applicable to both large and small communities, is the extent of newspaper circulation. This is because a person is likely to subscribe to the newspaper of any area of immediate concern to him. Figure 3-6 illustrates a hypothetical regional system of newspaper circulation districts.

If a number of service areas for individual activities or commodities are mapped for a city, their overlapping boundaries can be averaged to measure the *hinterland* (land behind) of the city. Figure 3-7 illustrates this method of hinterland delimitation between New York and Boston.

Although we can draw boundaries to show the area influenced by each settlement, we must remember that towns and

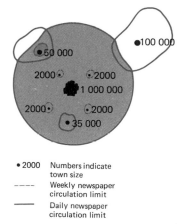

• 2000 Numbers indicate town size

---- Weekly newspaper circulation limit

—— Daily newspaper circulation limit

0   160 km

Fig. 3-6
Influence of a hypothetical city as shown by newspaper circulation.

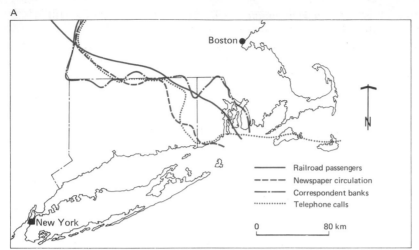

A

Boston

New York

Railroad passengers
Newspaper circulation
Correspondent banks
Telephone calls

0   80 km

N

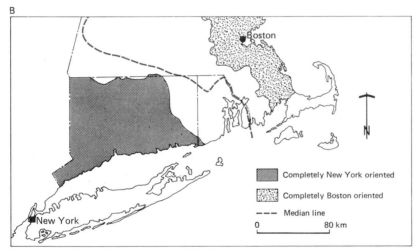

B

Boston

New York

Completely New York oriented

Completely Boston oriented

Median line

0   80 km

N

Fig. 3-7
Hinterland delimitation between
New York and Boston: A, service
areas mapped for four indicators;
B, a central line delimits the hin-
terlands.

cities and their regions do not exist by themselves. They are con-
tinually interacting with each other. Industries, stores, and banks
are likely to have branches or business partners in many cities with
frequent transactions and travel between them.

Interactions between Cities. Communities may grow by
competing with one another, as New York and Boston once com-
peted for the trade of the Eastern Seaboard. But they may also grow
by *complementing* each other. There are many examples of fairly
close associations between a steel-making center and a large diversified manufacturing city: Hamilton and Toronto; Sorel and Montreal; Gary and Chicago; and Fontana and Los Angeles.

Telephone calls and airplane flights are two ways of
measuring interactions between a pair of cities. Instead of such
direct measurements, however, it is possible to approximate the
degree of interaction by using the *gravity model*. This model, based

on Newton's gravitational theory, assumes that the interaction between two places is directly proportional to the product of their masses (populations) and inversely proportional to the square of the distance between them. Thus $I = \dfrac{P_1 P_2}{D^2}$. According to this model two large cities hundreds of kilometres apart might have the same number of interconnections as two small centers only a few kilometres apart. Is this a reasonable assumption?

In estimating the interaction of Dallas and Fort Worth, Texas, we obtain:

$$I = \frac{P_1 P_2}{D^2} \quad \frac{1\ 400\ 000 \ \times\ 600\ 000}{33^2} = 770\ 000\ 000$$

This large number supports the description of Dallas and Fort Worth as twin cities. However, to the novice, the number becomes meaningful only when it is compared to numbers for other cities. Such comparisons show that there is over twenty times as much interaction between Dallas and the much larger but more distant city of Houston than between Dallas and Fort Worth. Why might this be so?

The Urban Hierarchy. Geographers have looked at the interactions among towns and cities and observed that there is a hierarchy of urban places in North America. This hierarchy resembles a pyramid of numbers in a natural ecosystem, for there is a decreasing number of cities as you move up in the scale. Two major theories of urban location and growth, *central-place theory* and the *rank-size rule,* try to account for this urban hierarchy. These theories are based on the principle of least effort—humans will arrange their activities to minimize inconvenience, whether in distance, cost, or time. The pattern of town spacing in Christaller's central-place theory shows this principle at work. (Review Section 2.4.)

While central-place theory involves a hierarchy of size and location of towns, the rank-size rule does not call for an even spacing of towns. Zipf and others observed that a city's national rank is related to its size: that the second largest city (with a rank of 2) has one-half the population of the largest, the fourth city has one quarter of the largest city's population, the fiftieth city one fiftieth and so on. According to this rank-size rule, there will be only one very large city in a country, a few cities of intermediate size, and many small towns. In any country where the rank-size rule applies, its cities and towns can be graphed as a straight line as in Figure 3-8.

However, central-place theory predicts an ideal case and the rank-size rule is a generalization based on many observations. In reality, each will vary according to economic conditions in the country. For instance, in eastern North America, with rapid trans-

Fig. 3-8
An ideal rank-size distribution, with a slope of −1.00 (using logarithmic graph paper).

portation and plenty of money, the local service villages suffer and more shopping is done at large shopping centers in the city. In this situation there are fewer villages in the urban hierarchy. In an underdeveloped country, on the other hand, there is little spending money and few cars, and most shopping is for necessities at stores within walking distance. In these countries there is a much higher proportion of small towns than the ideal case.

Some of these differences can be illustrated by drawing urban pyramids for different countries. As outlined, changes in the urban geography will reflect the different economic and social conditions present. Some sample pyramids are given in Figure 3-9. Each step represents a functional and/or size class of cities. Towns of under 10 000 with only a few local services are the lowest class, manufacturing centers of 100 000 to 500 000 are the middle classes, and so on. The area of each level in the pyramid is proportional to the number of towns or cities in that class.

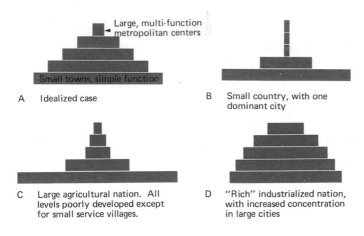

A   Idealized case

B   Small country, with one dominant city

C   Large agricultural nation. All levels poorly developed except for small service villages.

D   "Rich" industrialized nation, with increased concentration in large cities

Fig. 3-9
Some hypothetical urban size-function pyramids.

We have looked at several ways of measuring interaction between communities and several ways of showing the urban pattern that results from those interactions. In the past two centuries while this pattern has been developing, many factors have affected urban growth. These factors have not been at work equally in all cities, but have nevertheless combined to produce the complex urban ecosystem which is North America today.

For Thought and Research

1   Explain the terms "service area", "complementary cities", and "hinterland delimitation".

2   a) Account for the shape of the newspaper circulation districts around the cities of 35 000, 50 000, and 100 000 population in Figure 3-6.

   b) Where would your community fit into the diagram (Fig. 3-6)?

3 a) What is the connection between the literal meaning of hinterland and its economic meaning?

b) Use the gravity model to calculate the interactions between your town or city and at least five other towns or cities in your state or province. Rank your results with the highest interaction at the top of the column. Account for the ranking. If you disagree with the ranking, give your reasons.

c) Use the gravity model to calculate the interactions between: your community and the capital of your province or state; your community and the capital of your country; the capital of your state or province and the capital of your country. Account for the results.

4 a) A variation of the gravity model, Reilly's Law of Retail Gravitation is often used to estimate the hinterland boundary between two cities. Using the following formula, estimate the location of the retail boundary between your community (city A) and a neighboring town or city (city B). (*Hint*: The calculations are easier if city B is the larger.)

$$\text{Distance of boundary from city A} = \frac{\text{Distance between A and B}}{1 + \sqrt{\dfrac{\text{Population of B}}{\text{Population of A}}}}$$

b) Test your answer to 4 a) by asking a few people who live near an estimated boundary where they shop.

5 Marshall McLuhan called the world a "global village" because people can be in almost instant communication with any part of it. If this is so, is it still valid to use the gravity model to measure interactions between places? Why?

6 Explain how the idea of urban hierarchies is dealt with in:

a) central-place theory;

b) the rank-size rule.

7 Canada and the United States are both developed countries. Check the population figures for the top ten cities in each country to see if the rank-size rule fits. Try to explain any major city where the rule does not fit by looking for exceptional factors that may have affected the normal pattern of urban growth.

8 Examine Figure 3-9. Should all countries aim to achieve a shape like that of pyramid A? Defend your answer by referring to the advantages and disadvantages of each shape.

Recommended Readings

The following four books contain chapters covering such general topics as the size and spacing of cities, methods of measuring interaction, and regions around cities.

1 *The North American City* by M. H. Yeates and B. J. Garner, Harper and Row, 1971.

2 *Urban Geography, An Introductory Analysis* by J. H. Johnson, Pergamon Press, 1967. See especially pp. 100-102 for a comparison of central-place theory and the rank-size rule.

3 *Urban Prospects* by J. Wolforth and R. Leigh, McClelland and Stewart, 1971.

4 *The American City* by R. E. Murphy, McGraw-Hill, 1974.

The Urban Landscape

4

From earlier units you should now have an understanding of what an urban community is as a whole. In this unit we will focus on the internal ordering of such a community.

Suppose, for example, you live in a thriving steel city. Why did the steel plant locate along the waterfront? If a new plant were built where would it be located? Where do the employees live? Are there slums or areas of residential decay? Why do they exist? What functions and buildings are replacing slums, old warehouses, and open space? These and many more questions refer to the *urban landscape* of a community.

Before we can answer these questions about the *pattern* of urban land uses and the role of physical setting, we should have a knowledge of the *processes* (forces) affecting the development of urban structure.

4.1 PROCESSES AFFECTING URBAN STRUCTURE

In order to understand the processes affecting urban structure let us study the development of a city called Greenville. Throughout this discussion we will look at the emergence of commercial, industrial, residential, and institutional land-use patterns for three periods of time: early development (before 1840); later development (between 1870 and 1940); and recent development (since World War II). This is a true story; only the name has been changed.

EARLY DEVELOPMENT

In the early 1800s two major forces were shaping Greenville. These forces were concentration and segregation. *Concentration* is the process whereby many activities and people tend to be crowded onto a small amount of land. This is in contrast to economic activities such as farming, forestry, and fishing, where a small number of people and activities are thinly spread over a large area. The second process, *segregation,* refers to the separation of certain activities such as housing from other activities such as retail trade. How did these forces shape early Greenville?

Commercial activities are found in the oldest section of Greenville. People usually call this area the downtown. Why has this activity developed here?

The future downtown was owned first by an Indian Nation, followed in turn by a land agent and finally two farmers. Harmony with his environment was a goal for the Indian; profit was a goal for the land agent; open fields were the goal for the farmers. Each owner in this series expected different things from this land and with each sale the price increased. As the land became more expensive, the new owner would have to use the land more completely or more intensively in order to make his investment profitable. Very little can be done in our economic system to alter this trend to *concentrate* more activities on the same area.

Concentration continued to dominate the growth of Greenville. An immigrant to the area persuaded one farmer at the junction of the two major roads to sell some land for an inn and a blacksmith shop. Soon other services clustered near the inn and lined up along the two main roads. This ribbon development included two general stores and a shop for wind-driven water pumps. In short, the needs of the surrounding farming population determined the number and types of village shops clustered around the main intersection. Figure 4-1 illustrates this point.

Fig. 4-1
A concentration of activities and buildings develops to serve the needs of the surrounding rural population and travellers. (Courtesy Pioneer Village, Metropolitan Toronto and Region Conservation Authority.)

Circumstances favored the additional concentration of people and activities. First, Greenville was made the county seat. This governmental function attracted people from all over the region, which in turn encouraged new businesses to locate in the community. Among those that moved into the village were a flour mill, a farm-implement factory, and a bank. Why were these particular businesses attracted to Greenville when it became the county seat?

Second, people did not own cars and the only public transportation was the stagecoach. Because of this, people tended to do a great deal of walking within the growing town, and activities therefore had to be within walking distance. This encouraged business and commercial activities to remain concentrated around the nucleus at the junction of the two major roads.

This location, and any others which are accessible, provide a place where a concentration of people and activities may occur. For example, the prosperity of a retail businessman was related to the number of people who passed by his shop in Greenville. The most accessible locations became the most costly. If a business could not compete for these locations, it would be forced to accept a less desirable location. Thus a concentration of activities and people in one central area was encouraged by the lack of alternative competitive locations. Because transportation technology was in its infancy, only one location, the Central Business District (CBD), would be easily accessible to most of the citizens. The types of activities that could dominate the CBD were usually retail and service activities. Why could these businesses afford the rent while others could not?

A third factor encouraged concentration of activities in Greenville. People wanted to locate their businesses downtown but not everyone could be accommodated in the limited space available. This demand for space led to the development of buildings with more than one floor. Now one building could house a number of different functions or businesses. This layering of activities in one building is usually referred to as *multiple use*. What types of functions are accommodated above one-floor business establishments in your town? This multiple-use concept still seems to be valid in Greenville today, where a bowling alley is housed above a shoe store.

So far we have focused on the concentration of commercial activities, but the other activities were also clustered together. Greenville, in short, was a tightly knit package.

Industrial, residential, and institutional land uses in Greenville show how the second major process was shaping the town. This second process is the *segregation* of activities.

Those activities which could not pay the high rent of an accessible location in the heart of Greenville were separated from the central area. This list includes homes, a college, and factories which needed large areas.

Even among these less competitive activities there was a trend toward separation. Churches tended to congregate along several streets close to the central business area. Is there a Church Street in your community? Another example of segregation can be seen in the building of homes. Even in this early period several of the newer and larger homes were built away from the older homes and the noise of the factories.

Segregation occurs because some people and activities cannot afford to locate in certain areas of the city and because of personal values such as the desire for privacy, space, and the avoidance of noises and odors.

LATER DEVELOPMENT

During the period from 1870 to 1940 concentration and segregation of activities were still major forces shaping Greenville. However, a third force, dispersion, emerged during this period. *Dispersion* is the process whereby many activities tend to be widely spread or scattered around the edge of the city and beyond. The combined impact of these three forces on commercial, industrial, residential, and institutional activities was great.

Commercial activities showed a greater degree of concentration in the central area than ever before. Why? First, many people did not own automobiles and were tied to the electric streetcar and railroads running between communities. As a result there was still great pressure for space in downtown Greenville where these transportation facilities were focused. Second, with the invention of the elevator, buildings could reach even greater heights, and more and more activities could be concentrated in one building.

Industrial activities in general were consuming more and more land in Greenville. These activities were affected by all three major forces shaping the city during this period—concentration, segregation, and dispersion.

The main industrial concentrations occurred near railway lines. Because the inter-city road system was poorly developed, the railroad was a company's link with its outside market. Sites near the rail line were quickly occupied. Other manufacturers preferred to locate on the outskirts of the CBD. The high cost of this land forced companies to build multi-storey factories using elevators.

Segregation also shaped this land-use activity. The cost of buying or renting large amounts of land for industrial use usually ruled out the choice of a CBD location. Besides, the noise and smell made by some of these companies, such as rubber factories, would have met with opposition from the retail outlets in the downtown area. Any communication that was needed between the factory and a centrally located business could be handled by telephone, and therefore the need to locate in the CBD was reduced.

Dispersion occurred to the extent that some companies that needed large amounts of land were forced to move to railway sites near the edge of the city. It was checked by the fact that most of the laborers did not own cars and relied on the electric streetcar systems. In cities with ports, dispersion was reduced since harbor facilities create a natural focus for the concentration of manufacturing activities.

Residential development was also shaped by the same three forces. Concentration of higher-priced homes occurred. Business leaders and professionals tended to build their large homes in fashionable areas. This was partly due to their desire for large attractive house lots, and partly because of a desire to live near their friends. Here is a good example of segregation made possible by the ability to afford the best locations. The automobile soon enabled this group to separate themselves even more, as they could build farther away from the central area. Indeed, in the 1920s, as the automobile became more dependable and the roads more reliable, several of the wealthiest citizens moved outside the city into the country. This movement of the wealthy also illustrates the process of dispersion of residential land use.

Where did the general laborers live? During this period they usually lived close to the central city and their places of work. With limited incomes, the laborers could not compete with their bosses for housing. Under these conditions poor citizens tended to locate in housing areas which were separate from those of wealthier citizens. Segregation was a reality.

Dispersion was not as evident with this group as with the wealthier citizens. They were restricted largely to walking and streetcar travel. Their housing areas were, therefore, tied to the Central Business District or a streetcar system. Although a railway line connected several villages with Greenville, the laborers tended not to move out toward the end of the line in great numbers. Dispersion of working and middle-class housing would have to wait until mass automobile ownership became common and made commuting easier.

In summary, concentration of business activities in the Central Business District increased. Industrial and low-income residential development clustered around transportation facilities. High-income residential areas showed the greatest dispersion over the countryside. While both concentration and dispersion were pulling at the city of Greenville, segregation of land-use activities increased in all areas.

DEVELOPMENT SINCE WORLD WAR II

Fig. 4-2
Competition for space in the CBD raises land prices and, as a result, also raises building heights. Note the step-like increase in building height toward the CBD.

Since the Second World War the city of Greenville has exploded outward because of mass automobile ownership. At the same time concentration of some activities is still occurring. As both of these processes vie for dominance, the segregation of activities and people is more and more evident everywhere.

Commercial activities showed a great deal of change during this period. The Central Business District experienced a rapid rise in land values. Figure 4-2 shows the relationship between the height of buildings and the cost of land around the CBD. This rise in land values in the CBD is a continuation of earlier trends as competition for accessible locations still occurs. Indeed, the CBD is still a desirable location for commercial activities in Greenville. There is, however, great pressure to develop the remaining open space, now in public ownership, for commercial buildings. In addition, older buildings are being torn down and replaced by larger buildings which use the land more intensively. This process is called *redevelopment.*

For the first time the traditional concentration of activity has a real challenger. With the expressway system which now runs around the edge of the city, many people can easily reach places away from the central business area. New businesses and stores have now clustered together in shopping plazas. These clusters provide a convenient alternative to going downtown. This development of competing concentrations of business activities has tended to disperse the city outward.

Industrial activities, in cases where the investment in buildings is large, tend to remain in the same locations as in the previous period. However, many post-war developments have changed the character of manufacturing districts. Efficient long-distance trucking and better highways have given manufacturers an alternative to rail transportation. Many employees can drive to work. Modern industrial methods favor one-storey plants. In addition, there is limited space for expansion of businesses along the railroads in the city. Thus new industries, and old ones that are forced to modernize or expand, are locating on cheaper land near the edge of the city.

Although new forms of transportation allow industrial activities greater freedom in choosing a site, some cities restrict industrial sites to avoid conflict with other uses. This at least permits the organization of this dispersion in areas segregated or *zoned* for industrial uses. For example, Greenville's government decided to encourage all industries to relocate in one area which they called an industrial park. Here roads, rail, and water services were planned before many industries moved into the area.

Greenville's older manufacturing district is now aging. What will happen to it? Perhaps Figure 4-3 will provide an answer. The photograph shows an old factory in the foreground. The original activity has been replaced by a commercial outlet. In the background a new apartment building stands on the site of an old factory. Another example can be found where a new restaurant has just taken over an old factory and is appropriately called the Old Spaghetti Factory. Can you think of any other examples?

Fig. 4-3
An old manufacturing district. Note the invasion by new buildings with a different land use and the new function of this old factory.

The process now shaping the old manufacturing district is called the *cycle of deterioration*. Briefly, this refers to the life cycle of buildings. As a building reaches old age, it will either be remodelled by the occupant, torn down, or a new activity may filter into the area and take over the building for another use.

Residential districts for the higher-income families have continued to extend away from the central business area along established routes. Meanwhile, the poorer people tend to live on the more expensive land closer to the CBD. Why?

If you took a walk on the tree-lined streets around the edge of the CBD in Greenville you would see old single-family homes being used in many ways. Some homes have been renovated and used by professional services unable or unwilling to pay the rent for central office space. Other homes have not been maintained. Many have been converted into rooming houses. At any time, the right sale price may be offered and a developer will combine several lots and build new housing. Figure 4-4 shows what the result may be. In some cities the older homes have been remodelled and maintained by wealthier individuals. These changes illustrate the process of *succession* of land uses in a growing community.

Where do poor people move after eviction? Because they cannot afford to compete for better housing unless assisted by the government, these people tend to move into another building well-advanced along the cycle of deterioration. This situation also enables the CBD to concentrate additional activities by invading the aging area around it.

Wealthier citizens have intensified their exodus out of the city in search of attractive living space. The growth of the middle class, coupled with greater mobility, is a major factor behind the massive dispersion outward. In summary, this most recent period tends to show an intensification of the forces of concentration, dispersion, and segregation. For the first time the central core has powerful competition from plazas near the edge of the city along expressway routes. Plazas seem to be clusters of business activities that are also part of a massive dispersion of the city into the countryside. With regard to residential activity, the poor still seem to be concentrated in the inner-city, while the wealthier, having greater freedom to choose, tend to locate in redeveloped older sections and,

Fig. 4-4
A "hold-out". The lots behind this home were purchased by a developer who demolished the houses and built an apartment building.

most commonly, on the edge of the expanding city. Industry is still tied to investments along the waterfront and along railroads. But, in general, industry has moved to sites along highways and in industrial parks on the edge of the city.

CONCLUSIONS

The forces that shape a city include concentration of many activities on small sections of land. With various developments in transportation the central concentration of business activities can be maintained and enlarged. Such desirable locations are in great demand by retail firms and there is great competition for space. Usually the activity which can pay the required rent obtains the space. The exceptions to this rule occur in cities where social problems have made the CBD less attractive.

As the community organizes its activities, certain areas tend to develop special functions such as commercial, industrial, residential, and institutional districts. These areas are usually separated from each other, or segregated. The pattern the segregated sections will take depends on a number of factors. These include: the ability to compete for desirable space; the amount of space the activity needs; transportation and other facilities; the special needs of the population for their private space; the nature of the government's plans and laws to regulate the urban environment; and the cycle of deterioration in housing and manufacturing.

The city as a whole is being pulled in two directions at the same time. First, it is being pulled together as a tight package, usually around one or two central concentrations. This may result in a vertical movement as well. Second, it is being pulled apart or outward by increasing mobility, decay, and crime in the central area, and skyrocketing land costs. In the end, the man-made landscape of Greenville and other communities will be a mirror of man's attitudes. How man chooses to use these forces will be reflected in the urban landscape.

For Thought and Research

1   Describe and give an example of the processes of concentration, segregation, and dispersion.
2   Explain why each resale of a land parcel leads to a more intensive use of that land.
3   Identify and illustrate the major factors that create a concentration of commercial activities in the central area of a growing town.
4   Why did concentration remain the dominant force shaping Greenville and other communities almost until the Second World War?
5   Show how developments in manufacturing over the years illustrate the forces of concentration, segregation, and dispersion.

6 Explain why commercial nuclei (usually plazas) outside the CBD are able to compete with the CBD for customers.

7 How does the development of shopping centers illustrate the processes of concentration and dispersion?

8 Describe the cycle of deterioration as it relates to housing in a city.

9 Explain how the poor can live on the most valuable land while the rich live on less valuable land.

10 New inventions such as the telephone, railroad, automobile, and, more recently, commercial airplanes are changing the accessibility pattern of the city and, therefore, the man-made landscape. Discuss.

Recommended Readings

1 *The North American City* by M. Yeates and B. Garner, Harper and Row, 1971, pp. 213-398. This includes a good discussion on changes arising out of the development of the automobile.

2 *The Canadian City* by J. N. Jackson, McGraw-Hill Ryerson, 1973. This includes the foundations and evolution of the Canadian urban pattern, the historical components of urban analysis, and the Central Business District.

3 *Urbanism in World Perspective* edited by S. F. Fava, Thomas Y. Crowell, 1968. This is an advanced-level book dealing with urban theory from a comparative viewpoint.

4 *My Neighbor* by J. S. Woodsworth, University of Toronto Press, 1972. The modern city and the making of a city are included.

5 *The Geography of Urban Places* edited by R. G. Putnam, F. J. Taylor and P. G. Kettle, Methuen, 1970. A number of good articles dealing with aspects of urban landscapes are mentioned in this section.

4.2   THEORIES OF URBAN STRUCTURE

The internal structure of the city is very complex because the city is created by complex beings. Thus, in order fully to appreciate the city's structure and form, we must be aware of its origin and the effects of this origin. We must also be aware of its growth, function, physical site, and the human interactions that have created it.

In order to help us understand the complex urban landscape, researchers have developed *theories* or *models*. A model is basically a simplification of the real world; it does not show all the variations that exist in reality. For example, a map is a model. It shows an area of the earth's surface and, depending upon the purpose of the map, certain characteristics about that area. A model of the urban landscape performs the same function. It may be thought of as a tool used to develop explanations for characteristics that we observe. These explanations can then be tested to see if, in fact, they are suitable.

During this discussion of models of urban structure keep in mind that we use them to help us understand reality. However, since they simplify reality, they cannot explain all the variations. In fact, a model may not apply to all situations. As a result it may have to be discarded. When this happens, a new model is often created.

Most academic disciplines develop models in order to aid our understanding. Researchers of the urban landscape, following this tradition, developed three models during the first half of the twentieth century. They were developed to help understand urban structure and urban growth. Let us examine these in chronological order.

THE CONCENTRIC-ZONE THEORY

In 1925 Ernest Burgess, an urban sociologist working in Chicago, developed a theory to describe the development of a city. Burgess viewed the city as growing outward in the form of five concentric rings (Fig. 4-5).

Assumptions (upon which the theory is based)

a) The city grows outward in the form of five concentric zones or rings as long as there are no physical barriers such as rivers or hills to distort the pattern.

b) The city has a single center.

c) Growth is accomplished by a simple extension of each zone outward into the next zone.

Characteristics

The five zones can be described as follows:

ZONE 1: THE CENTRAL BUSINESS DISTRICT. The Central Business District is the heart of the urban community. It is here that the major commercial, social, and civic activities are concentrated. Burgess saw the Central Business District (CBD) as consisting of two parts. The heart of the district is characterized by office buildings, department stores, theaters, hotels, banks, and civic government buildings. In large cities each of these activities has its own distinctive district whereas in smaller communities these activities are all mixed together. Outside this heart or downtown core there is a district comprised of warehouses and light industry.

ZONE 2: THE TRANSITION ZONE. Surrounding the Central Business District is a zone of residential decay called the Transition Zone. It is a zone in transition because central business activities and factories mix and invade an area of aging residential dwellings. While some old buildings may be beautifully preserved, most are allowed to deteriorate because the owner, who may not live there, is waiting to sell his valuable space to the invading CBD activities.

Because the area is in a state of decay it is often the site of an urban slum. Low-income groups are crowded together into run-

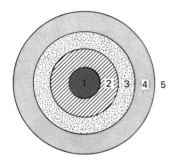

Fig. 4-5
The concentric zone theory.
Zone 1: Central Business District
Zone 2: Transition zone
Zone 3: Zone of independent
       workingmen's homes
Zone 4: Zone of better
       residences
Zone 5: Commuter zone

down flats and tenements. In many cities this is the area where newly arrived immigrants tend to live. During the early part of the twentieth century millions of European immigrants first experienced life in the New World from the transition zone. The poor and the new immigrants live in this area because the rents are low and because they are probably living close to where they work. Many unskilled workers are able to find jobs in the factories and warehouses scattered in the CBD. Also their transportation costs to and from work are kept to a minimum.

The poverty and crowded conditions found in this area of the city create a breeding ground for social disorganization and crime. A large proportion of the families living in this area are unstable and many end up in the divorce courts. In addition, this is the area where we find a large number of transients: the hobos, drifters, and bums who travel from one city's skid row to another.

ZONE 3: THE ZONE OF INDEPENDENT WORKINGMEN'S HOMES. This third zone is inhabited by blue-collar workers who have worked their way out of the zone of transition. Often these people are second-generation immigrants who have adapted to the North American culture and who have sufficient money to purchase their own homes. By living in this area of the city the workers are able to live within easy access of their work and yet benefit from the better housing conditions that are found beyond the zone of transition. Although the residential buildings are old, they are in a better state of repair than in zone 2 and there is less crowding. Most of the families live in their own homes rather than in tenements. Within this zone the family groups are more stable, there are fewer transients, and the crime rate is lower than in the zone of transition.

ZONE 4: THE ZONE OF BETTER RESIDENCES. Farther from the CBD is found an area of better homes. It is here that we find a large area of middle-class homes and small pockets of upper-class residences and apartment buildings. The homes in this zone are newer and more spacious than those in the third zone. While single-family homes are most common, apartment buildings and small business centers develop at strategic points such as street corners, main thoroughfares, and public transportation routes. This zone is approximately 15-20 min by public transit from zone 1.

ZONE 5: THE COMMUTER ZONE. This outer zone encircles the city and lies beyond its continuous built-up areas. Much of the zone is still open space and is often located beyond the city limits. Here small villages, surrounded by open country, gradually become dormitory towns or suburbs. A dormitory town is so called because the people who have their homes there actually work and find their entertainment in the large city. Because most people who live in the commuter zone work in the CBD, this zone is located within one hour's traveling time from the center of the city. Thus, good transportation facilities to the city are essential for the people who live in the bungalows on large spacious lots in the commuter zone.

Summary. Burgess emphasized the outward growth of the city so that each zone is not static. As the demand for more space increases, both industry and people move outward in a process of *invasion* and *succession*. Usually a ripple pattern originates in the oldest central ring. Business activities expand into the transition zone which forces low-income groups to move outward. This group then displaces the middle class and wealthy who, in turn, are forced to move outward.

THE SECTOR THEORY

In 1939 Homer Hoyt, a land economist, developed a theory based upon his studies of residential land rent. He discovered that many cities grow in sectors or wedges radiating outward from the CBD along major transportation routes (Fig. 4-6).

Assumptions

a) The city grows outward from the Central Business District.

b) A particular type of land use develops near the CBD and migrates outward to form a pattern composed of sectors.

c) Growth is toward open ground and the homes of community leaders.

d) Growth extends along the fastest transportation routes creating a star-shaped city.

Characteristics

Hoyt discovered that, once a type of land use was established near the city center (even if by chance), that type of land use tended to remain on that particular side of the CBD and grow outward in an expanding wedge or sector along a major transportation artery. For example, after an upper-class residential district has been established on one side of the CBD it will grow outward along a transportation route. This transportation route provides fast access to the CBD for the residents of this sector. In addition, since the wealthy are able to afford the best residential land they select areas of high ground or ravine lots that have a beautiful view and are away from the noise and air pollution of industry. On the other hand, the poorer residents of the city, who are less able to afford these good residential sites and who seek areas close to where they work, will tend to locate in a sector adjacent to an industrial sector or close to the CBD. At the same time, middle-income groups locate in sectors adjacent to high-income areas. In effect, the middle-income areas act as buffer zones between the upper- and lower-income areas.

As the wealthy move toward the outer edge of the city, they vacate the older homes found adjacent to the CBD (see the broken

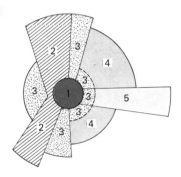

Fig. 4-6
The sector theory. Land uses develop around the CBD and expand outward in pie-shaped wedges or sectors.

Area 1: Central Business District
Sector 2: Wholesale light manufacturing
Sector 3: Low-income residential
Sector 4: Middle-income residential
Sector 5: High-income residential

line in Fig. 4-6). These older homes are then subdivided and occupied by lower-income groups. This process of old homes, formerly occupied by the wealthy, being gradually taken over by lower-income groups is called *filtering*. The homes filter downward in terms of the class of people that occupy them.

Summary. It is felt by many that Hoyt's model is an improvement upon Burgess's model because it takes into account both the distance and the direction of growth of the city in relation to the CBD. In addition, Hoyt pays attention to the effects of the transportation system on the development of the urban landscape.

THE MULTIPLE-NUCLEI THEORY

In 1945 two geographers, Chauncy Harris and Edward Ullman, developed a theory that would take into account new urban forms ushered in by the widespread use of the automobile. In addition, they wanted to create a more flexible model that would account for spatial arrangements not considered in the two previous theories (see Fig. 4-7).

They felt that several factors, not previously taken into account, should be given more consideration. For example, *site* should be considered because it can play an important role in the development and growth of an urban area. An upper-class residential area may develop away from the CBD because of a favorable setting. Thus, an upper-class district may not develop outward in a sector pattern as Hoyt said it would. In the same way, an industrial area may develop because of the availability of a large amount of flat land close to a harbor.

Urban structure may reflect an irregular and unpredictable pattern and thus not conform to the strict rules established in the Concentric Zone or Sector Theories. It may be predictable, however, in that we know the rich tend to select scenic areas and open space while industry tends to develop on flat open areas that are often poorly drained. This is a theory of tendencies based partly on site and partly on man's needs.

In addition to the site, Harris and Ullman felt that *historical* factors should be given more consideration. In London, England, for example, the area around the medieval commercial core has remained to this day as a center or nucleus of financial activities. The area around Westminster has provided the traditional focus for political administration. Generally speaking, they felt that whenever a nucleus develops it tends to remain a focus of activity.

Assumptions

a) In many cities the land-use pattern is built up around several growth points or nuclei.

b) In some cities these nuclei have existed since the city

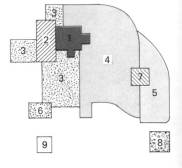

Fig. 4-7
The multiple nuclei theory.
1: Central Business District
2: Wholesale light manufacturing
3: Low-income residential
4: Middle-income residential
5: High-income residential
6: Heavy manufacturing
7: Outlying business district
8: Residential suburb
9: Industrial suburb

was founded while others develop as the city grows.

    c) The city has a cellular structure.

Characteristics

The urban landscape develops a structure resembling a cluster of cells each of which has distinctive characteristics. These cells have at their heart a growth point or nucleus. As noted, there are basically two types of nuclei. The first type develops at the beginning of the city's growth. These nuclei remain as growth develops in the spaces around them. The second type of nuclei develops after the initial growth of the city. These include new industrial parks on the edge of the city, suburban shopping plazas, outlying office complexes, or an airport.

There are four major factors that encourage specialist land uses to group around the nuclei. These factors influence the distribution of human activity in the city. The four factors are as follows:

CERTAIN ACTIVITIES REQUIRE SPECIALIZED FACILITIES. Activities that require the specialized facilities of a port will be drawn to the harbor area of a city in order to make use of the facilities. Heavy industry, which requires a large amount of flat cheap land, will locate where this type of land is available. Warehouses and light industries will locate on inexpensive land with good accessibility to clients. Commercial activities are attracted to the CBD and other highly accessible points in the city within easy reach of large numbers of customers.

CERTAIN ACTIVITIES GROUP TOGETHER BECAUSE THEY BENEFIT FROM COHESION. Financial and office-type activities group together in order to communicate easily with each other. Many types of retail outlets benefit from grouping together because this concentration of activity attracts large numbers of potential customers. However, not all retail outlets benefit from grouping together. Small grocery stores may in fact try to avoid competition.

CERTAIN ACTIVITIES ARE UNABLE TO AFFORD THE HIGH RENTS OF THE MOST DESIRABLE SITES. The poor, who are not able to compete with the wealthy for the best residential locations, may be forced to live in a decaying or aging section of the city. Activities such as wholesaling and storage of bulky items require great amounts of space at a low cost. Retail outlets such as pawn shops, second-hand clothing shops, and used-furniture shops also locate in less desirable areas because of their owners' inability to pay the high rents of the more desirable locations.

CERTAIN ACTIVITIES ARE DETRIMENTAL TO EACH OTHER. Upper-class residential districts avoid industrial areas because of the noise and air pollution. In addition, areas of wholesaling and storage, which require street-loading facilities, do not locate where pedestrian and auto traffic are found. The high degree of crowding that would result would be detrimental to the efficient operation of these types of activities.

Summary. Because the Multiple-Nuclei Theory was developed at a later date than the previous two theories it incorporates changes brought about by the widespread use of the automobile. The outlying business districts or shopping plazas grew up with the development of residential suburbs and both were made possible by the increased mobility provided by the automobile. In addition, with so many people living in the suburbs, it was not long before industry began developing in suburban industrial parks close to where the employees lived. These industrial parks are areas set aside and serviced for industrial activities.

Although the Multiple-Nuclei Theory describes the city as cellular in structure, it does not rule out the possibility that some areas may exhibit a concentric or sectoral pattern. For example, around the various nuclei activities may develop in a concentric pattern or along a major traffic artery in a sector arrangement.

The flexibility of this theory allows it to consider all three patterns: concentric, sector, and cellular. However, because it is so flexible and because it does consider the individual site characteristics and historical development of each city, it is not able to present a rigid generalization about urban form. As a result, perhaps this theory should be considered more as a guide to thought rather than a rigid model of urban structure.

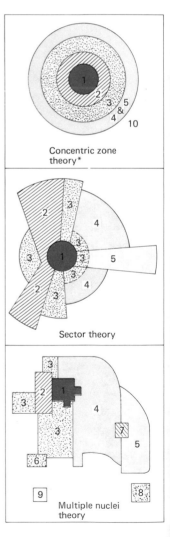

Concentric zone theory*

Sector theory

Multiple nuclei theory

COMMENTS ON THE THEORIES

As mentioned earlier these models simplify what is found in our cities (Fig. 4-8). Because they are not able to consider all the variations, each model does have drawbacks in terms of its application. Let us briefly examine some of the criticisms directed toward these models of urban structure.

Concentric-Zone Theory. Burgess's theory has been criticized as being too simple. In other words, it is so generalized that it does not take into account many important variations within the city. For example, many variations in land use will exist within each zone. Thus, a zone described as consisting of workingmen's homes will have factory districts, commercial areas, and areas of middle-class housing. These are not accounted for by Burgess. In addition, most CBD's are not circular in shape nor do factory districts completely surround the CBD in most cities. Because cities tend to grow outward along major transportation routes, they develop in a star-shaped rather than concentric pattern. Burgess's theory also fails to consider the development of outlying commercial areas such as shopping plazas and the industrial and manufacturing districts located around airports. Of course, these developments have taken place since Burgess developed this theory during the 1920s. Despite these and other drawbacks, the Concentric-Zone Theory can be loosely applied to many cities and it does aid us in understanding some patterns that can be observed in the urban landscape.

Sector Theory. When Hoyt first brought out his theory it was criticized as being too economic in nature. The theory failed to recognize the non-rational behavior of people and the element of choice. For example, an upper-class residential district may grow up and continue to exist in a particular part of a city for social reasons rather than because of its location. Since the wealthy are able to afford to live anywhere in the city, they may not follow the pattern established by Hoyt. On the other hand, lower-income groups, which do not have the same freedom of choice, may fit better into the sector pattern.

More recently criticisms have arisen as a result of changes in technology and social conditions. In terms of technology, the expressways that now encircle most large cities have opened up large areas beyond the built-up parts of the cities. This region is being developed for upper-class housing with the result that the pattern is not in the form of sectors radiating outward from the city. At the same time, social values are changing, with the result that middle- and upper-income groups are moving back into the city's downtown areas. Houses that have been occupied by low-income groups are refurbished and sold to upper-income groups.

Multiple-Nuclei Theory. Because this theory considers so many individual characteristics about each city, such as site and historical factors, it cannot present a rigid model for all cities. Rather, it is seen as a guide. Although this model has been the most well-received, it has been criticized for assuming that all cities originate and grow from one central nucleus or CBD. Many of today's large metropolises developed when several towns grew together. There are, therefore, several major growing centers. This theory, in addition to the other two theories, has been criticized for considering only ground-floor activities. All three fail to take into account the types of activities found in modern multi-storey buildings.

Summary of the Theories of Urban Structure. Burgess viewed the city as a series of concentric zones with the CBD at the center surrounded by industry and then by residential zones that formed ever-increasing circles outward into the countryside. Hoyt concentrated on residential development and discovered that, as the city grows, land uses that develop around the CBD have a tendency to grow outward in a unique way. This outward growth of particular land uses is in the form of sectors that grow up in various parts of the city along major transportation routes.

Both the Concentric-Zone Theory and Sector Theory were developed before the widespread use of the automobile. The automobile has provided urban dwellers with a greater degree of

Fig. 4-8
Summary of the three models of urban structure.
Areas of Land Use:
1: Central Business District
2: Wholesale light manufacturing (In the concentric zone theory this type of land use is found at the outer edge of the CBD and in the transition zone.)
3: Low-income residential (workingmen's homes in the concentric theory)
4: Middle-income residential
5: High-income residential
6: Heavy manufacturing
7: Outlying business district
8: Residential suburb
9: Industrial suburb
10: Commuter zone (concentric zone theory)

(Note: numbers have been changed in the concentric zone theory diagram in order to compare the land use structure in all three theories.)

freedom and mobility than either Burgess or Hoyt could have foreseen. Our dependence on the automobile and the resulting road and expressway development have caused distortions in the original models.

In an attempt to describe the effects of the automobile and to account for the changes taking place in our cities, the Multiple-Nuclei Theory was developed. The city was viewed as consisting of several growing points or nuclei, each of which grew up as a response to changing human needs.

Recent studies have indicated that we must not discard any of these theories. In fact, elements of all three help to describe the internal structure of our North American cities. Each model describes a distinctive pattern, and each pattern can be found in the urban landscape. Therefore, instead of thinking one model is better than another, we must consider them as complementing each other. Each one describes characteristics that, when added together, give a reasonably good idea of what is occurring in our cities.

Research is currently being directed toward a greater understanding of the structural development and growth of our ever-changing urban areas. With the help of high-speed computers hundreds of variables are being analyzed and correlated in search of a greater understanding and appreciation of the complexities of the urban scene. If different patterns can be found from these investigations of the changing urban form, then possibly a new model of urban growth will emerge in the future.

For Thought and Research

1 a) What does the term "model" mean?
   b) Why do models have drawbacks?
   c) Why are models created?
2 a) Upon what assumptions did Burgess base his theory?
   b) List the characteristics of each zone in the Concentric-Zone Theory.
   c) How do the zones grow?
3 a) Upon what assumptions did Hoyt base his theory?
   b) Describe the characteristics of the Sector Theory.
4 a) Why did Harris and Ullman develop the Multiple-Nuclei Theory?
   b) Why should site characteristics and historical factors be considered in the study of urban structure?
   c) What are the assumptions upon which the Multiple-Nuclei Theory is based?
   d) Describe the four factors that encourage specialist land uses to group around nuclei.
   e) Describe the changes that occurred in urban structure as a result of the widespread use of the automobile.
   f) Of what use is this theory if it does not present a rigid model of urban form?
5 Briefly describe the criticisms directed toward each theory.
6 Why can we not discard any one of these theories?

Recommended Readings

1 *Urban Geography* by J. H. Johnson, Pergamon Press, 1967. The theories of urban structure are discussed in Chapter 9.

2 *The American City* by R. E. Murphy, McGraw-Hill, 1974. Chapter 12 presents an indepth examination of the three theories of urban structure. This book has a companion exercise manual, *Exercises in Urban Geography* by R. E. Murphy, McGraw-Hill, 1968. See Exercise 10, "Theoretical Explanations of City Structures." This exercise demonstrates the models of urban structure using three American cities.

3 *Urbanism in World Perspective* edited by S. F. Fava, Thomas Y. Crowell, 1968. Urban ecological patterns are reviewed in Chapter 2.

4 *Urban Residential Patterns* by R. J. Johnston, McGraw-Hill, 1973. Chapter 8 discusses urban land-use studies.

5 *The Canadian City* by J. N. Jackson, McGraw-Hill, 1973. See Chapter 8.

6 *A Geography of Urban Places* edited by R. G. Putnam, F. J. Taylor, and P. G. Kettle, Methuen, 1970. Several relevant articles are presented in Section A.

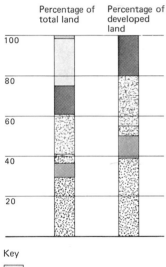

Percentage of total land / Percentage of developed land

Key

 Under water

Vacant

Other public

Road and highway

Commercial

Industrial

Residential

Fig. 4-9
Average use of land in 48 large American cities.

4.3   LAND USES IN THE CITY

We have seen from Section 4.2 that cities develop a recognizable structure or arrangement of land uses. We can now look more closely at some of the main land uses in cities—where people live, work, and do business.

Figure 4-9 shows that residential uses occupy the largest percentage of the urban land area, while the very important commercial areas occupy little space. Many people do not realize how much city land is covered by roads and other transportation systems.

Cities tend to have similar patterns of land use. Drive into almost any North American city. You will pass through a zone of motels, drive-in restaurants, and shopping centers. You will probably continue through a typical suburban residential area or perhaps through a modern industrial district. Before reaching the distinctive downtown area of tall buildings you will probably also notice zones of older housing and businesses.

This pattern is a common one because land uses in every city are influenced by similar factors. Land value is one of the major determinants of land use. The sprawling homes and single-storey industrial buildings of the suburbs are possible because of cheap land, while only tall buildings can profitably use expensive downtown space. However, land value itself is determined by a mixture of other factors such as accessibility, competition, and the type and density of land uses allowed by local zoning ordinances. Can you imagine how all these factors would work to change land value? Imagine the case of a newly constructed expressway interchange on the outskirts of the city.

Physical features also have an important influence on land use. For instance, hilltop locations are often taken for upper-income homes, and waterfront land is often used for heavy industry. Social factors are reflected in the local reputations of certain neighborhoods as prestigious or crime-ridden. These reputations will have a definite effect on land values and uses. Age is another factor often reflected in land use; newer suburbs have very different housing and shopping patterns from the older, pre-automobile districts. In every city all these factors will be at work, in varying degrees, to produce distinctive land-use patterns.

INDUSTRIAL LAND USE IN THE CITY

With the exception of a few specialized-function cities, industrial districts are a common feature of most urban centers. These industrial districts can be categorized into four main types on the basis of their location, scale of activity, age, market location, and raw-material and labor supply. Figure 4-10 illustrates their relative positions within a hypothetical city.

Manufacturing Industries near the CBD. In many cases one of the oldest and best-established industrial districts is found on the fringe of the Central Business District. Factories locate here for several reasons. Since this part of the city is usually close to working-class residential areas an abundant source of low-cost, often immigrant, labor is assured. Also, the businesses that locate there, such as the garment trades, job printers, and food processors, find an advantage in having close contacts with wholesalers, shippers, and warehousemen. The accessibility of the central location is also an advantage for the distribution of the products from these factories.

Location in this area is not without its problems, however. Congested streets and high rents make the downtown area less than perfect. In addition, the old multi-storey buildings of this area are ill-suited for modern industrial use. Thus costs rise.

Manufacturing District on the Waterfront. Almost any city located on an ocean, a lake, or a navigable river will have a major industrial district on the waterfront. Most of the factories in this area, such as flour mills, iron and steel works, cement plants, and oil refineries, are dependent upon raw materials that are bulky and non-local in origin. These materials are brought in by water or by rail in order to minimize costs. It is important to remember that not all the industries in the waterfront area need a location on navigable water. Many industries that create noise, dirt, or bad odors are forced into this area by municipal zoning regulations designed to restrict these industries to a section of the city away from residential and, to a lesser extent, commercial areas.

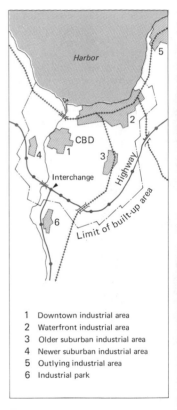

1 Downtown industrial area
2 Waterfront industrial area
3 Older suburban industrial area
4 Newer suburban industrial area
5 Outlying industrial area
6 Industrial park

Fig. 4-10
Location of industrial districts in a hypothetical city.

Several problems are encountered when one examines the waterfront manufacturing area. In most cases the city has completely encircled the waterfront district so that expansion is difficult or impossible. In many cities the residents have decided that ocean-, lake-, or river-front land in such an accessible area (usually at or near the city's center) is far too valuable for industrial use and would be better used for parks or housing. As a result, some waterfront industries are being relocated to outlying areas where large amounts of cheap land are available.

Suburban Manufacturing Areas. The largest number of factories in most cities is found in what are now, or were, suburban areas. The factories are normally small to moderate in size and are involved with what is called _light fabrication_. Older examples of this type of area are generally rail-oriented, while newer ones are usually road-related. When properly controlled by building codes and zoning ordinances, such areas can be of benefit to the city. They allow employment to be spread out and thus reduce pressure on the transportation system.

A special type of suburban industrial district is the prestige manufacturing area. Firms that produce low-bulk, high-value products such as computers, pharmaceuticals, and electronic devices often have beautifully designed, carefully landscaped factory-offices that enhance the companies' public relations image and beautify the neighborhood.

A recent development, mainly in the suburbs, is the industrial plaza. It is like a shopping plaza except that small manufacturing and wholesaling companies occupy the units. The companies share such expenses as heating and building maintenance so that costs are reduced. The industrial plaza is a benefit to the city since, if it is well-designed, it is an efficient use of land.

Outlying Industrial Areas. Some industries require so much land that it is impractical for them to locate in the city itself. Therefore they must find land beyond the limits of the city. Such industries as automobile assembly plants and iron and steel mills can require over 1 000 ha of land. They locate in areas where cheap flat land is available and access to suitable water, rail, or road transportation is available. When one such factory locates in an area it attracts its suppliers and sometimes its customers to the area, forming an industrial district.

The industrial park is a relatively recent type of industrial area found outside the city. It is a carefully planned industrial development designed so that the companies which locate there will have ease of transportation, efficient services, and cheap, available land for expansion. They are usually several hundred to a few thousand hectares in size and can be planned to be in harmony with the local area.

TRANSPORTATION LAND USE IN THE CITY

A surprisingly large amount of the land in a city is used for transportation. If housing, industry, and commerce are the flesh of a city, then the roads and other transportation networks are the circulatory system. Unfortunately the transportation systems of many of our cities are suffering from an advanced case of hardening of the arteries. In many cities the time required to travel 15 km in the rush hour is greater than it was in 1890, even though the automobile, bus, and subway have been invented. North American urban leaders are wrestling with the problem of deciding what form city transportation should take in the years to come.

Roads. The most basic element of any city's transportation system is its roads. There are several types of roads, as indicated in Table 5. Different cities have different criteria for classification but those presented in Table 5 should be typical of most cities.

TABLE 5   TYPICAL STANDARDS FOR CLASSIFYING ROADS

Type of road	Width of right-of-way	Function	Access and intersection characteristics	Speed limits
Freeway	50 m or more	To carry large volumes of traffic long distances at high speed	Access from other freeways or arterials; grade-separated inter-changes	90 km/h or more
Arterial	23 m to 45 m	To carry moderate to large amounts of traffic short to medium distances; to link collectors to freeways	Grade-separated interchanges with freeways; inter-sections with collectors	55 to 90 km/h
Collector	20 m to 25 m	To carry light or moderate amounts of traffic from local roads or point of origin to arterial system	Intersections with arterials and local roads	45 to 65 km/h
Local	up to 20 m	To carry light amounts of traffic from point of origin to collectors	Intersections with collectors	35 to 55 km/h

There are a number of reasons why transportation planners think in terms of not one but four complementary road systems. Obviously there is a desire to speed people on their journeys. Equally obvious is the fact that it would be impossible and undesirable for all of the roads in the city to be freeways. Few people would want cars driving by their homes at 100 km/h. Pedestrian safety is an important factor. Freeways owe their relatively high speeds to

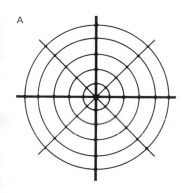

A

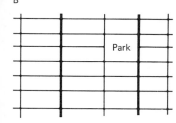

B

Park

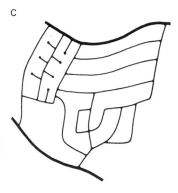

C

Fig. 4-11
Road patterns: A, radial-concentric; B, grid; C, garden.

their limited access, no stop signs or stop lights, overpasses, and interchanges. These take up room and are very expensive to build. On the other hand, not all roads could be of the local or collector types since a cross-town trip could take an hour or more in a moderately sized city. A balance of types must be reached.

The four types of roads that make up the street system can be arranged in two basic ways. The first of these is the *radial-concentric pattern* which consists of major roads radiating out from a central point, together with concentric circular roads around the central point (Fig. 4-11). Many of the great cities of the world including Washington, Paris, and London were laid out on this pattern during a classic period of urban design which died out with the Industrial Revolution in America in the mid-1800s. The radial-concentric pattern can result in a beautiful city with natural foci of attention at central points of the pattern. In a small town this might be the town hall or a park; in Washington, D.C., which is made up of several modified linked radial-concentric units, such buildings as the Capitol and Washington Monument are located at pattern centers.

The latter part of the nineteenth century was a time of practicality in American life. Unnecessary frills were eliminated, including the beautiful radial-concentric road pattern. In its place came the practical but generally unattractive *grid pattern* (Fig. 4-11). The grid pattern moves traffic efficiently since there are no points of congestion such as the focal points in the radial-concentric patterns.

The grid pattern also encouraged lots and buildings with right-angled corners. This is efficient but it caused monotony within the city. In fact, in cities with grid street patterns, points of interest are created where streets deviate from the pattern.

A third type of road pattern is found in the local and collector roads of some post-World War II suburbs. In areas like this, vehicle speed is secondary to such considerations as pedestrian safety, neighborhood quiet, and attractiveness. The result is the *garden pattern* which forces cars to slow down and produces quiet, attractive, cul-de-sacs and crescents (Fig. 4-11).

Mass Transit. Mass transit takes many forms in the city. These include subways, buses, streetcars, and commuter railways. It can be divided into two types according to whether or not a separate right-of-way is required. Generally buses and streetcars use ordinary streets and roads while subways and commuter trains operate on rights-of-way of their own.

Buses and streetcars do not operate efficiently on streets and roads, however. Traffic jams and turning cars slow transit vehicles, while the stopping of buses and streetcars, combined with streetcar tracks, obstruct cars. A solution to this problem is restricted bus lanes, and streetcar routes isolated from car and truck traffic.

Other Transportation Land Uses. Other types of transportation are important users of land in the city. Train terminals and bus stations do not take up a significant percentage of the city's land but both require an accessible location, usually near the city's center. In addition, rail lines, both for passengers and freight, together with rail yards, take up considerable space and, more important, divide the city into districts.

Often we tend to ignore a very important transportation land use in the city—parking lots. In most cities, a significant proportion of the downtown area is used for this purpose.

A land use that is taking up an increasing amount of the city is airports. With the advent of the jumbo jet and air travel by the masses, the need for large efficient airports has increased. These new superports, such as the ones at Dallas and Montreal, cost hundreds of millions of dollars and require thousands of hectares of land. They are so large that they must be placed as much as 80 km from the city center. Thus transportation to and from the airport becomes a problem. In some cities the trip from city center to airport at each end of a 500 km flight can take longer than the flight itself.

Transportation in the Future. The transportation scene in most cities is both confused and complicated. What happens to transportation will, to a large extent, determine what will happen to the future of many cities. There are a number of questions facing the planners and politicians of most cities. Should the transportation emphasis be placed on expressways or on mass transit? Should new airports be built or should other inter-city transport systems, such as fast trains and STOL aircraft, be developed? How, and at what cost, can pollution by automobiles be reduced? Can a less expensive alternative to subways be found? Should the civic government try to prevent people from driving downtown? If so, how?

RESIDENTIAL LAND USE IN THE CITY

Residential land-use patterns have been the basis for many of the models of city structure. Burgess's Concentric-Zone Theory (Section 4.2) describes a progressive improvement in homes from the blighted zone of transition to the better residences and well-to-do commuters' homes on the outskirts of town. Hoyt concentrated on the sectoral characteristics of certain residential types, particularly upper-income housing. However, both of these models pre-dated the post-war boom of suburbia, which is based on the automobile. Therefore, they do not present a total picture of residential patterns, even when combined.

One of the major aspects of residential life in modern North American cities is the division between city and suburb. This division arises because of the gap in construction dates. Many city areas consist of older housing stock, which was built to contain the higher population densities of the compact nineteenth and early twentieth-century city. The suburbs are relatively new and car-oriented. In the United States, many city areas have become increasingly black, as the white middle class has migrated to the suburbs. New York is the classic example of a city facing tremendous problems because of its old, run-down, and overcrowded housing districts and the accompanying social and racial difficulties. Many old slum dwellings in the city have been replaced by public housing. However, these urban-renewal projects have largely failed to solve the problems of the slums they replaced.

On the other hand, the suburbs are not without their own problems. Suburbia has often been criticized for monotony, with rows of identical houses occupied by almost identical families with young children. The life of the suburban housewife has been described as boring and isolated. A group of houses built all at one time does not constitute a community, especially if the developers neglected to include a park or other community recreational facilities. Suburban communities are characterized by low densities, with houses often occupying as much as 5 000 m² of land. These large lots are often made necessary by restrictive zoning laws which help to maintain class and race distinctions by making it almost impossible for poorer people to build homes in the area. The suburbs, which according to the 1970 American census now contain 36% of the population of the country (more than city areas), are still the home of young, car-owning, largely white middle-class families in single detached dwellings.

It is evident that housing characteristics reflect a complex mixture of factors, including the age of the housing, land value, zoning, and social processes such as racial segregation and changing family sizes. At present, the factor of changing family sizes has

Fig. 4-12
Apartment developments such as this have helped to add variety to suburbia.

had a direct effect in causing a boom in apartment construction. This has happened because the post-war baby boom has now resulted in large numbers of young adults. With the lower birth rates and larger numbers of working women, housing demand has shifted toward apartment life. Apartments now represent between one-third and one-half of new dwelling units constructed. Moreover, apartments are being built in the suburbs, which seems unusual to people used to the traditional central city location for these buildings (Fig. 4-12). New high-rise complexes are being built where accessibility is greatest, such as on vacant land near expressway interchanges or on redeveloped land near the city center. This trend to apartment construction is especially pronounced in Canadian cities such as the rapidly growing Metropolitan Toronto. What trends are evident in your city?

COMMERCIAL LAND USE IN THE CITY

The small percentage of city land occupied by commercial land use (usually 4-5%) is not a true indicator of the importance of these retail, wholesale, service, and financial establishments. Commercial areas are found in every part of the city. Geographers have studied commercial land uses within cities, and generally recognize three types of commercial areas: centers, ribbons, and specialized areas. A widely accepted chart of the components of the urban business pattern is shown in Figure 4-13.

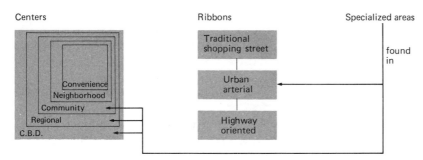

Fig. 4-13
Major elements of the urban business pattern.

    Centers. The pattern of business centers very closely resembles the central-place hierarchy among towns and cities in a rural area (see Section 2.4). This resemblance can be explained by the fact that both hierarchies are based on the shopping patterns of people. For example, the population served by a small town is similar to the number of people served by a neighborhood plaza and both will have stores that need only a low threshold population. Therefore, in the hierarchy of business centers, as in central places, we also find that, as centers increase in size and trade area, their numbers generally decrease.

    The lowest level in the hierarchy is made up of the small

street-corner shops serving immediate necessities. This convenience center contains, for example, a milk store and a smoke shop. At the next level is the neighborhood plaza containing such stores as a supermarket, bakery, barber shop, and beauty salon. These stores have a low threshold population, usually found within a few blocks. Store types that require a larger threshold population, such as a jeweler, a florist, or a small department store, will be found in community shopping centers. Most general shopping needs can be satisfied in plazas of this level. Community plazas can be found at major street intersections.

Of course, the larger business centers contain all the types of stores and activities found in the smaller centers. Thus, at the regional plaza, which is the largest plaza type, we find hardware stores and bakeries as well as the specialized stores requiring a high threshold population. Store types unique to these regional centers include bookstores, major department stores, and music stores. Some of the biggest suburban plazas of this type now offer strong competition for the CBD, since they offer over 100 stores as well as cultural attractions such as theaters. Also, they are at easily accessible locations such as expressway interchanges, and provide huge parking lots. Nevertheless, the highest level of the business center hierarchy is the CBD, which is the focus not only of the entire city but of the city's hinterland as well.

You may have noticed that this hierarchy of business centers does not seem to fit your community. You may live, for instance, in a new car-oriented suburb where the planners decided to eliminate the street-corner convenience stores in favor of more neighborhood plazas. Such an area may have only the top three levels of business centers. On the other hand, a low-income neighborhood may not have the income necessary to support specialized stores in a community or regional plaza and may, instead, have more of the lower-order centers. In this area there will be more convenience shops and neighborhood plazas featuring second-hand stores. As with most classification systems, this hierarchy represents only the average situation.

Ribbon or Strip Development. Commercial ribbons or strips of businesses along both sides of the street have always been present in cities. The shopping streets of older residential districts that developed along streetcar lines still exist. Usually, the type of store found on these traditional shopping streets is similar to those in convenience and neighborhood plazas, with grocery stores, bakeries, beauty salons, and cleaners. In some neighborhoods these ribbons may take on a particular ethnic character reflecting the surrounding population (for example, Chinatown). In some run-down areas, these streets become skid rows, with many bars, liquor stores, and rooming houses.

In newer, more car-oriented parts of the city we find urban arterial ribbons. Here businesses take advantage of their exposure to traffic and their easy accessibility. A customer on a weekend shopping trip will make a special trip to a car repair shop or to a furniture store in addition to the regular shopping. The customer may remember the large establishment that he drives by on his way to work; he may recall that it was on the main road and had plenty of parking. Discount department stores often take advantage of this type of location, hoping to entice customers to make a special trip to their stores. On recently developed sections of urban arterial ribbons we also find drive-in restaurants and banks.

On the outskirts of cities, highway-oriented ribbons are found. These are usually a collection of unplanned businesses trying to catch the eye of the passing motorist. Most of you have driven into a strange city along such a route, lined with motels, restaurants, and gas stations.

Specialized Areas. Specialized areas are the least recognizable of the three types of business area because they are found within the other two types; that is, in large centers and along some business ribbons. Specialized areas are made up of activities that profit by clustering together at easily accessible locations within the city. This clustering may be for the purposes of comparative shopping, as in the typical automobile row where several car dealers locate side by side to attract customers who want to price several models before buying. The importance of accessibility is illustrated by the grouping of medical offices over stores in shopping centers. In this way specialized medical districts have been formed, usually in an unplanned fashion.

There are several common locations for specialized areas all featuring high accessibility. Many of these areas are found along urban arterial ribbons as they attract customers travelling by car for special shopping trips. Examples include furniture districts and automobile rows. Other specialized areas are found within the CBD where many transportation routes meet. These areas include entertainment districts and very specialized shopping streets. Most large North American cities include a variety of specialized areas in outlying business centers, along suburban arterial ribbons, and in the CBD.

THE CENTRAL BUSINESS DISTRICT

The heart of any large urban area is the Central Business District (CBD). The health of a city may often be determined through an examination of the CBD. A healthy community will have a dynamic CBD that has the vitality and ability to meet changing conditions and situations.

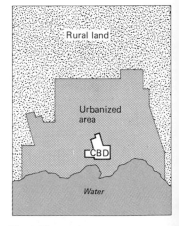

Fig. 4-14
The CBD is *not* usually found at the geographic center of the city.

The CBD is perhaps the easiest component of urban structure to recognize. It is the area of the city with the tallest buildings and the highest daytime population density. The CBD has the greatest concentration of offices and retail stores as well as the highest land values. It is also the focus of major urban transportation routes and the center of civic and social aspects of urban life.

The CBD is usually found near the original site of the city. While the city grows outward the CBD continues to develop near the original site because it remains the most accessible part of the urban area. This is due to the development of major traffic arteries linking the CBD with the outward growing areas of the city. Since most cities develop along a coastline or river, the CBD is usually found near one edge of the urbanized area (Fig. 4-14). Thus, although the CBD is the heart of the modern city, it is not usually found at the geographic center.

Why did CBDs develop in all our cities? The major determinants are accessibility and convenience. In order for businesses to survive they must be easily accessible to the public and to each other. For example, in reviewing the history of most of our cities we find that businesses began clustering at the most accessible point in the developing urban area. This was usually an intersection of major roads or next to port facilities. At that time there were no modern communication facilities. As a result, commercial establishments and financial institutions had to be close together. This allowed face-to-face business contacts and easy movement of paper between different organizations. As time passed, more businesses moved into the CBD in order to take advantage of the easy access to other establishments, the central location of the area, and the prestige of locating in what was the most highly desirable and, therefore, expensive location in the city. Although modern communication facilities have somewhat reduced the importance of face-to-face contacts and movement of paper, these factors are still important enough to cause clustering in the CBD.

The CBD, like all areas of the city, is in a constant state of change. This is quite visible when we observe older buildings being torn down and new higher towers being erected in their place. In addition to this vertical extension there is also a horizontal movement taking place. Generally speaking, the CBD expands in one direction and contracts in the opposite direction (Fig. 4-15). The area into which the CBD is expanding is called the *zone of assimilation*. This migration is usually in the direction of the best residences found in the city. The zone of assimilation can be recognized by the fact that most new development is taking place within it. It is the site of the newest professional offices, specialty shops, office towers, and downtown hotels.

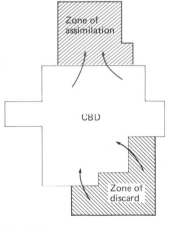

Fig. 4-15
Migration of the CBD.

On the other side of the CBD another boundary shift is usually taking place. This is the area from which the CBD is migrating. It is called the *zone of discard*. Little or no new development takes place, the land values decrease, and less desirable activities such as pawn shops, run-down movie houses, cheap bars, and low-grade restaurants develop in this zone. Although the zone of assimilation and the zone of discard are found in many cities, not all urban areas experience this phenomenon. In some cities there is rapid growth and horizontal extension on all sides of the CBD. In other cities, however, the heart of the city is in the process of decay and the CBD is shrinking, leaving many areas of discard around its outer edge.

The Core-Frame Concept. We have now observed the CBD as one component within the entire urban complex. In order to understand and appreciate its nature more fully, we must take a microscopic point of view. In other words, we must look at its inner structure. Generally speaking, the CBD can be divided into two broad zones: the core and the frame. This core-frame concept is based upon intensity of land use and types of activities found in the CBDs of the most North American cities. In this investigation of the CBD core and frame we will first examine the components of the core and then proceed to examine the structure of the frame. It must be remembered, however, that the boundary separating the core from the frame is difficult to determine exactly. Thus, the core should be thought of as gradually merging into the frame. (Fig. 4-16).

The *core* is the center of the CBD where the land is used most intensively. It is here that we find the greatest concentration of activities, the highest daytime population densities, and the focus of

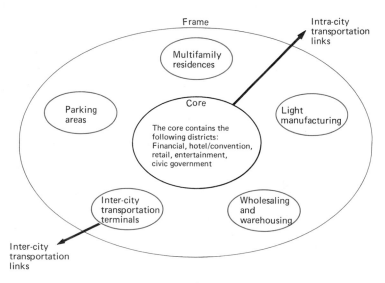

Fig. 4-16
Representation of the core-frame concept.

the city's transportation system. The core occupies only a small portion of the total CBD area because it must be kept relatively compact. This compactness is necessary because the main mode of travel in the core is walking.

It is in the core that we find the *peak land-value intersection*. This is the point in the city where land is most expensive. It is the street intersection where intensity of land use is greatest, pedestrian concentration is highest, and, frequently, where vehicular congestion is at a maximum. The location of this point varies from city to city although it is usually near the geographic center of the CBD. As one moves away from this intersection both land values and intensity of land use decline.

The core is composed of specialized-function areas; that is, it has several districts occupied primarily by one dominant type of activity. The typical CBD core may have financial, retail, government, entertainment, and hotel/convention districts. All of these functional areas are interrelated but have developed in various parts of the core for various reasons. Let us briefly examine these major functional districts.

FINANCIAL DISTRICT. The financial district is also called the district of offices. The predominant activities are related to business carried out in office buildings. The area includes: banks, lawyers' offices, brokerage houses, professional offices, and other related activities.

The largest buildings in the city are usually found in the financial district. As was previously mentioned, offices cluster together for the convenience of communication, face-to-face contacts, and the movement of paper. The development of the high-speed elevator allowed extended vertical growth and thus the high degree of office concentration. Some companies locate in this area because it is prestigious to locate in the CBD core where the action is. In addition, a company that builds a skyscraper with its name on it receives a great deal of free advertising since the building becomes a city landmark.

RETAIL DISTRICT. The CBD is the retailing heart of the city and the core contains most of the retail outlets. The retail stores in the core do a greater volume of business per unit area than anywhere else in the city. Because of the great accessibility of the core, the stores are able to attract customers from all over the city and from the neighboring small towns. The greatest concentration of shops is adjacent to the financial district and is therefore able to serve the large numbers of people who work in the office buildings. The retailing district is characterized by department stores, large numbers of men's and women's clothing shops, shoe stores, furniture stores, jewelry shops, and camera shops.

The retail stores generally occupy street-level locations in the multi-storey buildings found along major thoroughfares where pedestrian traffic is greatest. In this way they are able to advertise their goods and attract the maximum number of potential customers.

Have you ever noticed how some stores have a tendency to cluster together? There may be two or three department stores, fifteen women's clothing shops, ten shoe stores, and three or more record stores. By clustering in this manner they are able to attract large numbers of people. Studies have indicated that two department stores, for example, will attract a greater number of customers if they are located near each other than if they were located by themselves. This clustering of shops selling similar items allows customers to compare quality, price, and service.

Within the retail district of the core we find two basic types of outlets. There are the stores that attract customers and there are the stores that are parasitic in nature. The stores that attract customers from all over the city are the department stores and the specialty shops. Specialty shops are stores that sell specialized items such as clothes, shoes, cameras, and electronic equipment. Because the stores specialize in one type of good they require high threshold populations in order to survive. By clustering in the CBD they can draw upon the entire city population for customers. The parasitic stores are the non-specialty shops that sell day-to-day convenience goods. This type of retail outlet includes drugstores, small lunch counters, and smoke shops. The parasitic stores attract their customers from shoppers who have been drawn to the core by the department stores and specialty shops. These shops usually do not have a large frontage on the street since they require much less advertising space than the specialty shops.

HOTEL/CONVENTION DISTRICT. In close proximity to the financial district we find the hotel/convention area. This area is not usually a cluster of activities as are the financial and retail districts. Rather, the hotels and related convention facilities are often spread out around the financial district. It is in these downtown hotels that the out-of-town businessman finds accommodation and where large business gatherings are held. The central location of the hotels attracts customers who want to be near their clients in the business area and near dining and entertainment facilities. In addition, many tourists stay in this area of the CBD because it is close to the entertainment district, the shopping district, and cultural facilities.

A recent phenomenon of large cities is the development of hotels near the airport and motor hotels at major intersections along freeways. In both cases they provide convenience for travellers, easy accessibility to several areas of the city, and an alternative to the often noisy, dirty, and crime-ridden downtown core. Despite these recent changes, however, the downtown hotel is important to many visitors and residents alike.

OTHER FUNCTIONAL DISTRICTS OF THE CORE. The major entertainment district of the city is found in the CBD core because of the accessibility of the core area. Like retail outlets, entertainment activities require large threshold populations in order to survive. They must draw upon the entire population of the city as well as the people who work in the financial district. By locating close to the retail district the entertainment facilities also allow people to relax after shopping. Similarly, the businessmen and tourists staying in the downtown hotels are also a source of customers.

The CBD core is also the site for activities related to running the city itself, that is, the civic government. The city hall and the courts are located in the heart of the city. In a city with a healthy core, the city hall may act as a focal point not only for civic interaction but also as a place for social gatherings and recreation.

The other component of the CBD is the *frame*. In comparison to the core, the frame is characterized by activities such as wholesaling, warehousing, inter-city transportation terminals, parking lots, automobile sales, and multi-family residences. Because the land in the frame is in less demand than in the core, cost of land is lower and there is less intensity of land use. There is more open or vacant space, the buildings are not as high, and growth is more horizontal than vertical. Because the frame is larger in area, there is more reliance on vehicles for movement. In the frame there are many non-related areas of activities, whereas in the core most of the activities are interrelated. There is also a greater diversity of land-use activities in the frame, as it is larger.

The wholesaling, manufacturing, and warehousing activities are located in districts away from the most sought after locations in the core and are, therefore, possibly less familiar to most of us. Since these activities do not require prime land in the core they are usually near the edge of the CBD or at least located in such a way that they do not conflict or interfere with core functions. Often these frame activities are located in run-down buildings on small narrow streets near the zone of discard where land prices are more reasonable. Yet they are still in close proximity to their clients located in the core.

Summary. The CBD, composed of the core and frame, is a dynamic part of the city that grows both horizontally and vertically. The horizontal movement or migration creates a zone of assimilation and a zone of discard. Within the core most of the activities are in some way dependent upon one another. This tends to reinforce the desire of activities to locate here. In the frame there is a greater diversity of activities and less dependence among the activities. Most activities locate in the CBD because of its high degree of accessibility from anywhere in the city. In essence, the CBD is the heart of urban life.

For Thought and Research

1   Give examples from your town or city to show how each of the following factors has influenced land use: zoning; age; physical features; land value.

2   a) Rank the land uses in Figure 4-9 according to the percentage of developed land they occupy. Where does the rank not fit the importance of the land use and why?

b) Why is only 77% of the area of the average large city developed?

3   a) List the characteristics of eight types of industrial areas.

b) Identify an example of as many of the eight types as possible in your area.

c) List the types of companies found in each type of industrial area.

d) Classify the industries in each type of area as mainly basic or non-basic.

e) In what ways do industrial parks meet the demands of manufacturing industries for a good location?

4   a) What are the physical differences between the four types of roads?

b) What are the purposes of each?

c) Find an example of each in your community.

5   In a table compare the characteristics, advantages, and disadvantages of the three road patterns.

6   a) What road patterns are found in your area?

b) Can more than one pattern be combined? How?

7   a) Discover the load and operating characteristics of the types of mass transit.

b) Is the mass-transit system of your town or city public or privately owned? Does it make money?

8   Compare roads and mass-transit lines with respect to the following: space requirements, convenience, speed, and environmental effects.

9   a) Explain why the division between city and suburb exists in many cities.

b) Make a list of the advantages and disadvantages of life in the suburbs.

10   Why have many public-housing projects failed? What other methods of urban renewal exist?

11   Account for the boom in apartment construction, especially in suburban areas.

12   Give an example from your city of each type of business center and of each type of commercial ribbon.

13   On a graph similar to Figure 4-17, mark the approximate points that would be occupied a) by each level of the business center hierarchy (convenience, neighborhood, community, and regional) and b) by each level of the hierarchy of rural central places (village, town, and city).

14   Give an example from your city of a specialized area found a) within the CBD and b) on an urban arterial.

15   a) Why is the CBD not usually found at the geographic center of most cities?

b) What is meant by face-to-face contacts? Give examples and explain why such contacts are important.

c) What is meant by the term "movement of paper"?

d) Explain why there is prestige for a company to locate in the CBD.

16   a) Why is the migration of the CBD usually in the direction of the best residences in the city?

b) Define the following zones and give examples of the types of activities found in them: a) zone of assimilation; b) zone of discard.

c) Describe the characteristics of the peak land-value intersection.

17 a) Why do stores selling similar items cluster in the CBD?

b) Why is the CBD core such an attractive area to locate a retail business?

c) Compare the types of stores that attract customers to the CBD with parasitic type shops.

18 Describe the interdependence of CBD core activities. Give examples.

19 Briefly describe the functional districts found in the CBD core and frame.

20 Make a chart to compare the CBD core and frame under the following headings: intensity of land use; growth; parking space; mode of travel; and diversity of land use.

21 Why is the CBD described as the heart of the city?

Recommended Readings

1 *Suburbia in Transition* edited with an introduction by L. H. Masotti and J. K. Hadden, Franklin Watts, 1974. This collection of articles from the *New York Times* is thought-provoking and concerned about every aspect of the suburbs of today.

2 *The North American City* by M. Yeates and B. Garner, Harper and Row, 1971. This book contains very thorough, although advanced, readings on commercial land use, the CBD, residential land use, and industrial land use.

3 *The American City: An Urban Geography* by R. E. Murphy, McGraw-Hill, 1974.

4 *The Canadian City* by J. N. Jackson, McGraw-Hill Ryerson, 1973.

5 *Urban Geography: An Introductory Analysis* by J. H. Johnson, Pergamon Press, 1967.

Fig. 4-17
Trade-population graph.

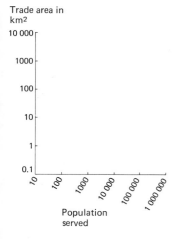

Trade area in km²

Population served

Man and the Urban Landscape

5

In our study of the urban ecosystem, we have observed some of the factors that have led to the location, type, and growth of urban communities. In addition we have looked at the internal patterns of the community itself. In all these discussions there has been present one element around which all activity revolved. This is the presence of man. The urban landscape, after all, is a creation of man.

Urban communities are located where they are because that place was considered best to serve some human need. Similarly, a community will grow or die depending upon its usefulness in the scheme of human interactions.

Our urban communities are an accumulation of many urban patterns. Each pattern was affected not only by the previous form of the city and its site, but also by the contemporary political, economic, social, and technological systems of its inhabitants.

A city grows and takes a certain form because of decisions made by individuals or groups of individuals working together within institutions and corporations. These decisions are many and varied. At the individual level they may include where to live, work, and shop. On a larger scale, such as city governments and corporations, the decisions may include where, what, and when to build or invest. The result of these numerous decisions is the growth and development of an urban community designed to maximize the satisfaction and safety it provides for all its citizens and to create the best possible environment for each individual living there. Has this ideal been achieved in your urban area?

There are times, as seen in previous units, when it is necessary to place primary emphasis upon a process and to view human interaction merely as the medium in which this process is operating. However, one must always remember that man is the focal point of the urban system. As such, it is now necessary to observe man's perception of and operation in the urban ecosystem of which he is the main protagonist.

5.1   MAN'S NEEDS AND DESIRES

As the previous units have demonstrated, the urban community is the result of influences exerted by a great many factors. In most cases these factors reflect the needs and desires of the human community that has created the urban environment.

If each of us were to make a list of our personal needs and one of those of mankind, the lists would undoubtedly be very long and both would reflect our own hopes and desires. Despite the fact that many of the needs would be similar there would also be many that are dissimilar in nature. This situation results because each of us places a personal meaning on our own and mankind's needs. For example, you may feel that it is important to accumulate a great deal of money during your lifetime and therefore assume that this need is important to everyone. Of course, not everyone agrees that this is an important aspect of life.

The needs that we all have vary with time, the conditions under which we live, the locality in which we live, our age, sex, financial position, religious outlook, cultural or ethnic background, and so on. In fact, as each person goes through life, his needs and desires are constantly changing, growing, or diminishing (Fig. 5-1). There are certain needs, of course, that do not change—the need for

Fig. 5-1
Changes.

fresh air and water, a certain amount of food per day, space to sleep and stand, and people with whom to communicate and interact. In terms of the urban ecosystem, we require a place to live, a place to work, shop, and recreate, and a means of transportation to and from various places. In addition, we require adequate water and sewage treatment facilities, police and fire protection, garbage collection, and a host of other services resulting from high-density living. Apart from these very obvious needs there are others which are equally important but perhaps less noticeable. These include the needs for building materials, petroleum products for building roads and running vehicles, and space for dumping garbage.

When considering the needs of man as reflected by the urban environment we must not only consider the needs of the individual but also the needs of groups and the relations between individuals and groups. Man has needs that result from his membership in groups. No man is an island who can live in isolation. Thus there are social needs which must also be satisfied. These social needs include such things as a feeling of belonging, friendship, acceptance by others, and the respect of other people. As a member of a group, a person not only has his own needs to consider but also his relations with others who have a direct influence upon him. Sometimes the needs and desires of a group differ from the needs of some of the individuals making up that group. Think of your own situation. Every day you come into contact with many people and many situations. In order to live with them it is necessary to consider the opinions, values, and individuality of others as well as your own and to reach a mutual understanding through discussion. Compatability, conflict, and compromise are an integral part of social interaction. Think of examples of each type of interaction in your daily relationships with others.

Relationships between individuals can be of a positive or negative nature. With few exceptions, man desires and needs the proximity of others. However, this proximity must not be extreme otherwise there will be unacceptable degrees of frustration, annoyance, and conflict. Some groups of people require a relatively large amount of public space and do not place a high priority on personal or family privacy. The opposite situation is also true as you will learn in the following example.

As an example of different perceptions of the environment and the demands placed upon it, let us consider the attitudes of a resident of a large North American city and a resident of Hong Kong. The very high population density and crowded conditions which are acceptable to a resident of Hong Kong may be totally unbearable for the North American. The perception of congestion and overcrowdedness is different for different groups of people throughout the world. What is your idea of crowded? Think of yourself in a

Fig. 5-2
Crowded?

NEXT TRAIN
5:20

OO

147

crowded bus or in an overcrowded room (Fig. 5-2). How do you react in such a situation? Perhaps the major task of human settlements is to provide people with as much privacy as possible (within acceptable limits) by limiting the distance or proximity between them, while still allowing the choice for interaction.

It is apparent that the needs and desires of one individual are not identical with those of other individuals. Certainly we all have basic requirements for survival, safety, and security regardless of who we are or where we live. However, when these are satisfied, higher-level satisfactions or desires are increasingly valued and become the basis of an individual's value and behavioral system. By this we mean that amenities become more important. What do we mean by amenities? Is a television set, an automobile, or a stereo system a requirement for survival? Some people might think so but of course none of them is. They are, therefore, amenities that perhaps could be described as those stimuli which lead to feelings of comfort, joy, or pleasure of varying degrees. The demand for amenities is related to social, cultural, educational, and economic factors. That is, at any income level the desires of an individual are reflected by his cultural experiences and the habits and attitudes of other people with whom he comes into contact. The individual learns, through his groups, the ideas, habits, and attitudes that society expects of him. Can you think of examples which show these different demands?

This discussion of needs and desires concerns both people who live in urban communities and those who live in rural areas. Although the remainder of this unit is focused upon people living within the urban ecosystem, it is important to remember that people living outside it also have needs and desires. These are often similar but they may be different because of the different factors affecting their lives.

We have looked briefly at a few of the basic requirements of human beings, and how some of these needs are reflected in the landscape. There are many more—the need to be one of the crowd yet remain an individual; the desire to be stimulated through sports, eating, or entertainment; the desire for privacy, to be alone but not lonely; the desire for friendship, medical care, recreation, and employment, to name but a few.

The urban environment does not always succeed in providing for the needs and desires of individuals. The size and the sometimes unfriendly, impersonal nature of the "concrete canyons" can lead to frustration and disenchantment. Why does this happen? Can we find any solutions?

Many of the topics that have been introduced in this section are considered in greater depth later in this unit. Many are not covered but will be left for you to ponder by yourself.

For Thought and Research

1   What factors determine our needs and desires throughout our individual lives?
2   What are some of the needs that are constant to all human beings everywhere?
3   What needs must be met in order for people to live in the urban ecosystem?
4   Relationships between individuals in a group can be of a positive or negative nature. Discuss this statement.
5   What is the difference between a basic need of man and the desire for an amenity?
6   What are social needs?
7   a) Why do the needs and desires of one individual differ from those of another individual?

b) Compare the needs of a person in his teens with those of an adult. Perhaps a talk with your parents will help.
8   Read your local newspaper and see if you can find examples of different desires or goals of various groups of people or individuals within your local community. Analyze them by determining who they are, what interests they have, the action they are taking, and the possible outcome of this action.

Recommended Readings

1   *Ekistics, The Study of Human Settlements* by C. Doxiadis, Hutchinson, 1968. A very large book with many thought-provoking sections.
2   *Taming Megalopolis, Vol. 1 What is and What Could Be* by H. W. Eldredge, Anchor Books, Doubleday, 1967. A book containing many papers on the present situation of cities and possible remedies to the many problems that exist.
3   *The Death and Life of Great American Cities* by J. Jacobs, Random House, 1961. Takes a people-oriented position on current redevelopment and planning practices.

5.2   NICHES IN THE URBAN COMMUNITY

Within every community, whether it be animal, plant, or human, there are niches into which individuals are accommodated. In the human community, and the large urban environment in particular, attempts have been made to create broad classifications to help the study of the social aspects of the city. As you are well aware, the population of urban areas is extremely varied and there is a tendency for different types of people to reside in different areas of the city. Within these areas distinctive community types can be recognized. These communities may be viewed as being the spatial expression of the urban community's social characteristics—its ecology. Let us examine some of the reasons for this pattern of residential differentiation and see how it relates to niches in the urban community.

People generally choose to live in a certain part of the city because it best suits their needs. What any individual or family considers best depends partly upon income, number of children, age, the type of people who live in the area, the distance from work, and other personal preferences. Because of this selection process people are not distributed within an urban area in a random pattern. Their distribution is based upon decisions that reflect the niches occupied by the individuals within society. If we are able to determine the needs and characteristics of a family it will then be possible to determine, with a reasonable degree of accuracy, where a family would like to live and where it probably will live.

One method or approach that is employed in observing the niches of urban residents is to view their *socio-economic status* or social characteristics. This term refers to three major aspects of urban populations that help to explain primary differences in group behavior. These aspects are: economic status (social class), family status (demographic characteristics), and ethnic status (segregation characteristics).

Economic Status. Economic or social status refers to the differences in education, income, and occupation between various groups. These differences create a range of status groups commonly referred to as upper-, middle-, and lower-income groups. This grouping of individuals is also known as the *class structure* or the *social hierarchy* of a society. Each society has some form of ranking or stratification and every individual of that society has a position in it. This position provides the basis for according certain privileges and rights to that individual. The person who is a doctor, for example, is accorded certain rights and privileges that are greater and held in higher esteem than those given to a person who is a garbage collector. Generally speaking, the more important an occupation is to the members of society, the greater the prestige that is given to it. In addition, the higher the level of education that is achieved, the greater the income or reward that is given. Thus a person with these favorable attributes is higher on the scale than a person without them. A person who is in a particular income group at a given period of time, however, is not necessarily confined to that group as there is a certain amount of interaction and mobility between the classes.

Section 4.2, dealing with internal patterns in the community, pointed out that different status groups are found in different areas of the city. As a result, not only is there a social distance between the classes but there is also a physical distance between them. Think about this for a while. This is accomplished by both voluntary and involuntary separation. Similar occupational groups tend to gravitate to distinct social areas. The most extreme separation of these social classes tends to be at the upper and lower ends of the social ladder. That is, there are very distinct areas of high-income residents and of poor people. In addition, these two areas of extremes are very rarely found in close proximity to one another. Usually the upper class and lower class are separated by an area of middle-class housing. This middle-class area acts as a buffer between the two social extremes. A map of this separation shows that it appears in the form of sectors radiating outward from the center of the city (Fig. 5-3).

Because upper-income groups are able to afford the best sites for living, they are generally found in areas of scenic beauty (Fig. 5-4). They are often located in areas that overlook a ravine or on high ground that is not subjected to pollution. In many North American cities the wealthy residential areas are located to the west of industrial areas. Can you think of a reason for this situation? (Consider the direction of the prevailing winds.)

The wealthy neighborhood is also located in quiet areas of the city, some distance from incompatible land uses such as factories. These locations have the added feature of easy and rapid access to the downtown area of the city by good arterial roads. On the other hand, the lower-income groups, less able to compete for the high-priced land, must settle for less attractive areas. As a result, this group is generally found in areas of mixed land use near industrial or commercial locations (Fig. 5-5). In these areas the lots are small and congested, and the land is often low-lying and poorly drained. Another reason for living near industrial locations is that this is where many of the residents work. Why would this be particularly important to them? In some cases the low-income districts are found on the city's outer fringes where land is inexpensive and suburban industrial development is located.

A very interesting phenomenon occurs when the lower-income groups are found near the central areas of the city. As you probably know, this is the area of highest land values in the city.

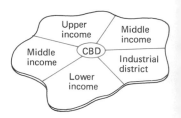

Fig. 5-3
Areas of economic status appear in the form of sectors radiating outward from the center of the city.

Fig. 5-4
The pleasures of wealth.

Fig. 5-5
The results of poverty.

Does it not seem strange that the poor often occupy some of the most expensive land in the city? How can this be? Surely the rents must be high in order to pay for the privilege of living on this expensive land so close to the city center. Is this the case in your community?

Economic status is an important category because it is a *social indicator*. A social indicator describes a set of characteristics which, in turn, reflects some of the living conditions and behavior of a particular group of people. For example, an area that registers high in economic status will probably have a low occurrence of malnutrition and have a small number of people who occupy each room in the dwelling. If the economic status is low the reverse is likely to be true. In addition to reflecting certain living conditions within an area, a social indicator is also important because it reflects behavioral characteristics about the population. For example, political attitudes, patterns of consumption, and group expectations are related to economic status. If a survey were taken of the residents in a very wealthy district in the city, they would probably have many characteristics in common. They may favor one political party over another, buy certain types of automobiles and clothes, and attend certain types of social functions. A survey undertaken in a poor district will reveal similar characteristics in the population but these will probably differ considerably from those in the high-class district. Very rarely will you find the wealthy and the poor attending the same social functions or having similar interests in food, politics, or literature.

Such differences are very important in advertising, store location, and political forecasting. Magazines that are geared toward high-income readers will have advertisements for expensive cars and exclusive fashion designs, whereas magazines catering to middle- and lower-income individuals will have advertisements for less expensive and less exclusive items. Can you give examples of behavior or attitudes in your city that are a reflection of economic status?

One thing that we must keep in mind when discussing social indicators is that they merely indicate the *most probable* living conditions and behavior patterns. They should not be viewed as absolute decrees of what will be found. They are tools that help us to explain some of the complex situations found in the urban community.

Family Status. The second component of socio-economic status is family status or the demographic characteristics of the population. This term refers to the age and sex differences of individuals and families and is related to the life cycle. The life cycle refers to the different stages that individuals and families go through—a child dependent upon its parents, a young single person, a young married couple without children, a family with children, and a family whose children have left. There are, of course, other combinations that can occur within this cycle. Why is the component, family status, important? At the various stages in this cycle the needs of an individual or family are somewhat different. For example, a young couple with no children requires very little space in their place of residence. Perhaps a small apartment will be sufficient. If the couple has children they will require more space and will, therefore, have to change their place of residence and move into a larger apartment or house. Similarly, when the couple is older they may no longer require the large amount of space that was needed when their children were at home. Again they may desire a new place of residence. Often, older people have higher incomes and have progressively advanced up the economic and social ladder so that their needs may become oriented toward status and leisure. They may desire a luxury apartment or wish to locate in a more prestigious part of town.

Different types of households (single people or families) have different residential needs, and thus locate in specific parts of the urban community. The city reflects these needs in the form of districts demographically distinct from one another. A visual expression of this pattern may help (Fig. 5-6). Generally speaking, this pattern takes the shape of concentric rings about the city center.

Each concentric ring or zone is composed of different family types because each area of the city offers different characteristics and living experiences. Thus, what is attractive to one family is not suitable for another. The area close to the CBD is often very attractive to single individuals or small families because it offers cheap accommodation in rooming houses or luxurious living in the high-rise apartment towers of the central city. It is close to downtown shopping facilities, business establishments, places of entertainment, and cultural facilities. Many older couples whose children have left are returning to this area to live because of the proximity to medical facilities and rapid-transit routes. The predominance of adult only apartment buildings and the lack of facilities for children such as playgrounds and parks also reflect the nature of the area. This area close to the CBD is referred to as an area of *low family status*. This term refers to the fact that the families are small, there is a large proportion of women in the labor market, and there is a high proportion of multiple dwellings such as apartments and rooming houses. These are a few characteristics that are represented by the term low family status. Can you think of others that would be applicable? A look at the information on housing and population characteristics for a few census tracts near the CBD may give you some insights.

These characteristics differ from families who are found in the zones further away from the CBD and in the suburbs. Larger families generally live in areas that have larger houses, more open space, playgrounds, and schools. The further one travels away from the CBD the higher the family status. This means that the families are larger, there are fewer women in the labor force, and there is a predominance of single-family dwellings toward the suburbs. Although this pattern is changing somewhat with the development of new apartment buildings in suburban areas near rapid-transit routes, the general pattern for North American cities is typically low family status near the CBD and increasing family status toward the suburbs.

Fig. 5-6
Areas of family status take the shape of concentric rings about the city center. Low family status areas are found near the CBD and higher family status areas are found toward the suburbs.

Ethnic Status. The final component of socio-economic status is ethnic status. Ethnic or racial groups often congregate or are segregated into particular areas of large urban communities in which they are a minority. This clustering is because new immigrants, or members of a racial group, may require interaction with fellow group members in order to exchange information, share cultural identification, seek help if there is a language or other type of barrier, reduce cultural shock, and to enjoy the company of people of the same background.

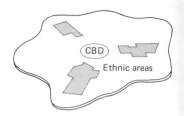

Fig. 5-7
Ethnic status. Ethnic areas appear in the form of clusters within the city.

Ethnicity is an important social indicator because it reflects different life styles and behavior from those found in other parts of the urban community. For instance, there may be higher densities of people per dwelling, different shopping behavior and entertainment activities, different family customs (the married children may move in with the parents), and more tightly knit community organizations. What are some other differences that are found in ethnic or racial districts?

As new immigrants arrive in the area where the previous immigrants first arrived (*ethnic reception area*), the older well-established members of the ethnic community often tend to move out in a pattern of invasion and succession. This process of invasion and succession is identical to that found in nature. In the case of an ethnic or racial group, members buy houses in areas of the city adjacent to the existing community. At first the ethnic individuals are in a minority in this new area. However, as more and more members move into this area it gradually changes in character and the ethnic population is greater than the non-ethnic. Thus, an area that was once only adjacent to the ethnic or racial community is now part of it.

Many ethnic areas tend to be located in parts of the city where rents are low and where work is close by, particularly in the case of groups with limited economic power. It is only after accumulating capital that the earlier immigrants are able to move out and make room for the new arrivals. In some cases one particular reception area has been used by several ethnic groups, one successively displacing another.

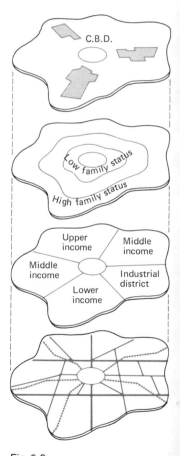

Sometimes an ethnic area may become a permanent feature on the urban landscape. This often occurs when the earlier immigrants do not move out because they enjoy their associations in the reception area. They may also have prestigious positions in the community. Those that do move often establish new ethnic communities in other parts of the city. In so doing, they can maintain their associations while having better housing. A good example of a permanent ethnic area found in most cities is the Chinatown district. On a map, ethnic areas appear in the form of clusters (Fig. 5-7).

Fig. 5-8
Urban ecological structure: a combination of social and physical aspects of the urban environment.

Some ethnic groups are large and consequently quite visible. In their part of the city they have developed a cultural landscape that is quite distinct from other areas. The various languages on advertising signs, the different varieties of food offered, the different selling techniques, and the general color of the area add a great deal to the variety, uniqueness, and interest of the urban environment. In some cities members of an ethnic or racial group do not have the freedom to locate where they wish. When people are forced to live in a specific area because of discrimination on the part of others a ghetto situation results. This forced segregation is a blight within the urban community because there is no freedom of choice. There is hostility rather than interaction between members of the ethnic or racial group and the rest of the community.

Summary. Studies from a number of cities suggest that the various components of socio-economic status form patterns. That is, economic status is reflected in a sectoral pattern, family status in a concentric pattern, and ethnic status in clusters or nuclei. If we superimpose these three indicators of social space on the physical space of the city, the human mosaic that makes up the city emerges (Fig. 5-8).

Whether we like it or not we all have a particular niche in society which can be seen in relation to other individuals who have similar or dissimilar characteristics. These niches are not static, however, and can be changed by an individual. By grouping some of the many characteristics that we possess, it is possible to come up with our socio-economic status. Remember, however, this is only a classification designed by researchers for study. Your individual identity remains your own.

Ethnic status

Family status   Social space

Economic
status

Physical space

For Thought and Research

1   Explain in your own words what a "niche" is as it appears in this section.
2   List and explain five ways in which man's actions are governed by his particular niche in society.
3   The three major components of socio-economic status are called social indicators.
   a) What is a social indicator?
   b) Why are they important in the study of man in the urban ecosystem?
4   Why do different social classes occupy different parts of the city?
5   a) Define the term "family status".
   b) Describe why and where families of different family status live in the city.
6   Why is ethnicity an important social indicator?
7   Describe how ethnic and ghetto areas expand.
8   What pattern is shown by each of the three social indicators?
9   a) On a base map of your own urban community locate various areas that have distinctive differences in socio-economic status, based on your knowledge of the city. If your knowledge is limited, census data may be useful.

b) Do the reasons given in this section explain the locations of these areas? Explain. A topographic or land-use map will be useful.

Recommended Readings

The following books contain information on man's niches in the urban community.
1 *Urban Society,* 5th edition, by N. P. Gist and S. F. Fava, Thomas Y. Crowell, 1964.
2 *Cities and City Life* edited by H. M. Hughes, Allyn and Bacon, 1970, pp. 59-67.
3 *Man and His Urban Environment: A Sociological Approach* by W. H. Nichelson, Addison-Wesley, 1970.
4 *Patterns of Urban Life* by R. E. Pahl, Longmans, 1970.
5 *Urban Prospects* by J. Wolforth and R. Leigh, McClelland and Stewart, 1971, pp. 94-107.

5.3   PERCEPTION OF THE URBAN ENVIRONMENT

Urban areas, like all environments, in some way affect those of us who live in, work in, or visit them. We respond to the environment around us by developing impressions or feelings through our senses. The sound of the wind through trees, the sight of a garden full of colorful flowers, the feel of soft grass underfoot, or the smell of dinner cooking on a barbeque may give us a feeling of satisfaction and contentment. On the other hand, the sight of garbage lying by the roadside, the sound of children crying, the crunch of broken glass, or the smell of automobile exhaust may give us an entirely different impression or emotional response. Both these positive and negative aspects affect our overall interpretation and perception of the urban environment.

Perhaps the greatest impact an urban environment has upon an individual is through its visual appearance. The personality of a town or city is revealed by its physical characteristics: the design of the streets; the architecture; the open space; the presence of trees; the location of industry; and its state of repair or disrepair. The aesthetic qualities of these characteristics will, to a large extent, affect the impressions of visitors and residents alike.

In addition, the image that a city presents will change with time and under the conditions in which it is viewed. The clutter of overhead wires may be removed if underground wiring is installed. Similarly, the nakedness of a new suburb will change when trees mature and create a canopy of green. The hustle and bustle of a main street may also be replaced by a more sedate scene on a restful Sunday afternoon. Thus, in order fully to assess and appreciate an urban environment it must be viewed at different times and under varying weather conditions.

This brief introduction to the impact a city landscape makes on our senses leads us to a more important aspect of perception. How do we see our urban areas? Is there a common image?

If someone asked you what your urban area was like, what image would come into your mind? In other words, how do you perceive your urban environment? Do you see clusters of tall buildings, tree-lined streets, telephone wires, a famous landmark, the place "where it's at", or traffic congestion?

You might say, "Everybody knows what a city is and what it looks like!" Maybe most people know what makes up a city but does everybody see it in the same way as you do? If you compare your image of the city with those of your friends, your parents, or someone who lives in another part of the city or countryside, you will probably find that they have somewhat different images. The city has different meanings to different people.

A slum dweller, for instance, may find the area in which he lives attractive because of the friendships he has and because it fulfils his needs. An urban planner might see it as an area of blight which must be replaced by a new development. Another slum dweller may see the city as oppressive because of his lack of mobility, status, or dignity. This may be due to his lack of money, lack of educational opportunities, his color, or ethnic background. A civil engineer may see the city as a maze of surface and underground utilities. A suburban housewife may see it as an attractive shopping area. All these images help define the structure and problems of a city.

Is it really important what images different people have of the urban landscape? Recent studies have indicated that people behave, interact, and react differently to the urban environment depending on how they perceive it. As a result each person tends to live within his own personal urban environment. Does this sound silly? Look at it this way. Draw a map of your immediate neighborhood (see Section 7.3). Compare it with one drawn by a classmate. Do you see any differences? The road pattern may be the same and the main landmarks are there. But were you aware of the unique house on the corner? How about the broken fence in Mr. Frost's backyard, or the sportscar two streets over? Some may see nightclubs while other see sports or recreational facilities. One's perception of the urban environment may also contain less tangible elements such as a feeling for a particular place or a distinctive smell.

Each map drawn by an individual will differ according to the characteristics of the person drawing it and his perception of his surroundings. Some of the characteristics affecting a person's image are his interests and awareness of the surroundings. In addition, the age, sex, education, and background of the individual play a part. As you can see, there are as many images as there are people.

However, there are many similarities between images. Remember, despite your individuality you are also a member of a group with many similar attributes: age, sex, culture, occupation, temperament, and familiarity with the same environment. Fortunately for us we do have common mental pictures or public images. Otherwise we would not be able to operate successfully within the environment or be able to cooperate with other human beings. Can you imagine trying to tell someone how to get to your house or where to meet you if this were not so? Thus each individual picture is unique but it does generally correspond to or blend with the images that other people have.

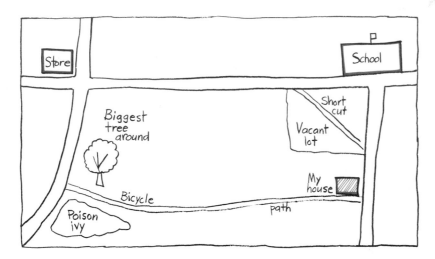

Fig. 5-9
"Map of my neighborhood". This map represents a student's image of what is in his immediate neighborhood.

When you drew the map of the city or your neighborhood, you put down on paper the image that you had in your mind (Fig. 5-9). In effect, this mental image was a mental map and represented the image you had of a particular space. You might now ask, "How did this mental map get there in the first place?" We form this image, or map, from our own experience within that space and from information received from outside sources such as the media and our friends. It is constantly being influenced and changed as we go through life and expand our experiences and knowledge.

The mental map you have of your own neighborhood is probably much more detailed than a road map. It might include such things as shortcuts or detours, a poison ivy patch, or even a familiar smell. On the other hand, if you try to draw a map of an area away from your normal pathways the map will probably become sketchy because of your lack of experience and involvement in the area and a shortage of information. Thus the degree of your perception varies with your familiarity and knowledge about a particular place.

Let's return again to the image of the large urban environment rather than a local neighborhood. We have talked about some of the elements that people may have in their mental maps. Let us now further clarify these elements.

Studies of the city image have shown that there are five main elements that people have in their image. These are paths, edges, districts, nodes, and landmarks. What do these terms mean?

Paths are those channels that a person generally travels (Fig. 5-10). They may be sidewalks, streets, walkways, or even railway lines. For some people these may be the most prominent elements of their image.

Fig. 5-10
Paths and edges. The paths are those routes that are commonly travelled. The edges act as boundaries to our movement.

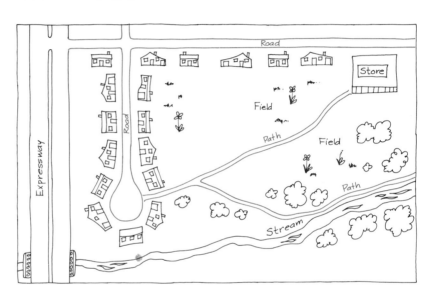

The *edges* refer to boundaries, both real and imaginary, found along customary paths (see also Fig. 5-10). These edges may be in the form of an expressway which prevents a pedestrian from moving from one spot to another, a wall, or the flow of traffic on a main street. They may also be psychological rather than physical such as the edge of an area occupied by a different ethnic group. What paths and edges can you see on your daily journey to school?

Districts are sections of the city. These are recognized as having some identifying character. Greenwich Village in New York, Cabbagetown in Toronto, The Loop in Chicago, and Gas Town in Vancouver are some examples. What districts can you see in the urban area with which you are familiar?

Nodes are strategic points on the urban landscape in the form of junctions or intersections. They are usually prominent features in a person's image because decisions must be made upon entering them. For example, upon entering an intersection a person's awareness must be increased because he might have to change direction or change his mode of travel (such as from a subway to a bus). Another interesting feature about nodes is that they may also act as symbols for an idea, life style, or condition. What comes to mind when the following nodes are mentioned: Hollywood and Vine, Los Angeles; Times Square, New York; Picadilly Circus, London?

Landmarks, like nodes, are reference points, but the observer does not usually enter them during his travels. They act more as guideposts. A landmark may be a building, billboard, sign, or store, to name but a few. They are usually prominent or distinctive in some way so that they can be easily distinguished from objects around them (Fig. 5-11). Some famous landmarks are: Place Ville Marie in Montreal; the Houston Astrodome; the Lincoln Memorial in Washington; Toronto City Hall; and the Eiffel Tower in Paris. What landmarks are found in your community? Why are they thought of as landmarks?

None of the five elements acts alone; they are usually all part of an individual's image of his urban area. The districts may contain many nodes, be limited by edges, be traversed by many paths, and contain many landmarks. In other words, a person observes the urban environment as he walks along paths. He is able to notice changes in districts because of distinctive qualities about them. Districts can also be separated from other districts by observable edges. Finally, an individual's sense of direction is usually aided by landmarks as he changes direction within nodes.

With this basic understanding of what constitutes a person's perception of the urban environment and how it is arrived at, we are now ready to look at some of the behavioral patterns of urban residents.

© CN Tower Limited,

Fig. 5-11
Landmarks act as guideposts or reference points.

For Thought and Research

1   What are some characteristics of your city that evoke a) pleasant and b) unpleasant impressions or feelings? What are the differences between your list and that of one of your classmates?

2   If someone asks you what image you have of your urban area, in effect, what are they asking you?

3   How does an individual form his image of the community in which he lives?

4   Why are there both similarities and differences between the images of individuals?

5   How might the following affect a person's perception of his surroundings?
   a) age;
   b) sex;
   c) education;
   d) ethnic background.

6   a) What are the five main elements people have in their image of the urban community? Give examples of each from your own community.

b) On a map of the city or your local neighborhood locate where you live. For a week mark all the journeys that you make. These will include journeys to school, to shop, for recreation, and for social purposes. At the end of this time note the following: Are you able to see any pattern? Are you able to distinguish any of the five elements mentioned in this section? If so, mark them on the map. Compare your map with those of classmates and determine how much of the urban community was covered by your class in the week.

Recommended Readings

1 "The Delimitation of the Town-Center in the Image of Its Citizens" in *Urban Core and Inner City* by H. J. Klein, Brill, 1967.
2 *The Image of the City* by K. Lynch, M.I.T. Press, 1960. This book should be read for a comprehensive understanding of perception of the city. Information on the five elements of images is thoroughly covered here.
3 *The Canadian City: Space, Form, Quality* by J. N. Jackson, McGraw-Hill Ryerson, 1973, pp. 82-100.

5.4 BEHAVIORAL PATTERNS: MOVEMENT WITHIN THE CITY

A. TRAVEL PATTERNS

In looking at the behavioral patterns of people in the urban community we are, in fact, examining a decision-making process. For example, you decide that an ice-cream cone would be enjoyable and then walk to the corner store to buy one. You have made a decision and then have proceeded to satisfy your desire by travelling across a small space within your community. If many people in your community travel to the corner store, a researcher might be able to draw some conclusions about the spatial behavior of the residents in your neighborhood. In other words, he would be looking for patterns of movement within the space of the neighborhood and the reasons for that movement. This very simple example gives us some idea of what is meant by spatial behavior and behavioral patterns. Having said this, however, you may ask yourself, "So what! How can this information be of any use?"

Information about the spatial behavior of people in a community and the reasons for such behavior is of importance to many people. This information can be used to give urban planners an idea of how best to plan new communities. This would improve the way we live by locating stores, hospitals, schools, and roads in the best place to meet the needs of the community. A retailer may wish to locate his store where the greatest number of people will pass by. Similarly, if a new plaza is to be built, it will be necessary to provide access routes. In order to provide the proper facilities, the planners must know something about the travel patterns of the people who will be attracted to the stores in the plaza. These examples represent only a few of the needs for information about behavioral patterns. After having read this unit, perhaps you will be able to determine other uses.

It is a difficult task to understand the behavioral patterns of people because we are dealing with a situation resulting from the interaction of many factors (Fig. 5-12). The situation is complex because each person is a complex entity having the freedom of choice. A person's behavior can be affected by many things. In the case of your wanting an ice-cream cone, it was probably a momentary impulse or whim that led you to that decision. In examining a more complex type of behavior we would have to consider such things as a person's personality, age, social status, and other socioeconomic factors. These things affect, either directly or indirectly, a person's perception of what is seen and what course of action should be taken. Essentially, the individual is attempting to best satisfy his needs.

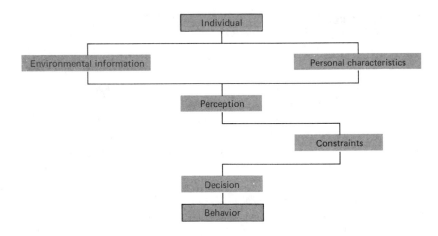

Fig. 5-12
Simple behavioral model. An individual's behavior is the result of decisions made on the basis of how he perceives the situation and how he accepts external constraints on his behavior.

In addition to being affected by these factors, an individual's course of action is also constrained by certain factors. These may include income, access to some form of rapid transportation, time, social values, and past experience. In the case of buying the ice-cream cone, if you did not have access to a bicycle or car, time to spend, and an inclination to travel some distance, you would have to be satisfied with the ice-cream cone from the corner store. Another store 8 km away may offer a wider assortment of flavors, but it is impossible for you to travel there because of the constraints placed upon you.

We have seen that the researcher is interested in spatial behavior (travel patterns) and the reasons for that behavior. Let us examine some of the problems involved in this type of research. Ask the members of your family what they plan to do on Saturday evening. If they are going out ask them where they are going, what type of vehicle they will use, the routes they will be taking, and when they will return. The diversity of answers to these few questions demonstrates how many possibilities are open. If you were to ask these questions of an entire urban community, the number of activity patterns you would discover would be enormous.

To make the situation even more complex, recent studies have shown that the direction of travel is not just related to the characteristics of the landscape; that is, to the street pattern. The individual's perception of the landscape is an even more important factor. A person may not always take the most direct route from one place to another because he perceives that another route is better for some reason (Fig. 5-13). One route may be faster and for that reason selected despite the fact that it is longer in terms of distance. This is often true in the case of expressways which allow an individual to reach his destination more quickly despite the fact that he will have to drive many more kilometres in the process. Similarly, a person may select a route that passes through a beautiful residential area rather than through an industrial one. As a result of this type of behavior an explanation of travel patterns cannot always be derived simply by looking for the most direct route on a map. We must be aware of two factors: the actual physical space and the human perception of that space. When these two factors are linked together by an individual they form a *mental map* which will influence his behavior.

Fig. 5-13
"Which route should I take today?"

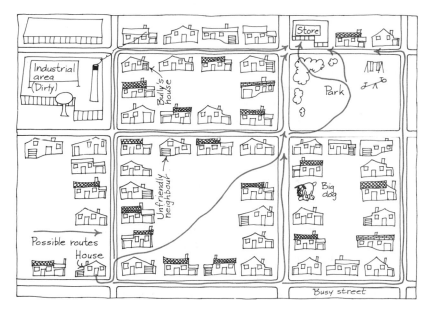

Let us now turn our attention to one specific type, that of travel behavior, in order to discover the general patterns involved and some of the reasons for these patterns.

Travel Behavior. While we are examining travel behavior remember that travel itself is not usually seen as an end in itself. The main purpose of travel is usually for a necessary or rewarding activity that occurs after the trip has taken place. The resulting activity is, therefore, a generator of travel. There are exceptions of course, such as a Sunday drive which in itself is a rewarding activity.

In order fully to comprehend urban travel behavior we must examine some of the major findings of recent research. We will briefly examine: trip purpose, direction of movement, trip length, trip generators, and, finally, the effects of people's images of the urban landscape.

In daily life, a person undertakes journeys to work or school, to commercial establishments, and to social and recreational pursuits. From the morning and afternoon traffic reports it is obvious that the highest concentrations of traffic occur immediately before and after the normal workday and are directed into and out of the central area of the city respectively. This day-to-day occurrence in our cities demonstrates the importance of the journey to work. Not only is work the most important purpose for travel from the home, it also indicates the direction of most travel—to the CBD. Of all trips that are undertaken in urban areas it has been found that 35-40% are made to the home and 15-20% to work. Thus almost two-thirds of all our trips end at one of these two places.

Fig. 5-14
Over-use and under-use of transportation networks.

The journey to work and its corresponding return trip are of vital interest to planners and traffic engineers because of the volume of traffic at two peak periods of the day. Modern transportation technology has enabled our cities to change from small compact units into vast sprawling metropolises. During this change, however, transportation networks capable of handling peak-load periods had to be developed. The result is a system that is overused twice a day and underused the remainder of the time (Fig. 5-14).

We have seen that the main movement of travel takes place toward the CBD. This movement occurs because travel is dictated by land use. In other words, the number of trips to a particular part of the city is determined by the amount, the intensity, and the kind of land use in that area. People gravitate to the CBD because it is the main area of commercial, office, and entertainment activity and is the most intensively developed land in the city.

Similarly, the number of trips that are made to areas away from the CBD decrease because of the decreasing intensity of land use. Thus, a person travelling toward his home in the evening rush hour will encounter most of the traffic close to the CBD and decreasing congestion as he approaches the suburbs. There are exceptions to this general rule, however, because there are areas of intensive commercial development outside the CBD. But here again the congestion will be great in this area and decrease as one moves away to areas of less intensive land use.

Another important feature of travel behavior is the length of the trip. Because most business activity takes place in the CBD and most people who work there live away from it, it has been found that the journey to work is generally the longest type of trip undertaken in the urban area. It is not unusual these days to find people living upward of 30 km away from their place of work. The advent of high-speed commuter trains, express buses, and expressways makes living far away from one's place of work not only possible but often desirable. Generally speaking, the more well-off an individual the greater the likelihood that he will live a considerable distance from his place of work. This may occur because he is better able to afford the increase in costs of the work-trip and he prefers the lower densities found on the edge or outside of the city. However, this situation does not occur in all cities. Why might this be so?

If the trip to work is the longest type of trip that is usually undertaken then what is the shortest? Most often the shortest trips are those taken in order to shop for day-to-day items. There is a tendency to relate the distance travelled with the reward obtained. Thus few people would travel 8 km in order to buy a package of cigars but many might travel that distance to look at a stereo system.

Up to this point we have been primarily concerned with the general travel patterns that are found in the urban area. In order to obtain a fuller understanding, however, we must also briefly examine travel behavior from a more individualistic point of view. Travel and travel patterns are related to human needs. While these will vary from family to family and from individual to individual, there are similarities. A person who has a great many interests and is involved in many activities will probably have a greater need to make trips within the city than someone who has less wide-ranging interests. Similarly, the number of trips made by individuals is related to income and car ownership because of the higher degree of mobility that results. In other words, the higher the socio-economic status, the greater the frequency of travel.

While on the topic of socio-economic status and travel behavior it is interesting to note that the total distance travelled by people and the frequency of their trips is more dependent upon their socio-economic status than upon their proximity to shopping facilities. That is, more is involved than just spatial factors. For example, a person of high economic status will more likely shop for an item at a store that caters to his group, even though that store is located some distance away. He tends to avoid a store just down the street that caters to a lower-income group.

Finally, in order to understand the transportation of individuals we must examine their image of the urban area. As an individual moves about the community on his journeys to work, to shop, to visit, or to recreate, he learns the spatial configuration of the area and evaluates places according to his perception of their uses for different activities. In addition, the overall image is related to where he lives within the city. A person living in the suburbs may view the city as a narrow wedge running from a focus in the central area of the city to his own neighborhood. Areas outside this wedge are generally less well-known because of infrequent visits to these areas. How might a person living in the inner-city view the city?

What is your image of the city? Which areas of the urban community do you know best? Where are your most frequent visits? Do you evaluate and rank certain places (parks, theater districts) as being more favorable than others for certain activities? By considering these questions, it may be possible for you to determine the patterns and reasons for the patterns of your own travel behavior.

For Thought and Research

1 Why is information about the spatial behavior of people of importance to city planners?

2 a) What characteristics of individuals affect their behavior?

b) Some factors constrain a person's behavior. List some factors that may constrain your travel patterns, and explain how they do so.

3 The direction of an individual's travel is not just related to the characteristics of the landscape, that is, to the street pattern. What other factor is important in determining a person's direction of travel? Give two examples of how this factor may influence a person's journey.

4 a) What route (or routes) do you take from your home to school? What are the reasons for selecting this route?

b) With your class, decide on a place where most of you go frequently and discuss the routes that are chosen and the reasons for this choice.

5 What does the phrase "generator of travel" mean?

6 Why is the journey to work so important in any study of travel patterns?

7 Describe the relationship between intensity of land use and travel patterns.

8 What factors affect the length of trips?

9 Discuss travel patterns as they relate to individual needs.

Recommended Readings

Most of the literature on travel patterns is very theoretical and statistical.

1 *Urban Geography: A Social Perspective* by D. Herbert, Praeger, 1973, pp. 238-243.

2 "Urban Travel Behavior" by J. F. Kain in *Social Science and the City* edited by L. F. Schnore, Praeger, 1968, pp. 161-192.

3 "Urban Transportation" by J. R. Meyer in *Exploring Urban Problems* edited by M. R. Levin, The Urban Press, 1971, pp. 275-299.

4 "Driving to Work" by A. F. C. Wallace in *Urbanman: The Psychology of Urban Behavior* edited by J. Helmer and N. Eddington, Free Press, 1973.

5 *The North American City* by M. Yeates and B. Garner, Harper and Row, 1971. See Chapter 15, "Intraurban Movements".

B. RESIDENTIAL MOBILITY

So far we have been primarily concerned with movement in the city from the point of view of travel patterns and behavior. There is, however, another side to the topic of movement which is often neglected despite its importance. This involves the examination of residential mobility, or, as it is also called, *intra-urban migration,* which is the movement from one place of residence to another within a particular urban area. Since approximately 40% of all the land within urban areas is used for residential purposes it is important that we understand some of the processes involved in this aspect of movement within the city.

Most of us are probably unaware of how often people tend to move from one place of residence or dwelling unit to another. In many cases we might spend all our childhood and early adulthood in the house of our parents and may think all other people live similarly. Despite our notions of residential stability it has been found that in North America 20-25% of the population moves every year. The majority of these moves, approximately two thirds, are intra-urban residential changes. Those figures are quite startling and they should raise many questions in your mind. Let us examine three facets of this situation by looking at the reasons for moving, the decision-making process, and the resulting spatial patterns.

Reasons for Moving. If we look at the country as a whole and observe people moving from one city to another, *inter-urban migration,* we soon discover that the primary reason for moving is the economic or employment opportunities offered in one city over another. These opportunities, however, are much less important on the smaller-scale intra-urban field of movement. What, then, are the major reasons why people move from one place of residence to another within the urban area?

Think back to Section 5.2 in which we examined the three social indicators of socio-economic status of urban populations. In this section we learned that an individual's needs change with his stage in the life cycle. This factor appears to be the most important in motivating people to move. When a young person becomes independent he or she will move out on his own into some type of residence. Upon marriage, another residence may be desired and arrival of children will again necessitate a move to another place of residence. This changing requirement for space in the place of residence accounts for approximately one half of the moves. The next most important factor appears to be cost; as income rises, the ability to buy or rent a larger or more prestigious residence increases. Tied in with this cost factor is the availability of housing stock within a certain price range.

Since intra-urban movement is affected by the stage in the life cycle of individuals and households, it is therefore correct to assume that certain groups will have a greater residential mobility than others. The greatest number of moves usually occurs in the 20 to 40 age group. Another prime influence on residential mobility is whether a person owns or rents his place of residence. There is greater mobility among renters than owners. What are the reasons for this situation?

Decision-Making Process. The next feature of residential mobility that we will examine deals with the actual decision-making process. In other words, what factors are considered and what steps are taken if a household (single person or family) is to change its place of residence. In this discussion we will assume that the move is made on a voluntary basis since this accounts for the majority of moves. In the case of involuntary moves, the options that are open to the household are, of course, reduced considerably.

Residential mobility, moving from one residence to another, is the behavior that results from a complicated decision-making process. In simplified terms, it involves two subsections: a decision to seek a new residence and the actual relocation decision. The first decision is the result of inputs that cause the household to want to move. The second decision is the actual selection of a new residence based upon inputs about dwelling units and neighborhoods throughout the urban area. Let us examine this in more detail.

A household exists within a certain space made up of the dwelling unit, the neighborhood, and other areas involved in the household's fields of activity. The environment within which the household exists is a constant source of stimuli: neighborhood activities, noise from traffic and children, air pollution, crime, plus many others. If these stimuli begin to aggravate the household beyond tolerable levels, a decision to move may be made. Other factors that could induce a household to move include the building of industrial sites close to the residence, a change in the location of the place of work, a higher or lower income and corresponding change in status level, the building of an expressway nearby, or a change in the ethnic or racial makeup of the neighborhood.

Once the decision to move has been made, the next phase, culminating with the actual relocation decision, begins with the search and evaluation of new locations. In order to reach a decision where to move to, the household will evaluate various areas of the city. This evaluation is based upon criteria that the household establishes. These criteria might include the size of the dwelling unit, cost of the dwelling unit, accessibility to place of work and shopping, proximity to schools, prestige of the neighborhood, and its ethnic composition. Can you think of any more?

In order to evaluate particular housing types and locations, the household must be aware of the possibilities open to it. Therefore it must conduct a search. Based on previous experiences the household will probably possess some knowledge of the areas of the urban community where it would like to relocate. This prior knowledge may come from the day-to-day activities of the household, from friends and acquaintances, or from a developer. In addition to this knowledge, new information may be sought from the media (television, radio, and newspapers), from real-estate agents, and from other sources. Upon completion of this search the household may decide upon a new location or it may decide to remain where it is.

Most movements from one place of residence to another are based upon this type of decision-making process carried out by individual households. Thus each year millions of these individual household decisions and movements are made within the cities of North America. If we now examine these movements, not in isolation as we have above, but as part of large-scale intra-urban movement, what type of pattern or patterns will we discover?

General Spatial Patterns. If any generalized pattern can be discerned, it is a movement from the center of the city outward. In essence, suburbanization is still an ongoing process in North

America. The urban fringe, still in a state of expansion, offers possibilities for new housing and low-density living (Fig. 5-15). With the decentralization of business and industry, new commuter transportation networks, and a deterioration of many city cores, the suburban locations present an attractive place to live.

Fig. 5-15
Most residential migration is directed toward the suburbs.

Some cities have been fortunate in that their downtown residential areas are being rejuvenated despite the general trend away from this area. This rejuvenation may be the result of large-scale urban-renewal projects, new apartments developed by private industry, or individuals moving into run-down houses and renovating them. This last method slowly changes low-income areas into middle- or upper-income residential areas.

It was mentioned earlier that there is greater mobility among people who rent than among people who own their place of residence. Since the rental market is usually in the central area of the city, as opposed to the suburbs, there is a greater frequency of moves within this area of the city than in other areas where home-ownership is a predominant characteristic. Areas of the city where there are apartment buildings would, therefore, probably have high mobility rates.

When households move they generally tend to relocate in an area of similar socio-economic status. Because areas of similar status are generally found in close proximity to one another, it follows that most moves will probably be relatively short in terms of distance. In addition, most districts tend to retain their socio-economic status despite the movement in or out of a large number of households.

As pointed out in the previous paragraph, residential mobility is governed to some extent by the social characteristics of the urban landscape. However, over a long period of time the nature of districts can be affected by this mobility. Some wealthy districts will become poor, some districts will be taken over by ethnic groups, and some will be lost to other urban land uses. In our discussion of ethnic status it was shown how the movement of people into an area in a process of invasion-succession can change the character of the area. In addition, there is another process that is important in the housing marketplace. The process is called *filtering* and involves the aging of homes and neighborhoods to the point where they become available to low-income groups. The old stately homes found near the CBD that have been turned into rooming houses or multiple-dwelling units are typical examples of this filtering process. Each day the urban landscape changes in some respect as individual households, each making separate decisions, fit into the larger mosaic of human interaction.

For Thought and Research

1 a) What is the most important factor that causes people to change their place of residence (i) on an inter-urban basis and (ii) on an intra-urban basis?

b) Describe how the factor in (ii) changes throughout an individual's life.

c) What is the second most important factor that accounts for intra-urban movement?

2 What are the reasons for greater mobility among people who rent a dwelling unit than among homeowners?

3 a) In point form show the steps involved in the decision-making process of moving from one residence to another.

b) Make a flow chart of this process.

4 If you had to move, list in order of importance the criteria that you would use to evaluate a potential location. Explain the reasons for your selection.

5 a) What is the generalized pattern of movement of intra-urban migration?

b) Explain the reasons for this pattern.

6 What areas of the city are characterized by high rates of residential mobility and why?

7 Describe the process of invasion-succession.

8 Describe the process of filtering.

Recommended Readings

1 *Urban Geography: A Social Perspective* by D. Herbert, Praeger, 1973, pp. 243-268.

2 *Urban Residential Patterns* by R. J. Johnston, Bell, 1971. See Chapter VII.

3 *The North American City* by M. Yeates and B. Garner, Harper and Row, 1971, pp.

5.5   SERVICING MAN'S NEEDS AND DESIRES

A.   PUBLIC UTILITIES AND COMMUNITY SERVICES

In most studies of urban communities one aspect is often overlooked or neglected. This is, how man's needs and desires are serviced. Perhaps this neglect occurs because we take so much for granted in a modern technological society. No longer does each individual have to be concerned with many of the fundamentals necessary for a healthy existence. Earlier in this unit we examined some of the basic needs that had to be met in order to survive. These included fresh water, sewage-disposal services, a marketing system for food, transportation facilities, police and fire protection, a place to live, and so on. Early in the history of North America these needs were of immediate concern to all members of society. Today we are able to take a less personal interest because we have established organizations to service these needs. Nonetheless, one should have a basic understanding of the things that are an integral part of everyday life.

Fig. 5-16
Outmoded and modern facilities. (Pickering Nuclear Generating Station photo courtesy of Ontario Hydro.)

In order to meet the demands of a constantly changing society it is necessary to be adequately prepared. Thus almost all cities have some type of planning agency. In any discussion of servicing man's needs it is vitally important to consider the planning aspects. If there is not proper planning, the needs of the community will not be met. Therefore, accurate planning and foresight are essential to successfully servicing man's needs and desires.

Communities are served by both public and private organizations. We will deal only with the public sector since it provides services fundamental to our existence. Essentially, public services are those services provided by some level of government in order to meet specific public needs. These services can be separated into two distinct categories: public utilities and community services. *Public utilities* can be thought of as components of the physical structure of the city and include such systems as water supply, sewage and refuse disposal, street lighting, electricity, and storm sewers. *Community services,* as we will use the term, refer to services that are separate from utilities. These include administration, communication, cultural, educational, medical, and recreational services, and fire and police protection. Under each of these headings there are numerous facilities provided to meet the service needs of the community. Under the heading recreational services, for example, we could include such facilities as parks, playgrounds, zoos, swimming pools, stadiums, beaches, bicycle paths, and golf courses. The facilities may be viewed as the physical manifestation of a community service.

How important are public services and their related facilities? In terms of land use alone, as much as one-half of the developed area within some urban communities is occupied by public institutions or used for public functions. To us as individuals the influence of the public sector on our lives is even more apparent. Most urban dwellers are born in a hospital financed with public money. They are educated in publicly supported schools and universities; they may die in a hospital and be buried in a public cemetery. During their lives they use the public transportation system, garbage-disposal services, sewage and water purification systems, public parks, and are protected by fire and police departments. The dependency of urban man upon his society is indeed very great.

An individual's needs and desires constantly change as he goes through life. The same is true, on a larger scale, of an urban community as it develops. The demand for more and a greater variety of public services and facilities increases as the population grows and the urban area expands. Facilities that were once sufficient become outmoded (Fig. 5-16). In addition to not meeting the requirements of this expansion, the older facilities do not meet the expectations or rising standard of living of the population. While some demands, such as the need for water and sewage systems, remain constant, demands for newer services are ever-increasing.

With the baby boom after World War II public services had to be expanded as more administrative personnel and schools were needed. As new concepts in education were introduced a greater variety of these facilities and programs had to be created. Changing technology created new needs for better sewage treatment facilities, water purification facilities, airport facilities, and new housing projects. A service that was once considered a luxury may now be seen as a necessity. The provision of a solid-waste disposal service in the form of recycling facilities falls into this category. At one time no such service was provided because few people saw a need for it.

Today, however, such a service is demanded in order to stop the waste of precious raw materials and to preserve the environment.

How do public services differ from services offered by private firms or individuals? Public services are provided through and monitored by the machinery of the government. Thus the political process is involved. Further, a unique situation exists with public services. The owner (the public) is also the consumer. Therefore, if a large number of consumers are dissatisfied, the policies may be changed through the election of new political leaders.

Another important difference is that the selection of an optimum location and profitability, fundamental elements in the private sector, are generally less important in the public sector. For example, a public transportation system may be operated at a loss in order to provide cheap and efficient transportation for members of the community. Because the system is losing money in order to meet these desired aims, the government may subsidize it. Such a situation would not last long if profit were the only aim. Thus, activities can be carried on by the government that no private firm could undertake unless it received government aid. In some cities, however, the government cannot or will not provide these subsidies.

Governments provide both tangible and intangible public services. We are mostly aware of the former because they are the most visible. Tangible services can be seen in the form of the facilities used to carry out the service. Sewage treatment plants, libraries, hospitals, parks, highways, and water purification plants are highly visible features on the landscape that reflect the provision of certain services to the community. Less visible and therefore somewhat intangible services are planning, zoning, and tax concessions. Although the results of these services appear on the landscape, the actual connection between the service and the physical manifestation of it may often be unclear (Fig. 5-17).

Fig. 5-17
A government service such as planning is intangible; however, the product of this planning, such as a school, is visible in the landscape and makes us aware of the intangible service provided by the government.

Regardless of the service offered, two groups of economic decisions are involved in providing it. The first consists of *investment decisions*—what to build, where, when, and how to finance it. The second consists of *operating decisions*—how, where, when, and for whom a service should be given, the quality and quantity of the service, and what charges will be made to the user. Of course, political influences have always been important, but aesthetic factors are having more influence every day on decision making. These decisions are not unique to governmental activities but they are perhaps more clearly seen because they are constantly discussed by the media.

The role of the planner in the implementation of new or expanded services and the subsequent building of facilities should not be underestimated. The planner should determine the real need of the community by realistically evaluating the opinions of the people who are to be served. This is not always an easy task if there are many interest groups or if the facility to be constructed is of a controversial nature. Second, the facility must be located or constructed so that it will adequately serve the community without becoming a blight on the landscape. Finally, a planner must be flexible and modify his own thinking to suit the changing desires of the community as a whole. Perhaps the most frustrating thing faced by the planner is the attitude of people who agree that a facility is required and is acceptable as long as it is not built close to where they live. This is often referred to as the ''yes, but not here'' syndrome.

Let us now look more closely at how man's needs and desires are serviced in an urban community by considering some specific examples. Since we are now familiar with many aspects of the travel behavior of urban residents we will begin by examining the transportation system.

Transportation System. The transportation system can be viewed as the circulatory system of the city. It moves people and goods to and from the community and provides the means for people to move from one activity to another. It is, therefore, the most important form of spatial interaction. There are basically three main aspects to this system.

TRAVEL PATHS. These travel paths are the structural components of the community and may occupy up to 30% of the total land area. They include main streets, side streets, freeways, mass-transit rights-of-way, and rights-of-way for railroads. The road and railway pattern plays an important part in helping to shape areas of the city. How is this done?

VEHICLES. A variety of vehicles use this circulatory system. They range from automobiles, buses, trucks, and streetcars to subways and commuter trains. Although automobiles make up at least 80% of the total travel on the freeways and streets of most urban communities, increasing importance is being given to mass-transportation systems because of extreme congestion caused by automobile traffic. This congestion of urban roads is leading many urban residents to the conclusion that the automobile is not suited to the urban environment in its present form. It is relatively inefficient in transporting people, particularly when one large car carries an average of 1.5 passengers. It would take a 15-lane freeway to carry the approximately 30 000 people per hour that one modern transit line (subway) can carry.

In most cases the number of trips made by bus or other rapid transit varies widely depending upon the density of population, the economic characteristics of the city, and the extent and quality of service offered by the system. For example, an area in the suburbs with a low population density clearly requires less service than an area with a high population density. Unfortunately, this limited service leads many suburban residents to use their automobiles and thus add to the congestion downtown.

TERMINAL FACILITIES. All too often it is forgotten that efficient transportation depends on good facilities at the terminals for handling incoming and outgoing people and goods. A suitable station or other facility may be required for handling large numbers of people. Parking areas must be provided where large numbers of cars start or end a journey. It is only through the proper integration of these three facets of urban transportation that the system as a whole will function effectively.

Water and Sewer Systems. Consider these questions for a moment. Why do you obtain fresh water when the tap is turned on even though the lake or river from which it comes is polluted? How does water get to the top of a tall apartment building? Where does the water go when you pull the plug after having a bath? Does human waste enter the lake or river from which the drinking-water supply comes? Such questions are important to all of us because they make us examine the quality of life.

We cannot escape the need for clean water, either for personal use or for use by industry. The demand for water is usually related to the population and industry of a given area. In a small town or suburb the average amount required may be 200 litres per capita per day. In a large city, however, the requirement may be 1 000 litres per capita per day. Although demand is measured in the number of litres per capita per day, this form of measurement also includes the demands made by industry, commerce, and fire-fighting units. This form of measurement, therefore, is a standardized measure that reflects population density and industrial development.

An urban community must consider not only the quantity of water that it requires but also its availability. It must decide where to obtain the water—from rivers, lakes, springs, or wells. If these sources are not large enough to supply a growing urban community, water may have to be brought in from places as far as several hundred kilometres away. New York City and Los Angeles are in such a situation. The water must then be treated so that it is clear, colorless, odorless, pleasant tasting, and free of toxic substances. In many communities, some residents prefer to buy bottled water that has not been treated with an abundance of chemicals. After the water has been treated it is then ready for storage at strategic points ready for distribution. This can be done in three ways.

GRAVITY SYSTEM. The source of water is at an elevation above the community so that the flow is caused by gravity. A town at the base of a hill may receive its water from a river that flows down the hill.

RESERVOIR SYSTEM. Water is pumped into a reservoir which is at an elevation above the community and the water flows by gravity through the water mains. These large metallic reservoirs are a familiar sight in many communities. In fact, in many places the name of the town is written on them to advertise it to approaching visitors (Fig. 5-18).

PRESSURE SYSTEM. Water is pumped into the water mains under pressure.

Generally speaking, most communities use a combination of all three systems in order to meet their varying needs. The pipes carrying the water generally follow the street pattern and are buried deep enough so that they are not affected by frost. Why do the pipes follow the street pattern?

We have seen how we obtain water but what happens when we have finished using it? Urban communities commonly have two types of sewer systems. One carries the liquid and solid wastes of a city for treatment and disposal. These are called *sanitary sewers*. All buildings (houses, office buildings, and industrial plants) served with water have sanitary sewers of various sizes leading to main sewers. The sewage from these locations is collected by gravity, although some pumping may also be required to move it to the treatment plant.

The other type of system is made up of *storm sewers*. Storm sewers are used to collect and carry away rainwater and other surface water to prevent flooding. In fact, they replace the natural drainage system destroyed by asphalt and concrete. Without these sewers the rainwater on the roads after a storm would drain away very slowly and cause flooding. After the next rainfall in your area locate the nearest storm sewer by following the flow of water on the road. In some areas storm sewers and sanitary sewers are combined. What are the disadvantages of this situation?

Fig. 5-18
A reservoir system.

Refuse Disposal. Another major service offered to urban residents is the disposal of refuse. Whereas the sewer system gets rid of the community's liquid and some types of solid waste, the refuse-disposal system gets rid of the bulk of solid waste. This includes garbage, ashes, industrial refuse, and any other material that is collected by public or private waste-disposal organizations.

The disposal of solid wastes is no easy task, particularly with the great number of throwaway containers used today. It has been estimated by the American Public Works Association that the average amount of refuse collected in urban areas is approximately 650 kilograms per capita per year. This amount varies from city to city, of course, depending upon local conditions such as the presence of home incinerators. But even so, it is an enormous amount of refuse. The disposal of solid waste has developed into a major cause for environmental concern. No longer is uncontrolled burning and indiscriminant dumping tolerable. As a result it will cost us more to dispose of our waste. Perhaps this will make us more conservation minded.

Once the refuse is collected from homes, commercial establishments, apartments, and industrial plants, it must be disposed of. There are several ways of doing this. The garbage may be disposed of by incinerators in the home or by grinding units in the kitchen sink. The waste from these kitchen disposal units flows into the sewer system and is later treated with other household waste. There are a number of possibilities open for the disposal of solid waste but the most effective are also the most expensive. In the past, open dumping was a very common method of disposal. Today there are still some communities that use the open dump but it is usually a breeding ground for flies and rodents and thus presents a health problem. In some areas of the world, organic wastes are composted to make agricultural fertilizer. Unfortunately this method is not very profitable and is therefore not very popular in North America. Perhaps the most practical of all methods is recycling. Although not all solid waste can be recycled it does have the advantage of preserving the limited quantity of resources in the world. Again the question arises whether or not it is economically feasible. Should this question even be asked in light of our limited resources? Finally, the refuse may also be taken to a large central incinerator where it is burned under controlled conditions to prevent odor and air pollution. The resulting residue may then be used as landfill.

Sanitary landfill is a term used to describe the method of waste disposal in which a trench or hole is dug and a layer of garbage or residue from an incinerator is covered by a layer of soil. This procedure may be repeated many times until the disposal site is full. In this way there is no odor, water pollution, flies, or rodents to make the operation unhygienic. The sanitary landfill procedure also has another advantage. Some communities located on flat terrain are now creating ski hills for recreation or a gently rolling topography that is more aesthetically pleasing.

In this section we have looked at three examples of how some of man's needs and desires are serviced. Some others that could be examined are the gas-distribution system, the location of underground facilities, electric-power systems, and steam-distribution systems for heating large numbers of buildings in a concentrated area such as the CBD. In addition there are many facilities provided by public or by a combination of public and private enterprise—restaurants, swimming pools, skating rinks, golf courses, and museums. The servicing of man's needs and desires within the urban community is an enormous task. As technology improves, people's desires change and as the community grows, so does the demand for more and different types of services and facilities.

For Thought and Research

1   a) What are public services?
    b) Describe the two categories of public services.
2   For each of the following community services list four types of associated facilities. For example: administrative services—city halls, courthouses, polling stations, municipal office building.
    a) educational;
    b) medical;
    c) safety or protection;
    d) cultural.
3   Describe how the public sector plays an important part in our lives.
4   Explain why there are constant demands for new services.
5   How do public services differ from services offered by private organizations?
6   What are the differences between tangible and intangible public services?
7   What is your reaction to the "yes, but not here" syndrome?
8   Briefly describe the three main aspects of a transportation system.
9   Describe the differences between sanitary sewers and storm sewers.
10 Describe the various ways in which solid waste may be disposed. In your opinion which is the best? Give reasons for your choice.

Recommended Readings

1 *An Introduction to Town and Country Planning,* 5th edition, by A. J. Brown, H. M. Sherrard, and J. H. Shaw, Angus and Robertson, 1969.
2 *Handbook on Urban Planning* by W. H. Claire, Van Nostrand Reinhold, 1973.
3 *Metropolis: Values in Conflict* by C. D. Elias Jr., J. Gillies, and S. Riemer, Wadsworth, 1969.
4 *Principals and Practice of Urban Planning* edited by W. I. Goodman and E. C. Freund, International City Managers Association, 1968. A comprehensive and very practical book.

5   *Planning and Human Need* by P. Heywood, Praeger, 1974.
6   *Urban Problems: A Canadian Reader* edited by R. Krueger and R. C. Bryfogle, Holt, Rinehart and Winston, 1975. See ''Urban Transportation''.
7   *Cities in Action* by E. Van Cleef, Pergamon Press, 1970.

B.   URBAN PLANNING

In the first part of this section we were primarily concerned with the provision of services and facilities needed to meet some basic human needs. There is a broader perspective, however, that we must take in order fully to comprehend the means of satisfying human needs and desires. This larger view entails the concepts of urban design. As previously stated, this service is of a less tangible nature. Urban planning not only involves planning streets, sewage systems, and disposal sites but also urban designs that will contribute to a healthy, stimulating community life. All too often in the past we have neglected this aspect of life in order to meet utilitarian needs. The title of this section, ''Servicing Man's Needs and Desires'', implies two things: first, the provision of services and facilities to meet certain human needs for survival; second, the provision of proper designs that will fulfil other essential needs. These may include aesthetically pleasing landscapes, areas for social interaction, a healthy environment for children, and solutions to current urban problems through proper design. In the following discussion several concepts of urban design and planning are presented. No comments either in favor or against are presented. It is up to you to decide the merits of each.

Garden Cities. In 1898 Ebenezer Howard published a book called *Garden Cities of Tomorrow*. In this book he put forward planning ideas that attempted to alleviate the congestion, squalor, and discomfort found in the cities around him. He proposed a merging of the town and the country by creating satellite towns surrounded by pastoral land. Each circular town would consist of approximately 2 400 ha and have a population of about 30 000. The town would be divided into six neighborhoods separated by radiating boulevards. The center of town would consist of public buildings enclosing a park and, in turn, surrounded by a greenbelt. Industry would be located on the outskirts of the town. Beyond the industrial belt would be another area of open space in the form of farmland (Fig. 5-19). Howard was the first person to introduce the concepts of greenbelts, satellite towns, garden cities, land assembly, and regional planning. These concepts have only become part of our language in recent years.

The Neighborhood Unit. In the 1920s Clarence Perry developed a concept in which each community or neighborhood within existing cities would be a self-contained unit. North Ameri-

Fig. 5-19
Ebenezer Howard's garden city: ''A City in a Garden''.

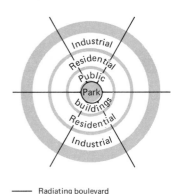

——— Radiating boulevard

▨ Greenbelt (open space, parks, farm land)

can cities expand by annexing land on their outer fringes. It was Perry's idea that as this expansion took place the new communities should be self-contained. Each community would be developed on about 65 ha and have a population of approximately 5 000 people. His model was based upon four principles.

a) Apartment buildings and shops should be at the outside corners of the neighborhood where traffic is the highest. In this way the inner portion of the neighborhood would be a quiet residential area composed of single-family dwellings.

b) Ten percent of the space within the neighborhood would be reserved for parks and open space.

c) The inner streets would not be for through traffic. They would be dead-ends or circular in nature so that all through traffic would have to take the major traffic arteries that bordered the neighborhood.

d) The elementary school would be the focus of the neighborhood and within easy walking distance from all the homes.

Radburn Plan. In 1928 Clarence Stein conceived a new form of development at Radburn, New Jersey. It would fit the needs of an automobile-oriented society. His primary aim was to separate automobile movement from pedestrian movement. In order to do this he planned large superblocks with a community park running through the middle (Fig. 5-20). The homes would be located on cul-

Fig. 5-20
The Radburn plan.

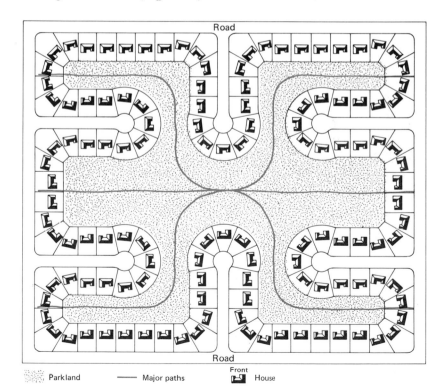

Road

Road

Parkland   —— Major paths   Front   House

de-sacs so that no vehicles could reach the center of the block. In addition, the houses would be turned around to face the garden and strips of parkland rather than the street. In this way the residents would be oriented toward the park and not the street. The park would be the backbone of the block and would be a focal point for the social activities of the residents. Although the town of Radburn was never completed, the residential sector was and has provided a model for developments in other parts of the world.

Broadacre City. In 1934 Frank Lloyd Wright, one of America's foremost architects and planners, developed the concept of an urban area that was spread out over a very large area. This

Fig. 5-21
"Complementing the environment" by Frank Lloyd Wright.

urban-sprawl approach was designed in order to make full use of the automobile. In order to travel between places of residence, work, and shopping it would be necessary to travel several kilometres in a vehicle. Each house would be low with clean uncluttered lines (ranch style) to complement the environment rather than clash with it (Fig. 5-21). The decentralization of activities was to complement the North American concept of wide open spaces and broad vistas.

Vertical City. In contrast to Wright, Le Corbusier, a Swiss architect and designer, proposed to build cities composed of very tall buildings. In 1922 he developed a plan whereby 3 million people would be housed in a vertical city of between 12.5 and 25 km². This concentration of people in towerlike structures separated by open green landscapes was designed to put life and vitality into the empty hearts of twentieth-century cities. The apartment towers would incorporate many of the urban functions found in a typical horizontal city. The middle floor of the building would be an interior street offering such facilities as stores, post offices, banks, and cinemas. In addition the buildings would be raised above the level of the ground on stilts so that the landscape would continue without interference (Fig. 5-22). This particular type of structural design is in use in many buildings in North American cities at the present time. It helps convey a feeling of spaciousness even in highly developed areas such as the CBD.

Fig. 5-22
Le Corbusier's "Vertical City" concept.

Arcology. Paolo Soleri, a contemporary designer, has designed a city for the future. It is a multi-storied structure of 25 storeys covering about 4 ha of land. It is self-contained and houses a population of 3 000 people. This design, like that of Le Corbusier, will promote interaction among the inhabitants and do away with the need for the automobile. The main modes of travel are walking, escalators, and elevators. Soleri calls this type of design for cities of the future "arcology".

We have now observed some of the possibilities offered for the design of our cities. These designs have been developed to meet the changing needs and desires of the urban community and to overcome some of the problems presently facing us. Although many concepts were developed in the earlier part of this century, they are only now becoming popular. What the future holds is unknown but each one of us can play a part in it if we have the will and determination.

If you were given the opportunity which design or designs would you select? Perhaps you would prefer a design based upon your own ideas. Exercise 7.28 gives you this opportunity.

For Thought and Research

1 Briefly summarize the six design concepts.
2 a) How feasible is Ebenezer Howard's design for contemporary society?
   b) Would you like to live in a garden city or satellite town? Explain your reasons either pro or con.
3 a) What are the advantages and disadvantages of the designs put forward by C. Perry and C. Stein?
   b) Compare these two designs with the designs of most of our modern communities.
4 Compare and evaluate the concept of urban design of Frank Lloyd Wright with those of Le Corbusier and Soleri.

Recommended Readings

1 *The Master Builders* by P. Black, Alfred A. Knopf, 1966. This book is basically concerned with architectural design; however, it does present the philosophies of Le Corbusier and Frank Lloyd Wright.
2 *Cities in the Suburbs* by H. Carver, University of Toronto Press, 1962. An extremely interesting book on urban design.
3 *The Search For Environment, The Garden City: Before and After* by W. L. Creese, Yale University Press, 1966.
4 *Metropolis: Values in Conflict* by C. D. Elias Jr., J. Gillies, and S. Riemer, Wadsworth, 1969. See Chapter 4, "Urban Design"; Chapter 5, "Planning"; and Chapter 7, "Housing".
5 *Planned Urban Environments* by A. Strong, Johns Hopkins Press, 1971.
6 *Cities in Action* by E. Van Cleef, Pergamon Press, 1970.

Alternatives for the Urban Environment: Benefits and Costs

6

What kind of city do most people want? What kind of city is it possible to have? Such questions are common today and reflect man's increasing concern for the urban environment of the future. In addition to greater concern, we also have a greater ability than ever before to control the nature of tomorrow's cities through urban planning. What kind of city do *you* want to live in? Is your concept of the ideal city realistic or is it an impossible dream? This unit should help you to answer these and similar questions.

6.1 DECISIONS! DECISIONS!

The urban landscape is the result of the many decisions made by individuals and groups of individuals. Your decisions as to where to live, work, shop, and recreate, how to get from place to place, and even when to do it affect the urban environment of today and tomorrow. Similarly the environment reflects the values you place on clean air and water, privacy, open space, trees, and even wastes.

If you choose a house on 5000 m² of land at the edge of the city, then you contribute to the growing trend to low-density living which is consuming farmland at an alarming rate. If you choose to take the bus downtown to work, then you reduce the demand on downtown roads and parking space. By not driving the car to work you reduce the amount of pollution in the air. If you choose to buy soft drinks in returnable bottles or restore old furniture instead of buying new, you reduce the amount of garbage burned or buried by your community. Demand for the raw materials needed for these products is also reduced. Yet, by the same action, you may cause unemployment in the industries that provide these products. The effects of your decisions are far-reaching. Now, you do not have to live on 5000 m² of land, or ride a bus, or recycle your wastes. These are only alternatives you can choose or not choose as you wish. But you should know that the decisions you make *will* affect the kind of environment in which you will live. (Fig. 6-1).

In addition to individual decisions, you influence the actions of industry and government. In Toronto, a group of concerned citizens stopped the construction of an expressway. In Los Angeles, a public referendum rejected a major public transit proposal. Are there similar examples in your community?

Fig. 6-1
Places to live—the choices are many.

Decisions made by others can affect your choices as well. These may be business, industrial, or governmental decisions. By accepting or rejecting the consequences of these decisions you also choose the nature of your urban environment. An industry locates in your riverside community. That industry pollutes the river with its wastes. You used to fish in the river as it flowed through the town park. Now you must either go elsewhere to fish, give up fishing, or start a campaign to clean up the river. The decisions that you and others make will affect the recreational environment of your town.

Suppose that your local planning office approves a change in the zoning laws which permits a high-rise apartment building in your neighborhood of single-family homes. Do you accept this decision or fight it? What effects would the apartment building have on you? Your response will affect the environment of your neighborhood.

Decisions also tend to come in packages. In choosing a residence we may eliminate a transportation alternative. Is a car a luxury or a necessity? It depends on where you live. The government made a decision and passed a law requiring all automobiles to have pollution control devices. This decision affects the quality of air you breathe, the viability of the internal combustion engine, and even the amount of precipitation in the city annually. Major decisions facing both the individual and the city today involve desirable and necessary living densities, mobility, growth, and environmental quality. The choices are many. To determine the *best* alternatives is often not an easy task.

How Do You Decide? The easiest and most frequently used method is to choose the alternative that provides the greatest amount of pleasure for the individual at the least cost for him. If choosing between two undesirable alternatives, you take the lesser of the two evils. Simple as it sounds, experience generally proves that determining what is better is not that easy. Pleasure cannot always be measured in dollars and cents. There are different types of pleasure that cannot be easily compared. Some pleasures are longer lasting than others. Similarly not all costs are monetary. Further, some costs are immediate; other costs may not be felt until sometime in the future. The decision can become even more complex when the effects of your choice on others is considered. You are faced with the age-old question of whether the individual's good can be placed above the good of society and the environment.

While decision making is not simple, determining rationally the best alternative in a given situation is not impossible. You will still be looking for the alternative that gives the greatest good for the least cost. However, to decide rationally you must consider the full implications of each alternative. This means that you must look beyond the immediate benefits and costs for you and consider long-range benefits and costs for you *and the rest of the world*. And remember, no decision is ever perfect for everyone.

Several methods have been developed which attempt to make decision making more rational. In *Alternative Analysis,* you determine all of the possible alternatives for any one decision, for example, your decision how to travel to school. You then determine all of the factors you would use to evaluate each alternative, for example, cost, time, weather, and air pollution. You then score each alternative by its relative desirability under each factor, with the best receiving the highest score. Table 6 illustrates how this is done. By summing the scores of each alternative for each factor, each alternative is evaluated and the best one selected. In this example, the bicycle received the highest score and, as a result, is the best alternative.

TABLE 6

	F₁ (Cost)	F₂ (Time)	F₃ (Air Pollution)	F₄ (Weather)	Score
A₁ (Walk)	4	1	4	1	10
A₂ (Car)	1	4	1	4	10
A₃ (Bus)	2	2	2	3	9
A₄ (Bicycle)	3	3	3	2	11

This method can be modified to reflect the differing importance of the factors considered. For example, cost may be considered very important while air pollution is of only minor concern. *Weighted Alternative Analysis* allows you to multiply the scores for each factor by a number consistent with that factor's importance. If cost is thought to be four times more important than time or air pollution and twice as important as weather, then the data of Table 6 are altered to those shown in Table 7. The best alternative is still the one with the highest score.

TABLE 7

	F₁ (x 4)	F₂ (x 1)	F₃ (x 1)	F₄ (x 2)	Score
A₁	16	1	4	2	23
A₂	4	4	1	8	17
A₃	8	2	2	6	18
A₄	12	3	3	4	22

A final method, which is the most detailed, is a *Benefit-Cost Analysis.* The balance sheet of costs and benefits that you construct will, of necessity, include a mix of items valued in dollars and cents, along with items to which it is difficult to give a monetary value. The noise that an expressway produces affects the sleep of nearby residents. What price do you put on lost sleep? Should we ignore such human costs?

The calculations of benefits and costs are also affected by the length of time considered. Too often, only immediate benefits and costs are estimated. A new expressway into the downtown area of a city may bring greater accessibility. In the long run, however, this may be cancelled by the destruction of functions in the downtown area which attracted people there in the first place.

The cumulative aspect of the individual's decision must also be included. Five thousand square metres of farmland converted to housing, by itself, is not of great importance. It becomes important when thousands of individuals make the same choice.

A decision is best if, after considering its full implications (non-monetary as well as monetary; the long run as well as the short; cumulative as well as individual), it has the greatest surplus of benefits over costs.

If you have tried Case Study 9.4, you know that deciding which is best is not easy. In many cases all that can be hoped for is that we know the full consequences of our decisions before we make them and are prepared to accept those consequences.

For Thought and Research

1 a) How do you get to school most days (walk, bicycle, drive yourself by car or motorcycle, get a ride with someone else, ride public transportation, or take the school bus)?

b) What other ways could you use if you wanted to? These are your real *alternatives*. Why don't you use them?

c) Which of the ways listed in a) are impossible for you to use, even if you wanted to? These are *non-alternatives*. Why are these means of transportation impossible for you?

2 List as many ways as you can in which your urban environment affects your transportation alternatives and non-alternatives.

3 In what ways does your choice of transportation affect your urban environment?

4 a) What effect has the government had on your transportation alternatives?

b) What action might the government take to improve your transportation situation?

5 a) Conduct an Alternative Analysis of your journey to school.

b) Conduct a Weighted Alternative Analysis of your journey to school.

c) For your chosen means of transportation list as completely as you can the benefits and costs to you and society. Be sure to consider the long-run, cumulative, and non-monetary effects discussed in this section. Use the following tabular form.

Benefits	Costs

6 Suppose that the government decides that the use of private automobiles wastes too much energy and creates too much air pollution. It plans to take measures that will curb the use of the automobile. How would you respond to this governmental decision? How might it change your life if adopted? How might it change the urban environment that you live in?

7 Most of the preceding questions deal with only one of your decisions—transportation. But there are many other decisions involving all aspects of urban life. Select what you consider to be another significant decision that affects you and the urban environment as a whole. Identify your alternatives and explain how your decision may affect the urban environment. Make a benefit-cost study of this decision.

Recommended Readings

1 *Guide to Benefit-Cost Analysis* by N. R. D. Sewell et al., Resources for Tomorrow, Queen's Printer, 1965. This booklet is the best guide to benefit-cost analysis available to date. It isn't simple but it is worthwhile reading if you want to know more about this frequently used technique of decision making.

2 *Man-Made America* by C. Tunnard and B. Pushkarev, Yale, 1963. Now in paperback, this prize-winning book examines selected problems of design in the urban landscape. Illustrations are excellent.

3 *Sick Cities* by M. Gordon, Penguin, 1963. Another look at the urban environment but with emphasis on man's behavior rather than on land. If the cities are sick, then so are we.
4 *Cities and Space* edited by L. Wingo, John Hopkins, 1963. A less emotional examination of the future use of urban land, with emphasis on the alternatives. Being a collection of essays, a cross-section of views are presented.
5 *The Last Landscape* by W. Whyte, Doubleday, 1968. This book is a practical handbook for obtaining a more liveable environment. It looks at the possible ways of solving some of the problems of the urban landscape.
6 *Design with Nature* by I. McHarg, Doubleday, 1969. This book applies ecology to urban design and presents a radically different method of urban planning.

6.2   HOUSING ALTERNATIVES

Where you will live is probably one of the most important decisions you will make in your lifetime. It is important to you because the fulfilment of such needs as shelter, security, and privacy are not only essential to your very existence but to the quality of that existence. If, for instance, the dwelling you live in fails to give you the privacy you need, the stress you will probably begin to feel may lead to irritability, headaches, and insomnia. Eventually this kind of stress, if great enough and continuing long enough, can lead to more serious conditions such as mental illness and heart disease. Of course, such serious disorders result largely from extreme deprivation of privacy. Each day the place where you live probably affects your life in dozens of smaller, less dramatic ways. An example is your journey to school or work. The length of that journey is a direct result of your choice of residence. Whether you commute across town or have only a five-minute walk is your decision (or that of the head of your household). The decision of where your dwelling is affects you daily in the time and effort required to make the journey.

The fact that housing is one of the major expenditures for the individual has an indirect effect on the way he lives. How much you spend on housing will determine how much you have left for other needs such as food, clothing, and entertainment. You can probably think of many other ways your dwelling choice affects you.

The decision you make is not only important to you, however. The dwelling you choose affects the people around you. Your dwelling requires resources—land, building materials, and public services. These goods and services are limited as far as the community is concerned. When they are allocated to your dwelling it reduces the supply of these items for all other possible uses. The land your building takes might have been used for agriculture, recreation, or industry. The lumber required for your home necessitated cutting down many trees. The cement meant gravel deposits had to be quarried. Money spent on roads, sewers, and water lines might have been spent on schools, parks, and welfare. Whether these uses are considered good or bad, they *are* effects of your decision on the community.

How important can the effect of one dwelling be, you may ask. Taken by itself, the effects of one dwelling would not be significant. However, as mentioned before, the urban environment is the sum of many individual decisions. If one person chooses to build a house on a 5 000 m² lot instead of a 2 500 m² lot, it costs the community only 2 500 m² more land. If 1 000 people make the same choice, 250 ha of additional land is required. When 100 000 people make this choice the additional land needed is 25 000 ha. Who pays if the cost of agricultural products goes up because so much land has been taken out of agricultural use? In this case, not only was double the land required but services such as roads, sewers, and water lines would have to be much longer. Does the individual bear the full cost of his decision or are there costs that society must bear because of his choice? The homeowner pays taxes, but will they fully reimburse the community for the added costs of his decision?

The decision you make, then, is not only important to you, but to your community as well. Similarly the decisions that are being made by others concerning their residences affect you. A dramatic example of this effect is the construction of a high-rise apartment building on a lot adjacent to a private home. The homeowner might find that his home no longer gets the afternoon sunshine because of the shadow cast by this building. He may feel uncomfortable in his own backyard because of the feeling that people are watching everything he does. Thus he has been affected by someone else's decision.

What have your decisions today got to do with the future urban environment? The availability of agricultural land, service costs, transportation costs, and open space for the future are being determined today by the kind of housing that is being built. All these things are related to the way in which we put land to use for housing (Fig. 6-2). The best measure of this is the residential density achieved; in other words, the number of dwellings we put on each hectare of land brought into residential use. A high residential density makes a city more compact. This affects the future of the urban environment by leaving more land for other uses such as agriculture. In addition there is more open space available for recreational use. Hence the cost of servicing the dwellings with roads, sewers, and water lines is not only reduced initially but future maintenance is also reduced. A more compact city means lower transportation costs. Of course, higher densities might mean less privacy, more urban stress, and an urban landscape with a different appear-

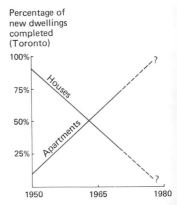

Percentage of new dwellings completed (Toronto)

Fig. 6-2
An increasing proportion of new housing is in the form of apartments and townhouses. What is causing this present housing trend? Will the trend continue?

ance. Higher densities is only one alternative. The various benefits and costs of the housing alternatives you have now, as far as the future urban environment is concerned, are the main focus of the rest of this section. However, since the individual is making his decision now, present benefits and costs are also considered.

It is probably against human nature to expect the individual to sacrifice his own desires for the good of society. Personal benefits and costs will probably remain the main basis of the housing decision. Still it does not hurt to know the broader implications of your decision. You are part of society. What hurts society or benefits society ultimately hurts or benefits you as well.

About now you might be thinking that a housing decision is important only when it concerns the building of new dwellings. True, if you move to an existing dwelling, no new demands are made on the community's resources. However, moving into an existing dwelling can increase the demand on the community's resources since developers may interpret your move as meaning that demand for that type of housing has increased. For example, if enough people move into vacant apartments, developers will probably build more apartments. Clearly, all housing decisions are important, regardless of whether or not they directly involve the building of new dwellings. Let us look, then, at the benefits and costs related to choice of dwelling. First, we will examine the question of loss of farmland to urban development and the possibility of future agricultural shortages due to this loss.

Density and the Loss of Farmland. The cumulative consumption of land by an urban population is a cost that must be considered. How we use land today and how much we use will shape the urban environment of tomorrow. If an increase of 2 million people is projected for an urban area by the year 2000, the density of residential development can greatly affect the land requirements of that urban development. Calculate the residential land requirements if the density is 10 people to the hectare and compare it with that of a density of 200 to the hectare. There is a difference! The low-density urban environment of Los Angeles and the high-density development of New York City illustrate the point. With four times as many people as Los Angeles, New York covers 40% less area.

However, even low-density requirements for population increases projected for the next 30 years will require only a small percentage of the vast land areas of Canada and the United States. The problem of land consumption is not with land generally, but with certain types of land. Cities are generally found in the center of good agricultural land. Growth converts even more agricultural land to urban use. If present trends continue, Los Angeles and New York will double their land extent by the year 2000, using over 12 000 km^2 of land to do so. Both cities are presently surrounded by good farmland. Still, the amount of farmland lost will be only a small portion of the total American farmland. New lands are being converted to agricultural use every year to offset these losses. There *should* be no problem, then, with a shortage of farmland. We can replace lost land in one place by draining swamps for cropland or irrigating desert areas for oranges. Technology can increase the yield per hectare with fertilizers, irrigation, pesticides, and even weather modification. So what's the problem?

California provides an excellent example. The leading agricultural producer in the United States, California has a unique combination of climate and soil conditions. It provides out-of-season fresh fruits and vegetables for the rest of the USA and Canada. But the best agricultural lands are only a very small portion of the state's total area. Low-density suburban development is converting much of these high-quality lands to urban use. Marginal lands are being converted to agriculture with expensive irrigation. But not only is this a costly substitution, it may not even be a lasting one. California's urban areas, especially Los Angeles, are short of water. When there is not enough water for both urban and agricultural uses, which use will suffer? The people of California may soon have to decide whether or not the state should continue to grow when the price of continued growth is costly water-supply projects and the destruction of prime agricultural land.

The rich fruit-producing area of the Niagara Peninsula in Ontario is undergoing a similar suburbanization. Unfortunately the well-drained soil desirable for peaches and grapes is also ideal for subdivison development. This fact, combined with its proximity to some large urban centers, results in hundreds of hectares of orchards and vineyards succumbing to the developer's bulldozer every year. The same thing is happening in the lower Fraser Valley near Vancouver.

In all cases, the important factor is not the quantity of farmland lost but the quality of land that cannot be replaced. For example, the fruit lands of the Niagara region of Ontario happen to be in an area of ideal climatic conditions. The combination of climate and soil is found only in this one small area in Ontario. The loss of that top quality agricultural land is a cost that must be assumed by urban development. The choice of low-density development aggravates the situation by consuming even more land per dwelling. This is a cost, however, that we cannot continue to ignore. The recent worldwide shortage of fertilizer is a warning not to place all our hopes on technology to replace the losses. We must soon decide whether or not the provision of four homes is worth the loss of a hectare of prime farmland. It is you who will have to pay more for peaches, oranges, and avocados as they become more costly to grow and are in shorter supply.

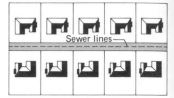

A   Rectilinear street pattern

Sewer lines

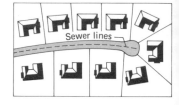

B   Curvilinear street pattern

Sewer lines

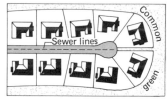

C   Clustering pattern

Sewer lines

Common green

Fig. 6-3
Design can reduce servicing costs.

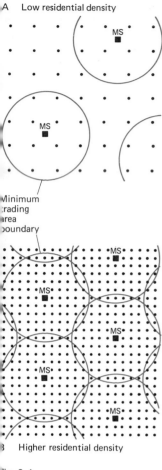

A Low residential density

MS

MS

Minimum
grading
area
boundary

•MS•

•MS•

•MS•

•MS•

•MS•

B Higher residential density

Fig. 6-4
Density of families determines distance to services (e.g., milk stores) and existence of choice for the consumer.

Density and Service Costs. The cost of consuming more land is not the only extravagance of low-density development. Each dwelling requires certain public services for its existence—roads, utilities, and community facilities.

The number of metres of roads and other services required for a certain population depends on how closely the dwellings are spaced. Lower-density subdivisions require more roads per dwelling than higher-density developments. It is not hard to see why. The more land you have to cross to service a residence, the longer the roads, sewers, and water lines must be. Figure 6-3 illustrates that, even with equal densities, road requirements can be reduced with better design. Shown are three possible layouts for ten suburban single-family homes. Notice that road requirements are reduced by making the street pattern curved instead of rectilinear. Reducing the private lots from 2 000 m² to 1 000 m² not only cuts road requirements in half but also provides space for park land. Densities are the same in all three layouts. In which subdivision would you prefer to live? Not only is a saving in road lengths passed on directly to the home buyer or renter in the form of lower housing costs, but dividends are also received in increased land available for other uses such as parks. Similar savings in construction costs are possible for water, sewer, and power lines. Generally, the closer the dwellings are spaced, the lower are the servicing costs.

All residential areas require community facilities such as schools, parks, and convenience stores. Each of these facilities requires a certain *threshold population* within a certain distance to warrant its existence. Figure 6-4 shows how a difference in density affects the number and spacing of these facilities. Clearly the average travel distance for residents to get to the facility decreases with higher densities. Also, the choice of destinations is greater in more densely populated areas. High densities mean lower service costs, and community facilities are more numerous and closer. How many would-be suburbanites consider these obvious benefits when selecting a lot for a future home?

Density and Transportation Costs. The fact that community facilities are farther away in low-density residential areas tends to affect transportation alternatives. In very low-density areas walking to the store becomes impossible; school buses become a necessity; the automobile becomes a necessity rather than a luxury (Fig. 6-5).

Density also affects whether or not a public transportation route will pay for itself. If there are insufficient people living along the route to provide enough users, service is discontinued or reduced. The greater the residential density, the more passengers there will be for the transportation service and the better it will be. Subways and other mass-transit lines require very high residential densities to be economically feasible. Your choice of residential density, then, greatly affects the transportation alternatives that you have. As will be discussed later, it also affects the cost to the community of providing these alternatives.

Density and Open Space. Loss of open space is generally thought of as a cost of higher densities. In fact, the decision to live in a single-family house is often made because of the amount of private open space that comes with it. Actually a high-rise apartment building may leave more land uncovered than single-family homes housing a similar number of people.

Open space is land that is not built upon. It may be natural green space or land that has been covered by pavement, patio blocks, or any other man-made surface. Lawns, streets, and parking lots are all open space. This space can be owned privately or publicly. It can be in large or small pieces. Giving it shape are the buildings that surround it. Generally the open space we value is green, but many paved areas add to the sense of space people need.

In a typical subdivision, about 70% of the land is not covered by houses. Except for roads, this land is almost entirely privately owned. About one third of each lot is dedicated to a front lawn which is usually ornamental and seldom used. It is required, however, to set the house back from the street. The backyard receives greater use, particularly the patio area. For many people the private space occupied by lawns is just so much grass to mow. And, unfortunately, these small private pieces do not provide space for popular activities such as walking, jogging, bicycling, golf, and tennis. Because of the large amount of private space and space devoted to roads, public open space provided for these activities is minimal. Should already low-density residential areas be further reduced in density in order to provide this additional open space? This would be unnecessary if private open space were partially reduced in favor of jointly owned public open space. The clustering technique of residential design can achieve this public space while maintaining or even increasing densities (see Fig. 6-3). A valuable benefit from clustering is the saving of attractive pieces of green space from construction. If a subdivision site contained a woodlot, ordinarily all of the land, wooded and treeless, would be developed for houses. With clustering, the houses can be grouped in open areas around the woodlot, protecting the natural beauty of the woods as a park. Similarly a stream valley can be maintained as a linear park rather than being buried in concrete under houses. Landscape architects call this "designing with nature".

Open space in high-density areas is important to provide residents with sunlight and ventilation as well as recreation. Buildings must be allowed a certain amount of space to ensure proper

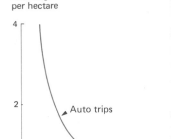

Fig. 6-5
A Chicago transportation study in the sixties indicated that as residential density declines, daily auto trips per family increase.

Dwellings per hectare

Trips per family

Fig. 6-6
Desirable spacing of buildings for maximum sunshine. A, too closely spaced to allow lower apartments to get sunlight; B, minimum lot size for apartment building (25 stories); C, almost the same density achieved with low-rise apartments (4 stories).

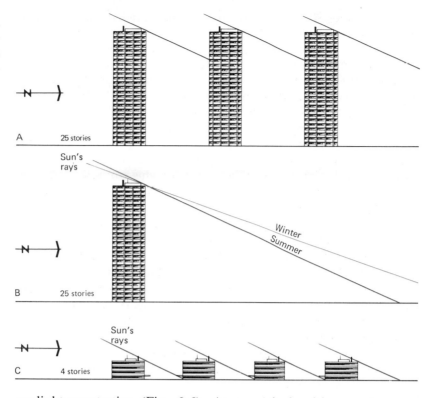

sunlight penetration (Fig. 6-6). As a result densities can be very similar for high-rise and low-rise apartment buildings. The amount of open space will be greater in the high-rise development, but the quality of that space may be lower. For example, open space around high-rise buildings tends to be inhospitable; large areas are devoted to car parking and ornamental lawns. Open space for recreation may get the little space that is left. But who wants to play tennis in total shade? And why must car parking use up open space when the cars could be parked underground?

High-density low-rise developments built in the European style around courtyards have much less open space than high-rise dwellings. However, the small courtyards can be inviting, being sunny, protected from the winds, and, generally, well treed. Unfortunately, this more human design for high-density development has been largely overlooked in North American cities since the invention of the elevator.

Density and Human Costs. Last, but not least, in the study of long-run and cumulative implications of our residential alternatives are the human costs which cannot be measured in dollars and cents. What effects do the density and scale of our urban environments have on man's health and happiness?

Studies of the behavior of rats and deer have been used to suggest that high-density living is dangerous to human health and happiness. Too much human contact can produce body stress resulting in disease, mental illness, family breakdown, and crime. All of these ills of society are on the increase. Is there any relationship between this increase and the trend to urbanization? It is probably not a simple relationship but the idea is interesting. Man's indifference to strangers in large cities has been attributed to his need to minimize human contacts for his own sake (Fig. 6-7). If urbanites got as involved with all their neighbors as rural dwellers do, the strain would be intolerable. The current exodus from the cities has been attributed largely to the need to reduce high-density stress.

Another group of researchers feel that high densities in themselves are not bad. Only when man or beast can find no temporary escape from the pressures do high densities cause problems. So long as the deer on an overpopulated island could swim nightly to the mainland for escape, they acted normally. When this escape was denied them, vast numbers of deer died of what researchers called shock disease. According to the same theory, man is comfortable in urban places so long as he can get away to rural and wilderness areas when he needs to. If low-density sprawl covers large areas as it does in Los Angeles, it becomes difficult to get out of the city. The suburbs may not necessarily provide more human benefits than high-density areas.

Man needs a certain amount of human contact. The popularity of urban life for many people is based on the ability to contact all kinds of people and do all kinds of things. In fact, studies show that there is suburban stress as well, caused by isolation and reduced experiences. The neurotic suburban housewife is a well-known figure. Is she a product of the suburban environment? Can man find a balance between privacy and isolation?

The scale of the urban environment also affects man's psyche. Do tall skyscrapers belittle man or represent his greatest achievement? What are the effects of the seas of monotonous subdivisions? More needs to be understood about how architecture and densities affect us. What stress does the necessity of a 20-floor elevator ride several times a day add to living? How much space do we really need? What constitutes privacy?

Not only do we have density alternatives but within these densities we have design choices. High density need not mean highrise buildings. Low density need not mean uniformly spaced monotonous sprawl. Clustering can maintain overall densities without converting every hectare into private lots.

In addition to the problems that housing choices create for the individual and the environment, the choices themselves may be getting fewer. Costs now threaten to put the ownership of a single-

Fig. 6-7
Crowds affect man's behavior. In what ways do people attempt to minimize contact with each other in crowds?

family house out of reach for the vast majority of North Americans. New housing starts show an ever-increasing proportion of town-house and apartment dwellings. If this trend continues, urban sprawl and its consequences will be lessened. However, the consequences of high-density living—stress, crime, and disease—may be even worse if care is not given to proper design of the urban environment. Group pressure on governments and developers may be necessary to ensure that immediate costs of construction are not the developer's only concern.

The design of the urban environment is up to you. The choice of a residence does affect your urban environment.

For Thought and Research

1 Find out how much land your dwelling consumes. If you live in a multi-unit building, be sure to divide by the number of units. At that amount of land per dwelling, what would be the residential density of the area in which you live? Why might the density you calculate be higher than the actual density of your neighborhood?

2 Explain how your choice of a single-family home can affect each of the following:
   a) your health;
   b) cost of food;
   c) transportation alternatives available.

3 a) Find out from your municipal office what restrictions there are for new residential construction in your community. For example, what are the minimum lot sizes for various types of residences, dwelling floor-space requirements, housing setbacks from the street, and residential densities allowed. Using this information calculate the maximum residential densities permitted for various housing types.

   b) Evaluate the standards that your community has for controlling residential densities. What are the desirable and undesirable effects of these standards? Suggest improvements in your local standards.

4 a) Find out from the local planning or municipal office the costs of roads, sidewalks, water, sewage, power, and telephone lines per frontage metre of residential land. Calculate the difference in cost of serving 100 lots with a frontage of 30 m and servicing 100 lots with a 20 m frontage.

   b) Who pays the difference in the cost of servicing, the buyer or the community as a whole? Ask a municipal official if the total cost of servicing new dwellings is paid for by the resident. Enquire specifically about the hidden costs of servicing and maintenance. What additional expense do longer roads and service lines cause? Who pays?

5 Observe the use of open space around an apartment building in your community. Note the following: number of stories, number of apartments (if possible), space used for parking, space devoted to lawns, and space for recreation. Is the area attractive? Do people use it? How does the structure affect sunlight, temperature, and winds at ground level?

Recommended Readings

If you wish to look further into the potential costs of farmland losses, the first two books are easy to read.

1 *The Destruction of California* by R. Dasmann, Collier, 1966.

2 "The Disappearing Niagara Fruit Belt", in *Regional and Resource Planning in Canada* by R. Krueger, Holt, Rinehart and Winston, 1963.
The following books enlarge on the topic of service costs and density.
3 *Man-Made America* by C. Tunnard and B. Pushkarev, Yale, 1963.
4 *The Shape of Towns* by K. Rowland, Ginn, 1966.
For more about the human costs of density alternatives see the following.
5 *The Last Landscape* by W. Whyte, Doubleday, 1968.
6 *The Hidden Dimension* by E. Hall, Doubleday, 1966.
7 *Design with Nature* by I. McHarg, Doubleday, 1969.
8 *Problems in the Bosnywash Megalopolis* by L. A. Swatridge, McGraw-Hill, 1972.

6.3   MOBILITY ALTERNATIVES

No urban dweller can doubt the need for mobility. What would your life be like if you never left your home? Yet mobility affects not only the quality of your life in the urban environment but also the quality of the environment itself. With restricted mobility, choices vanish and horizons narrow. Out of necessity people must live close to the people and places they need. With greater mobility, such as that provided by an automobile, people disperse. The environment takes on an entirely different appearance. Houses are spaced farther from each other. Industries and stores do not need to be nearby. The rapid spread of modern cities is largely due to the greater mobility of urban dwellers. Before the automobile cities were more compact.

Technology has been and will continue to be instrumental in increasing man's mobility. The car gets man farther in five minutes than he can walk in an hour, unless there is a traffic jam. Technology can increase potential mobility but not necessarily actual mobility. Technology also provides man with transportation alternatives. Some provide greater mobility than others. Some are privately owned while others must be provided publicly. Think of the means of transportation used around you (Fig. 6-8). Compare the mobility they offer and who provides them. The future promises even more choices. Each, you will discover, makes particular demands on the urban ecosystem.

The means of transportation you choose results in certain benefits and costs for the urban environment and society. The bicycle, unlike the car, does not require fossil fuels, nor does it emit poisonous gases into the atmosphere. But, like the car, it requires a path or road. In many cities, the ever-increasing number of bicyclists need separate bicycle trails and paths for safety. Each means of transportation makes demands. Each has benefits. Each has costs. Consider these every time you choose a means of transportation.

Why do we choose to travel the way we do and as much as we do? The next time you decide to ride the bus to school or to

Fig. 6-8
Transportation alternatives.

bicycle to the corner store, think of why you chose that particular alternative. What effect does the length of the journey have on the means you choose? Compare the choices you have for making a journey of two blocks with one of eight kilometres. Notice that the length of the trip limits the means of transportation you may find convenient or reasonable in price. The number of times a day or week that you must make the trip can also influence your choice.

Some trips you make are more important than others. Which of these would affect you more—the occasional trip to a downtown department store or the daily trip to school or work? You may enjoy the first trip more, but the daily journey to work or school makes a greater impact on your life. A trip of 30 min, twice a day, five days a week, consumes a great deal of your precious time. If it cost you a dollar a day to drive and park your automobile, the total cost per year becomes significant. Remember that you control the length of this trip by choosing your place of residence and sometimes even your place of work or school. If you work downtown but choose to live in the suburbs, 30 min away, then your choice is responsible for the longer daily journey. The amenities of the suburbs might compensate you for the cost of time and money spent to get to work. At the same time the demands placed on the urban environment are greater because of the distance you placed between your home and work. Not only does your decision cost *you* more, but it costs *society* more. More and wider roads are required. Large investments in mass public transit may become necessary if enough people make the same choice. Interestingly enough, many industries and offices are now relocating in the suburbs to be nearer to their employees. This exodus of employers from the inner-city benefits the suburbanite but hurts the city dweller. To keep his job he must now travel to the suburbs daily, if he can afford it. Low-income workers who cannot afford a suburban home or a car are the losers.

While the length and purpose of the trip may affect your choice of transportation, the reasons most commonly given for choosing a particular mode are usually expressed in terms of convenience, cost, likes, and dislikes. Ask your friends why they travel to school the way they do. Ask neighbors how they get to work and why. How often is cost or convenience mentioned? How often is their choice a matter of personal likes and dislikes? How often is lack of other alternatives mentioned? Certainly, if public transit is not available, you cannot use it. If you do not have an automobile, your only choice for distances you cannot walk is public transit. Some people dislike buses, others dislike driving. All of these things affect the transportation choices we make. They must also be dealt with by planners who wish to change transportation patterns.

When all our alternatives are examined, two appear most often in the present-day urban environment—the private automobile, and public transit systems. The majority of trips beyond walking distance are made by one of these two means. Because of their mass use, they exert a tremendous influence on the quality of the urban environment. How do they compare for convenience and cost? The answer is not a simple one. Costs to the environment and to society must also be considered.

Public Transportation. Regularly scheduled routes with fixed boarding points and a user fare are characteristic of most present public transit systems. Unless you are lucky enough to live right at a transit stop and unless the planned route goes exactly where you want to go, the use of public transportation involves the inconvenience of getting to and from it. Also, it often involves longer journeys than necessary. Examine Figure 6-9. Notice how the bus routes radiate out from the central business district. Transfers are made only in the CBD. What problem does the person have who lives in the location marked in this diagram if he has to take public transit to get to work? Why does the public transit system not provide a more direct route? What other alternative means of transportation would be more convenient? Perhaps the person could drive his car to a bus stop. However, if he has to drive a car to get to a bus, it is generally more convenient to take the car all the way. Only if no parking is readily or cheaply available at his destination would parking his car at the bus stop be a tempting alternative. Free parking at the bus stop would also encourage the use of the public transportation system. A source of inconvenience which must be eliminated for the public transit to compete with the automobile is delays caused by transfers and poor connections.

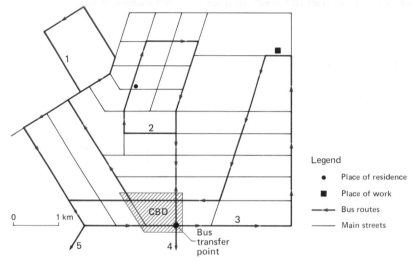

Fig. 6-9
Convenience and public transportation: sometimes taking the bus is not too convenient.

More frequent service to more places is essential to improve the public's image of public transportation convenience. But this costs money. Most public transit systems depend on ticket fares to cover costs. When a route fails to attract the number of passengers necessary to pay for the service they are getting, that route must either be subsidized from more profitable routes, fares increased, or service reduced. Subsidization can work to a certain extent but when too many routes go into the red, the public transit authorities are faced with the two other alternatives.

Where and why are the public transit systems losing money? As residential densities decrease, there are fewer and fewer passengers per unit area to be served. The chance of living near public transit decreases. The trip to catch the bus becomes more of an obstacle. Even if you get to the bus stop, destinations in suburban areas are more dispersed. The chances are greater that the bus will not take you where you want to go. Inconvenience, as we have said before, leads to even fewer public transit users. This low use is the reason why suburban public transit is usually losing money. In order to compete with the automobile in low-density areas, public transportation needs to become more convenient and have a more flexible service.

In high-density areas, more passengers per unit area makes routes profitable. Residents are nearer to transit stops. Destinations are more concentrated. The central business district provides a focus for transit routes. Figure 6-10 shows how transportation routes, in areas with high concentrations of people and activities, can focus on the center of activity, knowing that this is where people will want to go. In low-density areas, with dispersed centers of activity, public transit lacks a single focus and must expand service (tripled in this example) in order to serve the same number of dwellings.

When the volume of passengers on a route gets high enough, not only does service increase in frequency, making it more convenient, but the means of transportation employed may be improved. Streets have a limited capacity for moving people, even if they are devoted entirely to buses. Generally buses must share the route with automobiles. Traffic congestion slows buses and cars alike. Replacing buses with trains operating on their own private rights-of-way, such as in a subway or on an elevated track, dramatically increases passenger movement during peak hours. The new speed made possible by this improvement attracts even more users. The price of this increased capacity and speed is high. For example, a subway route can cost $10 000 000/km to build (1969, Toronto). Thus increased fares usually accompany such an improvement, even though passenger volume increases.

Rapid transit is a solution for high-density areas. In residential areas of fewer than 400 persons per hectare there are not enough passengers to make such services profitable. A strong central business district to act as a common destination for trips is also essential.

What are the benefits and costs for the urban environment of public transportation systems? Before looking at these, let us compare public transportation with the automobile for convenience and cost offered the user.

The Private Automobile. Ideally the automobile offers the ultimate in convenience, privacy, and flexibility for its user. It takes its owner wherever and whenever he wants to go, door to door, so long as there are roads and parking spaces. Its convenience suffers, however, when a great many other drivers wish to go to the same place at the same time. Bumper-to-bumper traffic and the search for a parking place are time consuming as well as frustrating. Parking in the CBD can be costly. Insurance, licence, and repairs add to the cost even after the initial purchase price has been paid (Fig. 6-11). How many drivers calculate the costs of insurance, depreciation, and repairs each time they choose to drive somewhere? When comparing the costs of taking the car versus the bus most people generally consider only gas and oil expenses. On this basis the

A high density community

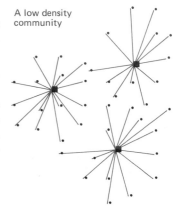

A low density community

Maximum distance customer is willing to travel for service

Fig. 6-10
Density, service centers, and transportation.

automobile is considered not only more convenient, but cheaper. Is it? Besides the non-calculated costs to the user there are the costs to the community of providing roads and parking for the automobile. Why should the user not pay for these? Who pays for the changes in the urban environment when trees and grass are replaced by cement and asphalt? Who compensates the pedestrian who must breathe choking fumes and the urban homeowner who must paint his house frequently because of air pollution?

For owner	Costs	Benefits
	Price	Convenience
	Depreciation	Comfort
	Insurance	Privacy
	Repairs	Time saved
	Gas and oil	
	Licence plates	
	Car washes	
For society	Costs	Benefits
	Road construction	High mobility
	Road maintenance	Employment (construction
	Noise pollution	and maintenance)
	Air pollution	
	Traffic control	
	Land removed from tax roles	

Fig. 6-11
The automobile: benefits and costs.

Public Costs of Transportation. So far public transportation and automobiles have been compared on the basis of convenience and cost to the user. On that basis the automobile is generally more convenient but usually more expensive. However, public costs (and benefits) are also involved. Roads cost money to construct and consume valuable urban space, as do subway routes. Is there a difference in cost or space consumed? Public transit systems sometimes receive subsidies from the municipal government. Roads are built with public money. Does one produce more air or noise pollution than the other? Which is the least costly to the urban citizen? Which provides the greatest mobility for the money? Which allocates the costs of mobility most justly? The answers to these questions should be as important to you as your personal convenience and cost.

The space taken up by a transportation route is very important in the urban environment (Fig. 6-12). Land used for transportation is land not available for housing, industry, commerce, or

Fig. 6-12
Note the land requirements of this expressway under construction.

recreation. While transportation is a vital service for these other functions, it is desirable to minimize the land required. Land for roads and railroads is generally removed from the tax base of the community. Hence too many roads tend to bankrupt a city. Newark, New Jersey, has discovered this fact. How much land is needed depends on the spatial requirements of each person being transported, the speed with which he is travelling, and how much of this service he demands. If each person wishes to travel in a medium-sized automobile by himself, then his spatial requirement equals that of the automobile. A road has to be a certain width in order to accommodate a line of automobile traffic. The maximum number of cars that could pass a certain point along the road in an hour would equal the hourly capacity of that lane of the road. If the traffic can move faster the capacity will increase. If more lanes are provided capacity will multiply by approximately the number of new lanes. If two people occupy each car instead of one, twice as many people can be transported along the same route. Similarly, if people choose to go by bus and if the bus can hold 50 passengers, then the spatial requirement of each passenger is one fiftieth of a bus rather than one car. Figure 6-13 illustrates the dramatic difference this can make. By switching from cars to buses, the capacity of the road can be increased without adding any lanes. Rail routes, on a narrower right-of-way, can transport still more people because speeds are greater and stops are fewer. There are, of course, other related spatial requirements for transportation that we have not considered—space for parking, garages, and terminals.

What is the true cost to society of driving a car downtown in rush hour? Since roads and transportation facilities are generally constructed to carry the peak capacity rather than the average, every car using the road during rush hours contributes to that peak. If, as a result, road widening or expressway construction is thought neces-

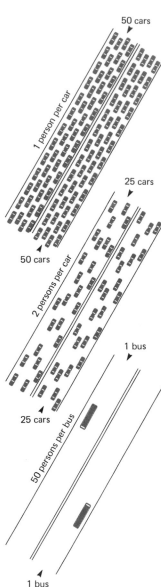

50 cars

1 person per car

25 cars

50 cars

2 persons per car

1 bus

25 cars

50 persons per bus

1 bus

Fig. 6-13
The efficiency of automobiles versus buses.

Fig. 6-14
Commercial land in the downtown areas of today's cities is being eroded by the expanding demands of the automobile—more roads, more parking.

City block 1945

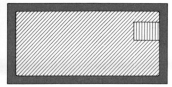

City block 1975

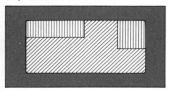

Legend

Transportation (streets)

Transportation (parking lots)

Commercial

sary, should the cost of such an improvement not be borne by those who use the route during peak times? How many rush-hour travellers consider the cost of expanding the route they take when choosing to go by car? Why should citizens who do not use these roads during peak periods pay for a wider road than they need? Perhaps all users of roads and parking spaces should pay a user charge just as the public transit user must. If the true cost of automobile use were calculated, public transportation would be more attractive and appear the cheaper alternative that it really is.

Other costs are also involved in transportation. For example, what is the cost of polluting the air with poisonous automobile or bus exhaust fumes? Should we not consider the cleaner air resulting from the use of electrically powered trains and streetcars? With petroleum reserves rapidly approaching depletion, can we afford the cost of using 5 l of gasoline to transport only one person 10 km? Construction costs per kilometre of expressways and rapid-transit lines are almost equal, but there is a difference in the value received. Compare space requirements and passenger capacities. Compare the noise and air pollution produced. Case Study 9.4 is an actual benefit-cost study of this matter.

In the past, road widening and construction benefited both private and public transportation because both used roads. Expressways are needed to keep automobiles moving but expressways do not serve buses. When expressways are built in the heart of an already developed urban area, it is necessary to convert large strips of land from other uses. They become concrete barriers, dividing neighborhoods from neighborhoods and producing a host of dead-end streets. An expressway is just as much of a barrier to traffic as a river flowing through the city, bridged in just a few places. And on what land is the road built? Often it is urban open space that is sacrificed. It provides the least expensive route in terms of displacement and expropriation. Increasing road and parking space in the inner-city is at the expense of the land uses that attract people downtown—stores and offices. Figure 6-14 illustrates the erosive effect that the automobile can have on the city center. Eventually the downtown is no more than a giant interchange. What price do we pay for this great accessibility? The pedestrian shopper—the consumer on whom business in the downtown depends—becomes alienated in a sea of automobiles. Automobiles inhibit his movement, disturb him with their noise, and make the air unpleasant to breathe. Is it surprising that the shopper finds the downtown less attractive and eventually goes elsewhere to shop? Ironically, even after all the road widening, the streets in most cities remain congested. The improvements simply encourage more people to use automobiles. Wherever expressways dump their users onto regular city streets, traffic congestion is a major problem. New extensions of the expressway soon seem to be the only solution. And so expressway begets expressway. Many projections of automobile needs to the year 2000 show that, in order to satisfy the needs, all the land in the inner-city must be converted to expressways. Who wants this kind of environment (Fig. 6-15)?

The urban environment that best suits the automobile avoids the concentration of activities in any one spot that creates traffic congestion. People are spread out over the land in low-density suburban developments. Central business districts are abandoned. This environment makes the alternatives of walking and public transit less convenient and more costly. The automobile eventually becomes the only alternative. You have only to look at the urban environment of Los Angeles to see what the future automobile-oriented city will look like. This city once had public transit, but its routes were torn up. Now rapid public transit in that city may be an impossible dream or a financial nightmare.

If you find Los Angeles attractive, as many do, then you can choose the automobile and the environment that goes with it with a clear conscience. If you do not like what you see, then you had better start considering the alternatives while you still have some. Can we find an alternative that provides the comfort, convenience, and flexibility of the automobile without its destructive effects on the urban environment? Can public transit be made compatible with low-density residential development? Is there a way of mixing automobiles and public transit to achieve a transportation system with the best characteristics of both while, at the same time, maintaining a good environment in which to live?

Some Proposed Solutions. If you think that some concentration is a necessary and desirable characteristic of the urban way of life, then expressways should not be allowed to penetrate and decentralize these concentrated areas. Automobiles and concentration are incompatible. This means that automobile traffic in the downtown area must be discouraged or prohibited. Pedestrian malls such as the one planned for Fort Worth, Texas, and existing in Ot-

A
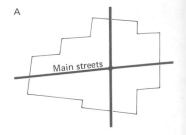

B
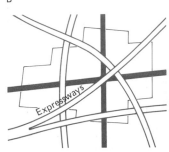

Fig. 6-15
Transportation in the inner city. A) 1945, before expressways; B) 2000, after expressways.

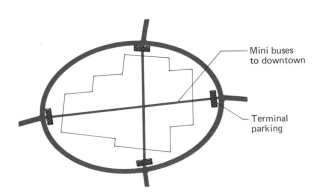

Mini buses to downtown

Terminal parking

Fig. 6-16
The ring solution. Compare the results with the total expressway solution in Figure 6-15B.

tawa, Ontario, are examples of areas where automobiles are prohibited. Restricted parking and charges closer to the real cost of parking space would also discourage people from driving downtown. Predictions that traffic jams will worsen if roads are not improved have been shown to be false. Traffic jams discourage people from using cars. It is road improvements that encourage more people to drive and thus perpetuate traffic conjestion. But if the downtown is not to strangle, alternative means of getting downtown must be found. Rapid public transportation is an obvious solution for heavily used routes. However it is no solution for low-density residential areas.

Leicester, England, solved the problem of suburban access to the central core by ringing the inner-city with an expressway (Fig. 6-16). From this ring, expressways radiate out to the suburbs. Terminals with large parking facilities are located along this ring, allowing the suburbanite to go the rest of the way into the city by fast public transportation. Removing automobile traffic from inner-city streets abolished the need for road widening. While having disadvantages, this plan is an attractive compromise.

Other alternatives include a dial-a-bus feeder system bringing people from their homes to major transportation routes, and privately owned mini-cars or capsules. The former has been tried in Toronto, Ontario. The latter is, at the moment, an urban planner's dream. These capsules would run manually in low-density areas and automatically through high densities on computer-controlled monorails (Fig. 6-17). High-speed movement with the bumper-to-bumper closeness possible with computerization makes large peak capacities feasible, reduces travel times, and increases road safety. Space requirements for the vehicle are the bare minimum, yet privacy is maintained. With the option of manual drive, door-to-door convenience and flexibility are maintained. Parking is still a problem but on a much smaller scale. If space is the problem, building over existing transportation routes might be a solution.

Fig. 6-17
The travel capsule solution. The capsule takes the individual right into the city and is stored in a high-rise garage within walking distance of work or stores. In the ring solution the individual must transfer from automobile to public transit. Compare the spatial requirements and convenience of the two solutions.

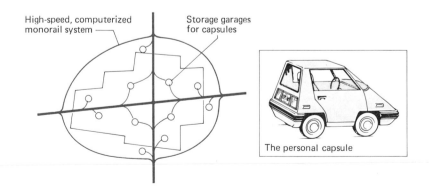

High-speed, computerized monorail system

Storage garages for capsules

The personal capsule

Another idea using the transportation we have today has been put into effect in Stockholm, Sweden. Stockholm already has a very well-developed rapid-transit system. Recent fare reforms allow passengers to buy monthly transit cards for one low fare. The card holder is entitled to travel as often as he wishes anywhere on the system.

We have discussed only some of the possible transportation alternatives you have. Each would provide a different urban environment for you. You must decide what kind of environment you want and what kind of transportation system will give it to you. Research Topic 8.6 will assist you if you wish to explore future urban transportation possibilities.

For Thought and Research

1 a) What demand does walking make on the urban environment? What are its benefits and costs for the environment?

b) Answer the same two questions for three other forms of urban transportation.

2 a) Commuting long distances to work is an alternative chosen by many urban residents. What is the cost to the commuter of a 15 km trip to work (one way), five days a week, 48 weeks a year if his car gets five kilometres to the litre and parking costs $2.50 per day?

b) Why might one be willing to spend so much time and money on commuting?

3 a) Study the public transit system in your community. How convenient is it? How long does it take to get downtown from randomly selected points in the city? Compare the times taken by public transit, car, bicycle, and foot. How would you improve the convenience of your public transportation? Is your proposal economically feasible?

b) Is the public transit in your community making or losing money? How have fares changed in the last ten years? How has the number of riders changed over the same period? Is there any noticeable relationship between fares and the number of riders? Has service increased or decreased during the same period?

c) Evaluate the success of the public transportation authorities in providing the community with an inexpensive (publicly through subsidies, or privately in fares) and convenient service. How do residential densities affect the transportation system? What can be done to improve the service or reduce costs? Has free public transit been considered?

4 a) How has the use of the automobile affected the urban environment? What kind of future urban environment best suits the further use of the automobile and why?

b) If people prefer the automobile should we try to force them to give up their automobiles and travel by public transportation?

5 Is it possible to build an urban transportation system that will fully satisfy all mobility demands? Explain your answer. What importance does this have for planning transportation systems in the urban environment?

6 How would the adoption of any one of the proposed solutions described at the end of this section affect the future urban environment? Explain your answer, including the ecological consequences.

7 a) Figure 6-18 illustrates two possible locations for freeways serving three centers of population. They may be within a larger urban complex or simply three neighboring communities. Evaluate the effects of the two alternatives on the urban environment and their ability to serve the three population centers.

b) Suggest a third alternative for the freeways' location and support your plan.

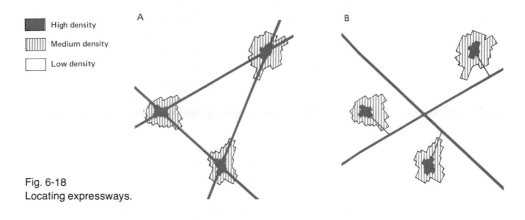

Fig. 6-18
Locating expressways.

Recommended Readings

1 "Traffic Jams—the Concrete Spread" in *Sick Cities* by Mitchell Gordon, Penguin, 1965.
2 *Auto vs Mankind* by K. Schneider, Norton, 1971.
3 *The Accessible City* by W. Owen, Brookings Institute, 1972.
Other books and articles on transportation alternatives.
4 "Urban Transportation Systems" by E. Davies, *Britannica Book of the Year,* 1969.
5 "Automobiles of the Future" by J. Flint, *Britannica Book of the Year,* 1972.
6 *Problems in the Bosnywash Megalopolis* by L. A. Swatridge, McGraw-Hill, 1972.
7 *Urban Problems: A Canadian Reader* edited by R. Krueger and R. C. Bryfogle, Holt, Rinehart and Winston, 1975.

6.4   GROWTH ALTERNATIVES

The impacts of all decisions in the urban environment cumulate to shape the growth of the future city. For instance, the density we choose to live in affects the size of future urban territory. The types of transportation we choose to use, how frequently we use them, and where the transportation arteries are affect the way the community will grow. Suburbanization and its low-density development has lead to *urban sprawl* over the countryside. As a result, some communities are beginning to merge with others, forming *conurbations*. For example, on the Eastern Seaboard of the United States several gigantic cities seem to be merging into one urban mass stretching from Boston to Washington, D.C. Some call this city of the future *Bosnywash,* others, *Megalopolis.* Will tomorrow's growth continue to spread thinly over the countryside or reach for the sky as in Manhattan? Should cities be allowed to merge? How do we control the size of tomorrow's cities?

The individual's power to control decisions on such matters seems non-existent. These decisions are made today largely by governments, developers, and corporations. Yet, groups of individuals like you have stopped the construction of unnecessary expressways and airports. Also, developers are controlled by planning agencies which try to represent the public interest. Planners have become increasingly aware of the need to involve citizens in the planning process *before* decisions are made. If you speak out, your voice can be heard. However, before you speak out you should consider carefully the alternatives that exist in order to make sure the urban environment of tomorrow is really the one you want. This section considers the alternatives for growth.

Waste Not; Want Not. When we develop land for urban uses are we getting the most out of every hectare? The intensity of land use we achieve determines how much land we need. For example, one-storey shopping plazas, factories, and schools are large land consumers. Do the benefits of one-storey buildings justify the amount of land this kind of construction demands? Some factories may require a one-storey building for efficient assembly lines and shipping. Yet they may build another one-storey building for their clerical staff. Might not the offices be built above the factory floor? With the high-speed elevators and escalators that we have today, could we not return to the vertical factories of the past for much light industry? Two-storey shopping plazas are gradually increasing in popularity. Distance between stores is not as far as it is with one-storey constructions. Shoppers find this more convenient. Could we have high-rise department stores in the suburbs? Now that school construction is virtually fire-proof, could we not return to two- or three-storey school buildings?

Perhaps an even more flagrant example of inefficient land use is the sea of parking lots surrounding apartments, shopping areas, factories, schools, and even parks. By comparing the area of land used for buildings with that used for parking lots, you may find that parking takes more land than the function it is serving. Instead of a parking lot serving only a factory, store, school, church, or park, it could be planned so that it serves more than one need. Industrial parking lots could provide parking space for a neighboring park. Combining a recreation center and a school not only means that the school can use the facilities of the recreation center, but it also means they can share a common parking lot, using it at different times. Theaters are now being built in shopping plazas to take advantage of parking that is already supplied for the stores but not being fully used during evenings and weekends. Parking need not be on the surface either. With land becoming increasingly more valuable it makes economic sense to provide underground or vertical parking in multi-storey parking garages.

The transportation arteries themselves are also large consumers of land, some more than others. Not only can this consumption be trimmed by the type of transportation we choose but also by multiple use of the transportation corridors. Buildings can be constructed over roads and railway lines. The rent from these activities on public land could even help pay for the maintenance of the transportation routes. Place Ville Marie in Montreal was developed over the city's downtown railway yards. In Japan they had another space-saving idea. They put the highway on the roofs of buildings. Beneath the road a linear complex of stores, restaurants, and specialty shops has been accommodated. The roof-top highway is half the cost of a typical skyway. Multiple types of transportation provided simultaneously on the same transportation corridor offer another imaginative use of space. For example, rapid-transit facilities can be placed on the median strip of expressways.

The technology is available now for most of the alternatives mentioned here. How long can we afford to squander land for single-purpose roads? "Waste not; want not" is still true. Our goal should be to cut out the inefficient uses of land. Our supply of land, after all, is not unlimited.

Green Space and Growth. No matter what intensity of land use is chosen for tomorrow's urban environment, we will be selecting, at the same time, the green space in and around it. Green space, which includes parks, vacant lots, and farmland, declines as urban development spreads. These areas of non-development give shape to the urban community by defining its limits. Without the contrasting green space, the urban landscape would be a shapeless mass of concrete. For the urban resident there would be no temporary escape from civilization. Clearly, growth decisions affect the quantity and quality of the remaining green space.

In order to ensure that needed green space is available in acceptable quantity and quality, we need to consider not only how intensively we will use the land but what land we will use and what we will leave as green space. Obviously someone must take active control over new urban development. But controlling the growth of a city is not an easy task. The problem is that growth often takes place outside the community itself and, therefore, is beyond its control. Only after the area has developed and been annexed can the city regulate its development. By this time the pattern of the community is already established. Obviously control of growth must take place before development. But how can this be done in rural areas? The following case study of a county on the edge of a growing city illustrates some of the problems involved in controlling urban development.

The county was situated on excellent farmland in a scenic area. The city was only 25 km away. As pressures increased to convert farmland to rural non farm homes, the country passed a bylaw demanding a minimum lot size of 0.8 hectares. This, it was hoped, would prevent subdivision development where ten houses to the hectare is common. Only a wealthy person looking for a country estate could afford to purchase 0.8 hectares. At the same time, feeling that they had the situation under control, county officials refused to join a regional planning board designed to plan the region around the city. Such planning, they felt, would limit their freedom. Reliance was placed on the farmer's desire to maintain the land in agriculture. What happened to this beautiful county? Farmers sold off a few hectares at a time along the roads. Because of the large lot zoning, subdivider speculation was discouraged. But, as a result, lots sold as cheaply as smaller lots nearer the city. Figure 6-19 shows the form this rural development took. These large lots were expensive to service. Their presence raised taxes in the area, forcing farmers to sell more land. Farms soon became too small for economic production. The natural beauty of the environment was destroyed. Finally, when there was little left to save, large-scale development was invited in to help reduce the costs of servicing. As this kind of sprawl takes place around a community, inner-city residents become further and further removed from open space. Eventually this county was annexed by the city.

What alternatives did the county officials have? They might have joined the regional planning board. With the power to determine what kind of land use would go where, growth could have been controlled. This county's growth could have been coordinated with the growth of other areas surrounding the city. However, even regional planning has its problems. Zoning development limits the owner's freedom to get the highest market value for his land. For example, a farmer who has his land zoned as permanent green space finds his land worth far less than his neighbor's zoned for industry. Regional planning still has not satisfactorily solved the human and legal problems involved in this kind of zoning. Cities have used this zoning technique to obtain cheap green space. But, without a fair purchase price for land, courts have declared these actions unconstitutional. Unfortunately the massive cost of purchasing green space at market value is beyond most cities' financial abilities.

Zoning, however, is not the planner's only tool. By demanding from a developer proper preservicing of lots with roads, water, and sewer lines, subdivision development can be controlled by the service provider, the municipality. Proper use of this control can make suburban development more compact. Had the county in

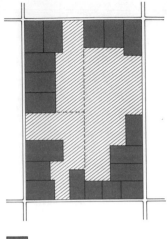

■ Rural nonfarm lots

▨ Farm land

Fig. 6-19
Piecemeal rural nonfarm development of a section of farmland.

Fig. 6-20
A belted city. Horizontal growth of the city is prevented by a belt of green space.

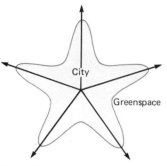

Fig. 6-21
A star-shaped city. Wedges of green space give it this shape.

Fig. 6-22
An eco-city. The natural characteristics of the land are used to locate green space.

our example taken this alternative the same amount of housing might have been allowed in a small portion of the county instead of being sprinkled throughout it.

Even when zoning control is established around a city, decisions still have to be made. What pattern of urban development and green space is desirable? The answer will determine the nature of tomorrow's city. Let us consider some possible patterns.

Belted City. With this plan, the city's spread is limited by a belt of green space surrounding the city (Fig. 6-20). New growth must either go beyond the belt (30-80 km) in new *satellite towns* or be more concentrated in the city. London, England, is the best example of this kind of planning. The experience of London has shown, however, that green belts are not the end to the problem. While satellite towns have grown beyond the belt, pressures for development inside the greenbelt are ever-increasing. Already development along major routes across the greenbelt has been demanded. The permanence of this open space is still in doubt. Some feel that too much green space was preserved. Also, because the geometric shape was the criterion for greenbelt zoning, much of the land saved was of little recreational value.

Star-Shaped City. Growth in this plan is channelled out of the city along major arterial routes. Wedges of green space are left in between (Fig. 6-21). The growth of the city is limited only by the distance people will commute to the city. Satellite-town development is also encouraged on each arterial route. The plan for Washington, D.C., used this concept. But, even before the plan was revealed, development was already taking place in areas planned as green space. Also, like the belt plan, the green wedges zoned more land as open space than could realistically be obtained or protected.

Eco-City. Geometric planning like that of the two previous grand designs tends to ignore the quality of the land zoned as green space and its potential recreational value. Beautiful parkland may be zoned for development because it did not fit the design. More land than necessary may be zoned as green space. The eco-city plan overcomes these difficulties (Fig. 6-22).

Nature does not conform to geometry. As a result, green space should be defined by natural characteristics rather than by geometry. Nature dictates that stream and river valleys subject to flooding should not be developed. Lands that erode easily or that charge ground-water reserves should be left in their natural state. Woodlots act as a sponge in rainstorms and prevent or lessen flooding and erosion. Some soils are not suitable for septic-tank developments because they do not provide adequate drainage. You may be able to add other areas that are unsuitable or undesirable for development. Eco-planning designates all land poorly suited for development or especially suited for agriculture or recreation as permanent green space. Development is then channeled onto the remaining suitable land. Green space determined in this manner is generally of greater recreational and amenity value. Unlike the arbitrary belts and wedges of the other plans, its retention can more easily be justified as being in the public good, even if land values rise. Best of all, as it is in smaller and more widely spread parcels it is accessible to more people. Further, the generally smaller overall quantity of permanent green space can be more realistically obtained and maintained.

Another Alternative. All previous alternatives assume that growth *will* take place. Obviously we have another alternative. We could choose to limit population growth either on a national basis through birth control or locally by discouraging growth in some places and encouraging it in others. The physical environment can only take so much concentration of human beings in one spot. Beyond this point, water supplies may be insufficient or pollution may become dangerous to human life. Why build expensive pipelines to take water to people? Why not encourage communities to develop where water exists naturally? What price in environmental quality are we willing to pay for growth?

For Thought and Research

1 a) Calculate the overall density of your community by dividing the total area of the community by its total population. Why would you expect this figure to be lower than most actual residential densities in your community?

b) From the planning agency for your community find out what population they expect to live in your community by the year 2000. If this kind of estimate is not available you could make your own. Plot on a graph of suitable scale the population of your community for the last 30 years. Project to the year 2000. This will give you an estimate of the population growth that might take place. Of course yours, like the planner's, is only an estimate. Many things can happen to change the rates of growth.

c) Calculate the land requirements of your community by the year 2000, assuming the population projection is correct and the community density remains the same.

d) Is it safe to assume that community density will be constant over the next 30 years? What are the trends in overall density in your community? Look at the densities of new development. Calculate past overall densities using census information. If you find the density is changing, how will this affect the land requirements you projected for the year 2000?

e) Consider the land surrounding your community. What effect would using the land for urban development have on the future environment? What will be the costs to society of its conversion to urban use?

f) What alternatives are there to the growth that you have projected for your community?

2 Why do people prefer single-family homes on large lots? What are the benefits and costs of this trend to the future urban environment? What may prevent this trend from continuing?

3 Examine the space consumed by a local shopping plaza. How much land is in the parking lot? How often is the parking space used to capacity? When is the space virtually unused every week? To what uses might this parking potential be put that would not interfere with shopping use?

4   Obtain a plan for your community's growth. On the basis of the discussion in this chapter evaluate the feasibility, cost, and quality of environment planned for.

5   Map the green space already protected by municipal or other government ownership in your community. Compare the amount of land they have with the land they would make permanent open space in the plan. Determine the cost of acquiring this land by finding out the average present value of a hectare of land. The assessment office would help you get this kind of information. You might also find out how much land value has increased in the last ten years. How much more would you expect the land to cost if it is not purchased now but ten years from now? Considering the results of your inquiry, will the city be able to purchase all the land they wish to? In what other ways might they prevent the land from being developed?

Recommended Readings

1   *Trends and Projections of Future Growth in the United States 1970-2000,* Dept. of Housing and Urban Development, US Government, 1969.
What alternatives do we have in dealing with growth in our urban areas? The following six sources provide controversial possibilities to think about.
2   *Last Landscape* by W. Whyte, Doubleday, 1970.
3   *A Question of Priorities* by E. Higbee, Morrow, 1970.
4   *The Shape of Towns* by K. Rowland, Ginn, 1966.
5   ''Ecumenopolis—Tomorrow's City'' by C. Doxiadis, *Britannica Book of the Year,* 1968. An abridged version of many longer works by the same author.
6   *World Cities* by P. Hall, McGraw-Hill, 1966.
7   *Problems in the Bosnywash Megalopolis* by L. A. Swatridge, McGraw-Hill, 1972.

6.5   ENVIRONMENTAL QUALITY

In medieval cities a citizen had to be careful when he passed too close to a row of houses for fear that chamber pots or garbage containers might be emptied on his head. Today we are much less obvious about disposing of our urban waste, but environmental damage caused by air, water, noise, and sight pollution continues to increase.

Water Quality. As Figure 6-23 indicates, a city converts much of its daily water intake into sewage. Since sewage facilities are largely invisible, most residents do not see this as a problem. To them, the only need for the future in terms of sewage disposal is to continue to build facilities to handle an ever-increasing volume of liquid wastes. To others, however, present methods are unsatisfactory. A high percentage of cities provide no treatment at all. Many merely remove solid matter (primary treatment) while others use secondary treatment (removal of undissolved solids and disease-

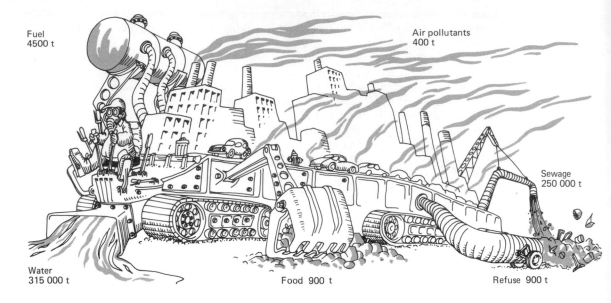

Fuel
4500 t

Air pollutants
400 t

Sewage
250 000 t

Water
315 000 t

Food 900 t

Refuse 900 t

causing bacteria). Collectively they pour billions of litres of pollutants into our lakes and rivers every day. We must choose between these lower-cost treatment methods with continued water pollution and the more expensive tertiary treatment which will help keep our waterways clean.

However, urban water pollution is not caused just by inadequate sewage treatment. Industrial waste is a major source of pollution. Industries of all types are creating thousands of new chemicals every year which compound the water purification problem. The people of the city of New Orleans, inheriting waste water from countless cities and factories upstream, drink water with more than 30 chemicals remaining in it after treatment. A difficult decision must be made by our cities. Industry provides local employment, business, and tax revenue. Therefore cities compete to attract industry. Thus, if a few environment-conscious cities impose fines or controls on liquid wastes, some industries might relocate. Until public opinion is sufficiently strong to bring about federal and provincial or state laws controlling industrial emissions, our water will not be clean. Each of us must ask ourselves: "How important is clean water to me?"

There are alternatives to our present methods of using water. Used water from drinking fountains could be collected separately from other used water and re-used as an industrial coolant or for ornamental fountains, pools, and small recreational lakes within the city. Salt water could be converted to fresh water. Against these costly alternatives we must compare the results of our present habits. Diseases caused by drinking water or by merely

Fig. 6-23
Man at the controls of the urban processing machine.

swimming in it are increasing at an alarming rate. Life in many rivers and lakes is already dead or dying and may take decades to restore. Are the world's oceans to suffer a similar fate? The future costs of water pollution may be greater than we presently think.

Air Quality. Although water pollution may be a problem in communities of all sizes, air pollution is common only in the larger industrialized cities. There are several main sources of air pollution—the automobile, thermal-electric generating plants, and industry.

The car has become a matter of controversy in many cities. Many North Americans choose to drive to work for reasons of convenience, comfort, and often time. We must realize, however, that cars pour large quantities of carbon monoxide, hydrocarbons, and nitrogen oxides into the air, lowering our life expectancy and increasing the threat of diseases such as emphysema, chronic bronchitis, and lung cancer. In cities such as Boston, Toronto, and San Francisco, citizens' groups have successfully battled against expressways. The choice has been made in favor of the environment. Federal laws, following California's example, have attempted a compromise by controlling exhaust emissions, at a cost of several hundred dollars per car. However, so long as the number of automobiles used in cities continues to increase, air pollution will remain with us.

While the automobile produces about half of our air pollution, another major source is the coal-burning thermal-electric generating plant. This source of pollution cannot easily be removed, however. Clean-burning natural gas can be used instead of coal, but diminishing reserves are likely to make this an expensive alternative in the future. Most water-power sites are already developed to capacity. Nuclear power leaves clean air, is becoming more competitive in cost, and has the advantage of a long-term uranium supply. However, it presents the threat of radioactivity near the plant and the problem of disposing of dangerous wastes. So far, none of these alternatives has been attractive enough to replace the offensive coal-burning plants on a wide scale.

Many cities are almost as reluctant to combat industrial air pollution as they are industrial water pollution. As in the case of industrial water pollution, the pressure of public opinion on higher levels of government is needed to produce laws controlling industrial emissions. Each of us has a voice in such matters; we need only take the initiative to exercise it on behalf of the environment.

Solid Waste. Our cities have many choices for the disposal of solid wastes. These are summarized in Table 8. At present, low cost, simplicity, and lack of public initiative have made sanitary landfill and incineration (without use of the resulting heat) the most common methods. Will we be more original in the future?

TABLE 8

Method	Advantages	Disadvantages
Sanitary landfill	Low cost Can renovate wasteland for parks (e.g. Mt. Blackstrap ski hill near Saskatoon) Simple—almost all types of refuse can be buried	Possible pollution of ground water as rainwater drains through garbage Unsightly, occasional blowing paper, and odors Potential sites near the city are being used up. Other sites are not under city control and may be politically unavailable
Incineration	Can be located close to sources of refuse Sites easily acquired Surplus heat can be sold to near-by factories or used to generate electricity for sale to ease load on power plants	Non-burnables and ash must still be buried Produces air pollution (fly-ash, smoke, odors, sulfur oxides and other gases) Air pollution controls are expensive
Recycling	Re-use of paper, glass, and metals helps to conserve national re-sources Recycled products can provide revenue to offset other dis-posal and collection costs Lessens volume of refuse to be disposed of by other means (paper is largest component of modern refuse)	Reluctance of people to take the time to separate their refuse Separate collections necessitate more city trucks and greater expense Must be used in conjunction with other methods since not all materials can be recycled
Wet garbage grinders	Decreases volume of refuse to be collected Improves sanitation (raw garbage is a health hazard)	Adds more solids to the sewer system Suitable only for kitchen wastes, a small part of total refuse
Dumping in ocean	Inexpensive Uses no valuable land	Water pollution may prove severe Can wash in to shore (e.g. Long Island)
Long-distance hauling	Uses land in uninhabited areas for landfill to decrease land costs and public offence	Very expensive
Compost-ing	Converts garbage into usable fertilizer Sale of compost can offset some of the cost	Requires up to two weeks curing before compost is ready for use Not suitable for all types of refuse

Climate Modification. How we decide to handle our urban wastes—solid, liquid, and airborne—will have a major effect on the quality of our environment. We may be aware of this, but how many of us realize how much environmental modification we are causing merely by building cities at all? Before you read on, jot down your answers to the following questions. Are winds stronger in the city or in the countryside nearby? Are cities warmer than rural areas in the summer? in the winter? Do cities get more or less sunshine than rural areas? Is it more likely to rain on a particular day in an urban area or in a nearby rural area?

Almost every climatic factor is altered in a city. Fossil fuels are burned to produce heat. This heat helps to make city temperatures an average of 1-2°C higher than in surrounding rural areas. But, in summer, when fuel use is low, the temperature difference is even greater. This puzzling fact can be explained by the fact that brick and concrete buildings store heat during the day, and release it gradually to keep producing heat in the city around the clock.

We city dwellers rob ourselves of sunshine in several ways. Tall buildings cut off sunlight at ground level. Polluted city air provides more particles as nuclei for water droplets to condense around. Thus cities near large rivers, lakes, or oceans have 10-20% more days per year with fog than similar rural areas. Pollution and related fogs act as a blanket to deflect sunlight. In northerly latitudes, when the sun's rays are at a low angle in winter, a city can lose as much as 40% of the sunshine that reaches nearby rural areas.

The effect of cities on winds and rain is even more complex. Cities have lower average relative humidities (amount of water vapor in the air) than rural areas, but may have 5-10% more rain. The first fact may be explained by the lack of open water surfaces in cities to produce evaporation. The second fact can be attributed to the greater air mixing and the larger number of condensation nuclei that exist in polluted air. Both of these produce more rain. Another contradictory situation occurs with urban wind patterns. Average wind speeds are lower in cities than in rural areas due to the sheltering effect of the buildings. However nighttime winds are stronger in cities than in rural areas. What would cause this?

These climate modifications may not seem very important. But, when considered in terms of the massive urbanization of so much of the world, the long-term implications may be serious. The world ecosystem maintains a balance between atmospheric characteristics, temperature, and precipitation. Until we are more certain of the long-term effects of replacing green plants with concrete, draining all surface water before it can evaporate, burning fossil fuels to produce heat, and pouring dust and gases into the atmosphere, we should be more cautious about indiscriminate expansion of cities. Our only other alternative is to introduce costly programs to rehabilitate the urban environment.

Noise. Noise, defined as unwanted sound, has always been a fact of life for the city dweller. However, the average urban noise level has doubled in the past 20 years, and threatens to double again in an even shorter time period. Noise pollution is more serious than many people think. Besides the obvious problem of gradual loss of hearing, high noise levels can cause anxiety, high blood pressure, increased mental illness, and even a higher crime rate.

Figure 6-24 illustrates some of the noise levels produced by modern civilization. The common unit for measuring sound is the decibel (dB). The decibel scale begins at zero as the faintest sound audible to the normal human ear. An important feature of this scale is that with every six decibel increase, the sound becomes twice as loud. Thus a noise of 100 dB is not 20% louder than a noise of 80 dB, but ten times as loud. It is apparent from studying this chart that there are many common noises over the danger level. In spite of the costs of sound-reducing equipment, laws designed to control noise pollution are essential for a better-quality urban environment in the future.

Aesthetics. Perhaps the most subtle aspect of environmental modification is the loss of the beauty and freedom of the green countryside. Unless future generations can adjust to finding sufficient beauty and recreational opportunities in a world of concrete, brick, and steel, we should be more hesitant to "pave paradise" at our present speed. Psychiatrists and ecologists warn of the dangers of overcrowding and of the human need for wide open spaces. This need is testified to by clogged rural highways and parks on weekends and by the rush to own a house and garden in the suburbs. We are a materialistic, cost-oriented society, but we must learn to consider personal and psychological costs that cannot easily be converted into dollars. Crusaders against water and air pollution in our cities are beginning to be heard, but sight pollution is not yet a major issue. In the future our decisions about environmental quality must include the aesthetic environment as well as the physical one.

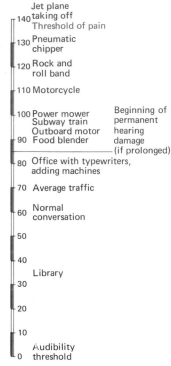

Fig. 6-24
Some typical sound levels on the decibel scale.

For Thought and Research

1 a) What pollutants are removed in each type of sewage treatment?
    b) What type of sewage treatment is used in your community? Why did your local department of sanitation or public works choose to use this method?
2 a) From the alternatives presented in Table 8, design an ideal refuse-disposal program for your community.
    b) Compare your design with the methods actually used and account for the differences.
3 Use the format of Table 9 to compare the city and the country climate in both summer and winter.

TABLE 9

	Sunshine	Temperature	Precipitation	Winds
Summer				
Winter				

4 What effect would the banning of automobiles in cities have on each of the following? Explain your answers.
   a) sunshine;
   b) humidity;
   c) rain;
   d) the need for parks in the city;
   e) noise pollution;
   f) average life span.

5 Obtain a decibel meter and measure the following noise levels.
   a) at a downtown intersection;
   b) at a rock concert;
   c) in the school hallway between classes.

Recommended Readings

1 *Our Precarious Habitat* by M. A. Benarde, Norton, 1970. Includes informative chapters on sewage, water pollution, waste disposal, air pollution, noise, etc.

2 *Environmental Pollution* by W. A. Andrews et al., Prentice-Hall, 1972. A guide to the study of water and air pollution as well as related readings and research topics such as sewage treatment and noise pollution.

3 *Sick Cities* by M. Gordon, Macmillan, 1963. A forceful book condemning our cities for the condition of our water, air, garbage disposal, and parks.

4 *Climate Canada* by F. K. Hare and M. K. Thomas, Wiley, 1974. Contains an excellent chapter on urban climates and a bibliography on the subject for further reading.

5 *Challenge for Survival* edited by P. Dansereau, Columbia University Press, 1970. Papers from experts concerned with the preservation of our land, air, and water environments in heavily populated areas.

6 *Urban Problems: A Canadian Reader* edited by R. Krueger and R. Bryfogle, Holt, Rinehart and Winston, 1975. Includes some excellent sections on pollution, aesthetics, and the challenge of the future.

7 *The Fight for Quiet* by T. Berland, Prentice-Hall, 1970.

8 *The Tyranny of Noise* by R. A. Baron, St. Martin's, Press, 1970.

Field and Laboratory Studies

7

7.1   USING AIR PHOTOS AND TOP MAPS

Topographical (top) maps show the general physical features of the landscape, the elevation, and the main human activities in an area. These maps can be used to supplement the very detailed information shown on aerial (air) photographs. For example, a top map will show the elevation of a hill that can be seen on an aerial photograph. Air photos may be either oblique or vertical. Oblique photos are taken from a point not directly above the subject, whereas vertical photos are taken from directly above the subject.

A top map is read using the names and colors on the map plus the key which identifies the symbols used. On the other hand, air photos do not have a key and the reader must recognize the shapes of objects, their texture, and their ability to reflect light. For example, a forest will appear dark, while a paved lot will be light grey in color.

You should understand that this is only a small sample of the sorts of activities that can be done with topographic maps and aerial photographs. For example, using vertical air photos, one can use tracing paper marked in a grid to calculate the percentage of the land area used for forest, for parking lot, for grassed open space, and so on. A specially photographed pair of overlapping vertical pictures forms a set of stereo photographs, which can be viewed with a special viewer to see three dimensionally. Comparing a revised top map of a city to an older version will enable you to see details about urban growth and change. Topographic maps and aerial photos can be used with almost any section of this book, and are most useful in studying your local area. Check with your teacher to see what maps and photos are available at your school.

AIR PHOTO STUDY #1

Figure 7-1 is an oblique aerial photograph of a modern suburb. Examine it carefully and answer these questions.

a) Identify the following land uses: single-family housing; townhouses or row houses; low-rise apartments; industry; railway; a community shopping plaza; a school.

b) Find evidence in the photo to prove that this area relies on automobile transportation.

c) Find evidence to prove that this area is still being developed.

d) At about what time of day was the picture taken? Give proof from the photo.

e) This suburb was built as a planned community. Draw a sketch map to show the planner's original land-use design for the community. Is it a good plan?

Fig. 7-1
Oblique aerial photograph of a modern suburb. (Northway Survey Corporation Limited photo.)

AIR PHOTO AND TOP MAP STUDY #2

Figure 7-2 is the top map and Figure 7-3 the corresponding air photo of Halifax, Nova Scotia. Examine these figures carefully and answer these questions.

a)   What is the elevation of the star-shaped citadel in the centre of Halifax?

b)   Why is the southern tip of the main peninsula not built up? Account for the light-colored border around this area and the bare patches inside the forested zone.

c)   What are the large buildings near the southeast corner of Halifax used for?

Fig. 7-2
Topographical map of Halifax. (This is a section from the topographical sheet 11 D/12, scale 1: 50,000 published by the Surveys and Mapping Branch, Department of Energy, Mines and Resources, Ottawa. Original in colour.)

d)   Suggest areas in Halifax where each of the following may be found and give reasons for your answer: a low-income residential area; the homes of the wealthy; heavy industry; the CBD.

e)   Find evidence that the map is more recent than the photo.

Fig. 7-3
Aerial photograph of Halifax. (Original photo supplied by the National Air Photo Library, Department of Energy, Mines and Resources.)

7.2 DEFINING A NEIGHBORHOOD

"Neighborhood" is a word with which everyone is familiar. However, few can define it satisfactorily. Yet the neighborhood plays an important role in man's existence in the urban environment. What makes a group of dwellings a neighborhood? What is the role of the neighborhood in the lives of the people who live in it? In this investigation you will be tackling these difficult questions. The answers may lead to further questions.

Materials

a) a dictionary

b) a map of your community

Procedure

a) Find out how a good dictionary defines neighborhood. If possible, use this definition to identify the boundaries of your neighborhood on the map.

b) Decide what the word neighborhood means to you. List the characteristics of a neighborhood. On the basis of your definition mark the boundaries of your neighborhood on the map. Use a different color from that used in a).

c) Discuss your definition with others. Do they agree with your view of neighborhood boundaries? Can you agree on a common definition of neighborhood? How could this change the boundaries of your neighborhood?

d) Test your skill at determining the boundaries of neighborhoods by going through the process again using a neighborhood other than your own. Is it more or less difficult to define your own neighborhood as opposed to others? Why is this so? You might compare your view of this neighborhood to that of someone who lives there. If there are differences try to explain them.

Discussion

a) In trying to define a neighborhood you have probably considered the relationship between people and their neighborhood. What is the value of having one? Do we need one? What activities happen within the neighborhood? What activities usually occur within the larger community around it? Discuss these questions with others.

b) Discuss the relationship between the neighborhood and the urban community as a whole. Are neighborhoods more or less important as the community becomes larger? Suppose the community as a whole needs an expressway, how could a knowledge of neighborhoods help in locating that highway? How else might a knowledge of neighborhoods be of value in urban planning?

c)   By this point you have probably noticed that neighborhoods differ in many ways. You may have even decided that some function better than others. To evaluate whether neighborhoods are good or bad is more difficult that just defining them. Research Topic 8.1, Design of Neighborhoods, will help you develop skill in evaluating neighborhoods.

7.3   MAPPING YOUR COMMUNITY

We see many maps in our everyday lives—weather maps, road maps, globes, directions to a friend's cottage, and so on. But we do not see maps being made, and, as a result, are often clumsy in our own attempts to translate the reality of streets and distances into readable maps. This field study outlines the steps involved in making a simple land-use map of a small neighborhood.

Materials

Each pair of students requires the following:

a)   compass

b)   tape measure

c)   notebook, ruler, and pencil

Procedure

a)   Before going on the field trip, define the limits of your neighborhood. This may be done on the basis of personal experience, by arbitrary choice, or by carrying out Investigation 7.2.

b)   Choose one boundary street as a base line. It must cross the entire neighborhood. Take a compass reading of the orientation of this street. Record your result.

c)   Divide your group into pairs of students. Station each pair at a cross street. Record the orientation of each street and measure the distance between each pair of students. The group leader should record this data on a sketch map as shown in Figure 7-4.

d)   Each pair then proceeds along its street to the opposite boundary of the neighborhood (if possible). Recording may be done in a stenographer's notebook or on similar paper,

Fig. 7-4
Sample sketch map of a community study area, showing starting points and initial measurements.

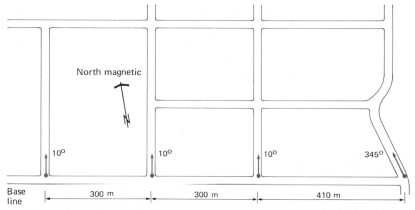

using the vertical center line to represent the initial orientation of the street. The following information should be recorded: width of street; changes in direction and shape of street; land use(s) along each side (using a scale such as 5 cm on the map to represent 100 m along the ground). Be sure to place all buildings, driveways, and other physical features in the appropriate places.

e)   Repeat steps a) to d) until all streets have been surveyed.

Discussion

a)   Assemble all completed maps into a single large mosaic on the classroom wall. You may now choose to add a color scheme if you want to illustrate different land-use regions, for instance.

b)   Mark a legend and scale on the final map.

c)   A useful exercise would be to reduce further the size or *scale* of your map to a scale such as 1 cm = 100 m. In doing this reduction you will probably find that further abstraction from reality is needed to make the map readable, such as the use of small symbols for different buildings and land uses.

d)   What are the advantages of each size of map?

7.4   AN URBAN TRANSECT

The word "transect" means to cut across. Your town or city undoubtedly has many streets that do just that: cut across the town from one side to the other. This field study involves an in-depth study of land-use changes along one of these streets. You can look at the land uses themselves, analyze the reasons behind each type of land use, record your study in slides or photographs, and decide whether one long street would give a stranger driving through an accurate picture of your town's character. The study can be done by one person or by a group. It may also be combined with or compared to Investigation 7.8, which also involves working along a transect or line across the city.

Fig. 7-5
A, a detailed transect across a small town; and B, part of a generalized transect along a city street.

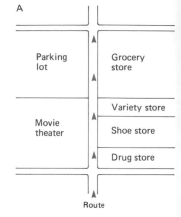

Materials

a) map of the city

b) camera

c) notebooks

Procedure

On a map of your town or city choose a representative street that crosses the entire town. Remember that a street on the outskirts will give a different picture of the city than Main Street will; choose a street that will avoid these extremes.

In a small town, a detailed survey may be conducted. Draw a line down the center of a piece of paper to represent your transect line and write in the land uses on either side of this line (see Fig. 7.5A).

In a city, a generalizing or classifying procedure must be followed.

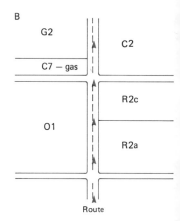

a) As you drive or walk along the route, list the main type of land use in each section (see Fig. 7.5B). Choose land-use designations from the following list:

R— RESIDENTIAL
    1—upper-income
    2—middle-income
    3—lower-income
        a— single-family
        b— semi-detached
        c— row housing or townhouses
        d— low-rise apartment
        e— high-rise apartment

C— COMMERCIAL
    1—strip—stores line sides of street
    2—plaza
    3—office buildings
    4—entertainment—restaurants, theaters, bars, etc.
    5—hotels and motels
    6—financial—banks, trust companies

7—individual stores—stores standing alone, gas stations, etc.

G— GOVERNMENT OR INSTITUTIONAL
    1—educational
    2—medical—hospitals, medical offices, nursing homes
    3—government buildings
    4—utilities and transportation

I— INDUSTRIAL
    1—light manufacturing
    2—heavy manufacturing
    3—chemical and petroleum
    4—warehousing

O— OPEN SPACE
    1—parks
    2—recreational—golf course
    3—vacant lots

b)   Take a representative picture at specified intervals, for example, every kilometre.

c)   Mark on your map any change in local government jurisdiction, landforms, and other factors that may affect land use.

Discussion

a)   Assemble your finished transect into one long strip map. It is recommended that colors be used to make land-use patterns more noticeable. Thus all residential areas could be shaded in red with the printed designation code (e.g. R1a, R3e, etc.) on top. Other possible colors include blue for commercial use, grey for government, brown for industrial, and green for open space.

b)   Look for patterns in your map. You may find that plazas are always in areas of high-rise buildings, or that detached houses are found only on the two ends of the transect. You should be able to classify areas according to the dominant land use.

c)   Try to find reasons for these patterns. Look for factors affecting them, such as land price, politics, zoning, economic history, and topography. Finally, you should be able to characterize the entire street and decide whether it gives an accurate cross-section of the character of your town or city.

7.5 URBAN FIELD MEASUREMENT

During urban field studies, measurements of land uses are often necessary. You may want to know how much land is used for parking in a shopping plaza. You may want to measure the frontage of suburban homes. You may want to find out the residential density in your neighborhood or in a nearby apartment complex. In this investigation you obtain practice in making such measurements.

Materials

a)   tape measure or metre sticks

b)   600-700 m of string

Procedure

a)   Linear measurement (measurement of length) can be carried out by using tape measures or metre sticks. If you need to be accurate in your measurement, one of these measuring aids should be used. Test your estimate of the width of a lot or building by using one of these measuring tools. Estimate the length first. Make an accurate measurement. Compare the results. How accurate was your estimate? Repeat with different areas. Does your ability to estimate improve with practice?

b)   A handy means of measuring is pacing. Less accurate than actual measurement but more accurate than visual estimates, pacing requires no equipment. This can be a great advantage on urban field trips. Everyone's pace is different, but, with practice, you can take paces that are fairly consistent in length. To test your pace length, lay out a line 5 m long on the ground. Pace this known length, counting the paces required to walk the line. Repeat this several times. Calculate your average pace by dividing the total distance walked by the number of paces. Do not attempt to take the largest paces possible. Your normal walking pace will be easier to maintain. Once you know the length of your pace you can convert paced distances into standard units of measurement. Again, select several distances to be measured. Pace the length and convert the result into standard units of measurement such as metres. Measure the distance accurately. Compare your results. If your results are not very accurate, retest your calculation of your pace length. Once you can estimate the length of an object over 5 m in length within a metre of its actual length, pacing can be used instead of tape measures for most of the measurements you will have to make on an urban field trip.

c)   Besides lengths, estimates and measurements of area are also needed. The most common unit of area in the metric system is the *hectare* and, in the British system, the *acre*. Look up the number of square metres in a hectare. On a flat open field, using string construct a square that is 1 ha in area. What is the approximate area of a football field?

Area is harder to estimate than length, but once you know how big a hectare is, you should be able to make better judgments of area. Test the accuracy of your area estimates by first estimating the area of a certain piece of land and then measuring it. Repeat until you can come fairly close to actual measurements with your estimates. By educating your eye to measure and by using the regularity of your pace to improve your accuracy, you can make better and more accurate observations in the field. At times, accurate methods may be required. But, in most instances, educated estimates are sufficient and require less time and no equipment.

7.6   VISUALIZING RESIDENTIAL DENSITIES

One of the main purposes of being able to visualize a hectare of land is to enable you to visualize residential densities. What would a residential density of five dwellings to the hectare look like? What does the residential density of your neighborhood appear to be?

Materials
a)   300-400 m of string
b)   graph paper
c)   ruler

Procedure
a)   Lay out a square of land, 1 ha in area (see Section 7.5).

b)   Subdivide the hectare into five lots. This gives you a residential density of five dwellings per hectare, if each lot has one dwelling.

c)   Subdivide your lots again for a residential density of ten dwellings per hectare, and twenty dwellings per hectare.

d)   After visualizing these densities in the field, use graph paper to make a scale representation of the hectare and the lot sizes for each of these residential densities. Using the same scale, represent a house 9 m × 12 m on each lot size.

e)   Calculate the percentage of each lot not covered by the house for each of the residential densities.

f)   On the small lots how might the houses be arranged to get the most useable open space?

g)   Draw a second square to the same scale, also a hectare in size, with no lot subdivision. Apartments of the same size as the houses are to be built. The city states that an apartment must have a minimum of 50 m² land surface. Determine how many apartments can be built on this lot.

h)   Determine the percentage of the lot not covered by the dwellings if the apartments possible on the lot are in a two-storey apartment building. Show this on your graph paper. Repeat the calculations if buildings of 4, 6, 8, 10, and 20 stories are used.

i)   Compare the open space remaining at each of the dwelling densities and with each of the apartment design alternatives. How useable is the open space in each of the cases in h)?

j)   Why is it necessary to have a standard such as a minimum of 50 m² land area per apartment?

k)   Examine the residential density in your neighborhood. Is it uniform in density or is it a mixture of different densities? Calculate the density of a single-family housing area, an apartment complex, and an area of town houses. Estimate the proportions of the lots that are not covered by the dwelling. Determine how this land is used and what proportion of the land is in each use. Evaluate the quality of residential environment achieved by each different residential density you can find. How useable is the open space? How attractive is the environment?

7.7   MICROCLIMATE STUDIES IN A HIGH-RISE AREA

In one high-rise apartment complex in Chicago, residents on the upper floors can often find out what the weather is like at ground level only by listening to the radio. They may literally find themselves above the clouds. Although microclimate differences are not this extreme around most buildings, many apartment dwellers are probably aware of the fact that the weather does vary from the ground floor to the penthouse. However, they may not be aware of the nature of this variation nor its extent.

Materials

a)   tape measure

b)   2 thermometers

c)   2 wet and dry bulb hygrometers

d)   2 anemometers

Procedure

Divide the class into two sections. Section A will survey the effect of height on microclimate while Section B will study the ecological effects of a high-rise building on the neighborhood.

Section A

a) Obtain permission from residents of apartments where you wish to conduct tests. Your choice of apartments will depend on the size of the building, but you should include apartments facing in different directions and at intervals of five to seven storeys. Clearly, students who live in the apartment should make these arrangements.

b) For each apartment, record readings of temperature, relative humidity, wind speed, and wind direction outside a window or, preferably, on a balcony. Note the time of day and the intensity and duration of sunshine. Ask the resident to estimate the time of day when peak periods of sun and/or temperature normally occur.

Section B

a) Draw a sketch map of the area similar to the one shown in Figure 7-6.

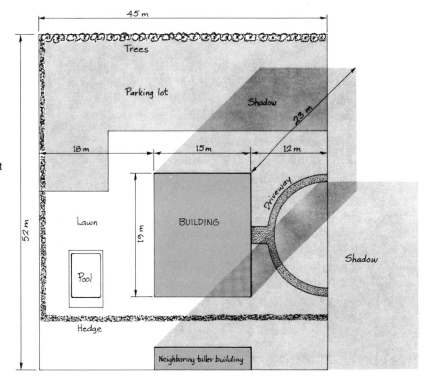

Fig. 7-6
A sample sketch of an apartment site, as seen from above.

b) Measure the dimensions of the shadows, building, and property, and add these to your diagram.

c) Measure temperature, light intensity, relative humidity, wind speed, and wind direction from the ground in the parking lot, under some trees, on an open grassy area, and in two or three other locations where you suspect you might get differing results. Record the data on your diagram or on a data sheet.

d) (Optional) In summer, you may wish to compare the density of grass cover close to the building to growth 100-200 m from the building. In winter the depth of snow cover might be compared in a similar manner.

Discussion

a) Summarize all your findings, using graphs or charts where possible. Account for any significant changes in microclimate that occur with the height or exposure of the apartment.

b) What variations in temperature, relative humidity, light intensity, and wind conditions occur around the apartment building? Account for your results.

c) What ecological effects does the shadow of the apartment building produce? If a city was made entirely of closely spaced high-rise buildings, what would its climate and vegetation be like?

Note

Information on the measurement of relative humidity, wind speed, and other abiotic factors can be obtained from *Terrestrial Ecology*, another book in this series.

7.8 MICROCLIMATES ACROSS THE CITY

In a small area there can be slight variations in climatic readings, which together make up the microclimate. When we listen to the daily weather forecasts, we usually hear a single prediction for the city. We can test the weather predictions and discover more about factors influencing climate by studying the microclimates along a selected line through the city.

If you wish to complete this study in one or two hours you need about four students per 1 500 m of the transect across the city.

Materials

Each pair of students will require:

a) tape measure

b) thermometer

c) anemometer or other wind velocity gauge

d) metre stick

e) sling psychrometer, wet and dry bulb hygrometer, or other humidity gauge

Procedure

A. Pre-field Preparation

a) On a large map of the city lay out a line crossing as many different environments as possible. For example, this route or transect could run beside water, and through a high-rise area, a shopping center, a forested lot, open parkland, an industrial complex, and a low-density residential area.

b) Divide this line into sections approximately 700-800 m long. A section covering several environments should be shorter than one containing long uniform stretches.

B. In the Field

a) Each pair of students should leave a pre-arranged marker at the beginning of its assigned section and walk toward the next marker to ensure that the entire transect is surveyed.

b) The following readings should be taken every 100 m. The interval between readings may be lengthened in a long uniform section and shortened if frequent changes occur.
   1) temperature 1 m from the ground;
   2) temperature 0.5 m from the ground;
   3) relative humidity at 1 m height;
   4) wind speed at 1 m height.

c) Record the readings on a sketch map of your transect using a scale such as 1 cm = 100 m. You should also record possible environmental factors that might have local influence on climate, such as an especially large tree or building, a nearby stream, or an open field.

Discussion

a) Make a set of parallel graphs along one wall of the classroom, one for each climatic indicator and one for environmental factors, as shown in Figure 7-7.

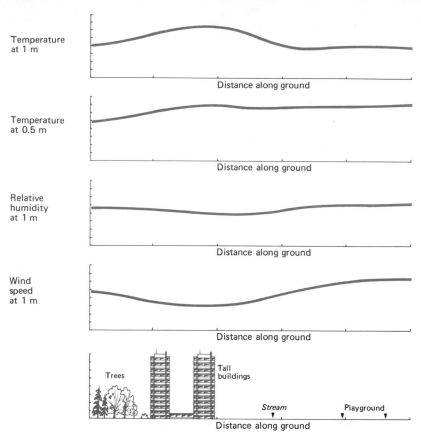

Fig. 7-7
Microclimate transect studies.

b)   Compare the graphs. How much variation occurred for each indicator? Where did the most significant changes occur and why? What factors seem to be most important in determining microclimate?

7.9   THE EFFECT OF A PARK ON THE URBAN CLIMATE

Man has dramatically reshaped the natural environment as he cut, paved, and built his urban habitat. What are the implications of this reshaping for the climate of a community? Has the climate been affected? How has it been affected? Is there a variation in climate from a suburban to a central district? How might climatic variation affect industry, housing, and living? There are many questions to ask and many answers to be found. In this field study we are concerned with the effect of a park on the urban climate. An increased understanding of how man can interact with his environment may be gained. Perhaps this knowledge can be incorporated into a plan for designing a better community.

Materials

a)   sling psychrometer
b)   anemometer or other wind gauge
c)   data sheets and pencils
d)   watches

Procedure

A. Pre-field Activities

a)   Obtain or draw a large sketch map of the park and surrounding area within a radius of several street blocks.

b)   Identify and locate the major natural and man-made features, including types of buildings.

c)   Using a dot planimeter sheet locate approximately 20 stations in the surrounding area.

d)   Determine the times for sampling and the number of readings to be made at each station.

e)   Assign a pair of students to each station.

B. Field Activities

At the appointed times each station will measure and record:

a)   the relative humidity;

b)   the air temperature;

c)   the wind speed and direction. If the winds are gusty or irregular, record the speed range, that is, the difference between the highest and lowest readings.

C. Follow-up

a)   Update your sketch map of the study area by adding natural and man-made features you located.

b)   Confirm the locations of the field stations and record at each station the data for the various times.

c)   Compile the data for all the stations so that everyone has a copy.

Discussion

a)   Describe the microclimate of the park area using the data obtained.

b)   Identify any variation in weather conditions throughout the park.

c)   Are changing weather conditions in the park occurring at the same rate at all places? Why?

d)   Answer questions a) to c) for the urban area surrounding the park.

e)   What differences, if any, exist between the microclimate of the park and that of the surrounding urban area? Why?

f)   What role does a park play in determining the nature of the urban climate?

g)   As a town planner you wish to make several changes in this part of the urban landscape. What might be the possible effects of the following changes on the urban climate: a high-rise complex near the park; enlarged lake in the park; reforestation or wind breaks?

7.10   MENTAL MAPS OF THE CITY

A paper map is an *abstract representation* of a section of the earth's surface with certain desired elements emphasized and less important elements eliminated. Similarly a mental map is such a representation in the mind of the individual.

Each person has a different mental map of the city, depending on his experiences. Not surprisingly, one's mental map of a familiar area will be very different from that of an unfamiliar area.

Materials
a)   supply of squared paper
b)   marking pens

Procedure
a)   Choose two distinct populations to compare. Examples might be the students in your class and the students in another school in a different part of the city; the fathers and mothers of your classmates; or downtown shoppers and suburban shoppers.

b)   Choose an area of the city or town to be studied. Each group should be reasonably familiar with the area. Suggestions are the downtown area, a local shopping area, the local neighborhood, or the entire town, if it is small enough.

c)   Ask each of your subjects to sketch, from memory, a map of the subject area.

Notes

a)   To avoid bias, use exactly the same instructions when interviewing each of the subjects.

b)   Avoid answering questions about the exercise until after the subject has drawn his map.

Discussion

a)   Back in the classroom use a tally sheet for each of the sample populations to tabulate the number of times various elements of the urban area being studied have been mentioned. Using the definitions outlined by Kevin Lynch in *The Image of the City,* M.I.T. Press, 1960, divide the items mentioned into nodes, edges, pathways, and landmarks.

b)   Compare the number and type of mental map elements mentioned by the two groups. (It is of little use to study individual maps.) How do the two groups see the subject area? Are there any significant and surprising inclusions or omissions? What does this reveal about the way each of these groups experiences the city? What implications for transportation, zoning, land use, etc. would these findings have for local planners and politicians?

7.11   MOVEMENT OF PEOPLE IN THE CITY

Continuous movement of people is one of the chief characteristics of life in the city. We hear traffic reports on the radio indicating almost daily traffic jams. Massive parking lots surround shopping centers. Many millions of dollars are spent yearly on expressways, buses, subways, and commuter trains. We know everyone is moving but do we know precisely where they are going?

The amount and direction of desired movement in the city has an obvious significance for those who must plan the transportation systems of our cities and towns. In this exercise you will investigate the nature of urban journeys and the relationship between these journeys and the existing and future transportation system.

Materials

a)   street map of your city or town

b)   transportation map of your city or town showing major roads, expressways, and public transportation routes

c)   ruler, marking pens

Procedure

a) Choose a sample population to study. It should include at least 30 people (it can be more) who live in a relatively confined area. Most important, it should be chosen so that it reflects, at least in general, the composition of the larger population it represents. Your sample could be selected from your family and neighbors.

b) Ask each person in your sample to list the number, type, time, and final destination (nearest major intersection) of the trips he or she makes in an average week.

c) Draw a line connecting the origin and final destination of each trip in your sample and indicate the number of such trips made during the week. Generalize as necessary if your map starts to become too cluttered. (Lines of increasing thickness can be used to indicate multiple trips.) Remember that you are mainly interested in overall patterns, not individual trips.

Discussion

a) You have now constructed a map of the *desire lines* of your sample population. These are simply straight lines that indicate the direction of trips taken by the members of your sample, not taking into account the actual route followed. Compare your desire-line map to the transportation-routes map. Does it appear that the existing transportation system is a result of the desire lines of your community or is it likely that the members of your sample moved to the area in response to the existing transportation system? How could the transportation system be improved to serve the needs of your local area?

b) How are the desire lines distributed throughout the day? What significance does this have for those planning the local transportation system? How could the desire lines be redistributed over time and space to make better use of the existing transport facilities? Is this possible?

Further Investigations

a) Compare the desire-line patterns of groups of people living in various parts of the city.

b) Attempt desire-line studies among the people who work or shop in a given location to determine the pattern of residence and travel to the location.

7.12 EFFICIENCY OF VARIOUS MODES OF TRANSPORTATION

Modern forms of transportation like cars, subways, and buses have high potential speeds. However, their efficiency in the city is often greatly reduced by congestion. Exactly how efficient and speedy are the various types of transportation in the city? How do the bicycle rider and the pedestrian fit into the urban transportation scheme? How could travel in the city be made faster and more enjoyable?

Materials

a)   bicycle

b)   motorcycle

c)   automobile

d)   public transit system

e)   watches

Procedure

a)   Read Section 5.4, Part A, Travel Patterns, before beginning this investigation. It discusses several types of trips within the community: the journey to work; the journey to school; the journey to shop; the journey to recreate. Choose one or more of these to test.

b)   Determine a typical trip of each type being tested. For example, a journey to work may be from a particular home in the suburbs to the sixth floor of a downtown office building during the evening rush hour. A journey to shop may be from the eleventh floor of a high-rise apartment to a nearby large shopping center.

c)   Have at least one student attempt each trip using each of the transportation forms practical in your town or city. Make these trips duplicate as closely as possible the conditions under which such a trip would normally be taken. Remember it is *not* a race. You are trying to duplicate average trips made by average people.

d)   Record the time needed for each trip, together with other details about the trip such as comfort, reliability, cost, and safety.

Discussion

a)   Prepare a chart similar to Table 10 for each of the trips attempted. When calculating costs be sure to consider both

direct (gasoline, parking) and indirect (insurance, depreciation) costs.

TABLE 10

Transportation form	Time for trip	Average speed (km/h)	Cost per trip	Cost per km	Comments (convenience, reliability, comfort)

Type of trip _____   Length of trip _____
Origin of trip _____   Destination _____

b)   Which form(s) of transportation is (are) most practical for
        the trips tested?

c)   How important are the qualities of speed, convenience,
        cost, and safety in determining the choice of transportation?

d)   In general, what transportation medium appears to be best
        suited for journeys of various types and lengths?

e)   Does the availiability of transportation facilities dictate the
        type of transportation used or does the demand for transpor-
        tation facilities result in their development?

f)   What is the mechanism for transportation planning in your
        area? Is it efficient? Does it answer the needs of the commu-
        nity?

7.13   PARKING FACILITIES IN THE DOWNTOWN AREA

A major problem associated with the automobile is that of providing
parking facilities, either on-street parking or off-street lots. The
amount of space available for parking is fixed, but the number of
cars using the space will depend on the length of time that the cars
remain parked. One of the major means of controlling parking, and
thus controlling the use of the car downtown, is to raise the price of
downtown parking.

Materials

a)   notebooks

b)   pencils

Procedure

Conduct a survey of parking areas along one or more transects radiating out from the area of peak land value in your city. In this way changes in the amount, type, and cost of parking can be noticed as one moves away from the city core. The following should be noted in the survey:

a)   type of facility—publicly or privately owned; a lot or garage;

b)   location (to be mapped later);

c)   capacity (in terms of spaces);

d)   number of cars parked in 24 h;

e)   parking charges;

f)   all areas used for on-street parking, including meter rates and time limits.

Discussion

a)   All parking-lot locations and on-street parking should be mapped on a large-scale map of the CBD and its environs. From this map, estimate the percentage of the land area in each city block used for parking.

b)   Draw graphs to show the change in cost and types of parking as you move away from the peak-value intersection. Explain the changes shown on your graphs.

c)   You may have noticed some areas where parking lots have had a poor effect (in terms of aesthetic appeal) on surrounding land use. You can include such comments in an evaluation of parking facilities in your city. Are facilities adequate, well priced, properly planned? How effective is parking cost as a deterrent to the use of cars downtown? Can you recommend any policy changes to your local parking authority or city council?

7.14   THE INDIVIDUAL'S ORBIT WITHIN THE CITY

This investigation illustrates the area within which the individual carries on his day-to-day activities. The individual is most familiar with this environment because of day-to-day contact. You may find this area to be surprisingly small, even for people who seem to have a great deal of mobility.

The individual's orbit has significance for urban design attempting to accommodate human needs. The effects of the environment on the individual's orbit can be found by comparing orbits in different situations. By studying your orbit you may learn things about your own relationship to your environment that you never thought about before.

Materials

a) a detailed street map of your community

Procedure

a) Before you can determine your orbit it may be necessary or desirable to increase your awareness of your own movements in the community. You probably have never given this much consideration. One method for doing this is to keep a travel diary, recording all movements outside your house or apartment. Movements within an apartment building but outside your own apartment should also be recorded. All movements can be recorded or you may only be interested in studying particular types such as social visiting, recreation, or consumer purchasing. Decide this first, and then record all pertinent trips, noting the following information: time and date of trip; means of travel; destination—name and location (the nearest street intersection); purpose of trip (social, consumer, work, school, recreation); stops along the way and their purpose. The length of time this diary is kept depends on the nature of the orbit you wish to plot. If a weekly orbit is desired then all activities engaged in for at least one week are included. Obviously the diary must be kept for at least a week and, preferably, for several weeks. Two weeks is a realistic time for a weekly orbit, considering the impractical nature of longer times.

b) A less exact but frequently used method for obtaining orbit data is simply to rely on the individual's memory of movements within the city. Once the diary has been used for a short period to raise your level of consciousness of your movements, you may supplement this with your recollection of trips made at least once a week.

c) Assuming that you are now aware of your movements within the city you can proceed to plot your orbit by following these steps:
1) Make a list of the activities you do at least once a week that require you to leave your home. You may classify these activities under general headings of social visits, consumer purchases, and recreation. The frequency with which you travel to each destination should be noted.
2) On the outline street map of your city plot the locations of all the activities noted. Accuracy to the nearest street in-

tersection is all that is necessary.

3) Join each destination to your origin (your home) with a straight line. Different colored lines can be used to distinguish the frequency of visits, if you wish (e.g., daily, biweekly, and weekly).

4) Outline your orbit by joining your most distant destinations. You can construct daily, biweekly, and weekly orbits, if you wish.

d)   Variations on orbits constructed can be made by plotting only one type of destination, such as social visits.

e)   Orbits associated with transportation types can be constructed by coloring origin-destination lines for specific types of transportation used for each trip.

f)   Once you have your orbit drawn the important phase of explaining the pattern revealed begins. What is its shape like? Does it extend farther in one direction than another? Why might this be? Compare daily, biweekly, and weekly orbits. Compare transportation orbits. Explain any significant patterns.

g)   The most significant analysis takes place when you compare your orbit to the orbit of others (classmates, friends, neighbors, people in different urban environments, and people of different age groups). How do the sizes of orbits compare?

h)   What factors seem to affect the size and shape of the individual's orbit in the city?

i)   Is there any relationship between the individual's orbit and what he may consider to be his neighborhood within the community?

j)   If you were a city planner, how would you use the information you have gathered about orbits in your community?

7.15   ALTERNATIVES TO HIGH-RISE BUILDINGS

A group of investors have purchased a one-hectare site in the heart of an old but well-preserved neighborhood near the downtown area of a city. The surrounding homes are three-storey townhouses, now mostly subdivided into apartment flats. To recoup their investment in the land, the builders feel they must build at least 240 dwellings on their land. A high-rise apartment tower seems to be the best building type to accomplish this. The homeowners around this building site do not want a 40-storey apartment building towering over them. They fear that it will destroy the character of their neighborhood and lead to further apartment towers. Your assignment is to work in the neighborhood's behalf to plan a redevelopment of the block that will meet both the needs of the developers and the needs of the neighborhood residents.

The specifications are:
1) a one-hectare rectangular site;
2) 240 dwellings;
3) dimensions of each dwelling are to be 10 m × 10 m × 2.5 m, including halls, elevators, etc.;
4) adequate sunlight and ventilation for all dwellings.

Materials

a) corrugated cardboard or styrofoam sheets

b) desk lamp

Procedure

a) Choose a convenient scale for a model of your redevelopment project, considering the building materials you will be using.

b) Build a model of a 40-storey apartment tower for comparison.

c) Build your design. Keep it simple by keeping dwellings rectangular.

d) Demonstrate adequate sunlight by simulating with a desk lamp the lowest noonday sunlight angle in your area. No apartment should be shaded from the sun by other buildings.

e) Be prepared to justify your plan on the basis of suitability to the neighborhood, quality of open space, adequate sun and ventilation, and rental value of dwellings, as compared to the 40-storey apartment building.

f) Present your plan to a panel of judges who play the role of the developers. The developers must keep their best interests in mind and evaluate the alternatives presented, selecting the one they consider best. This decision should also be justified.

7.16 ECOPLANNING A NEW RESIDENTIAL DEVELOPMENT

On the accompanying three maps of a piece of land proposed for urban development (Fig. 7-8), you are given data on the natural situation of the site (its vegetation and soil conditions) and the urban situation (proposed plans for the site). It might be a site on the edge

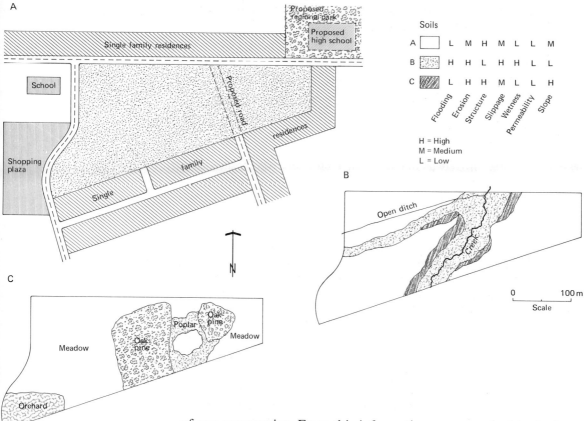

Soils

		Flooding	Erosion	Structure	Slippage	Wetness	Permeability	Slope
A		L	M	H	M	L	L	M
B		H	H	L	H	H	L	L
C		L	H	H	M	L	L	H

H = High
M = Medium
L = Low

N

0   100 m
Scale

Fig. 7-8
Characteristics of land proposed for urban development:
A) urban situation; B) soil characteristics; and C) vegetation.

of any community. From this information you are asked to design a plan for development. Feel free to alter proposed roads and zoning, but justify your changes. Note that, for traffic-flow reasons, the major road proposed through the woodlot must be built, but its path within the site may be altered. You may go into as much detail as you wish but your plan should show what land you would develop and what land you would keep as green space.

Materials

a)   tracing paper or acetates

Procedure

a)   Examine the situation carefully. The total area is 6.5 ha, of which 2 ha is woodlot. The development is to consist of single-family dwellings, 15 to the hectare. Five percent of the total area must be open space. No land is required for schools. You cannot change roads or buildings that already exist. Consider the effect of the residential development to the south on the residential area you are planning. What improvement to these residences is necessary if the stream running through the new area is to be of satisfactory environmental quality?

b) Examine the soil conditions and determine those unsuitable for urban construction.

c) Examine the vegetation and evaluate each type for urban development. You might find a benefit-cost analysis a useful tool in this kind of evaluation. Remember that, as the planner, you will have to convince the owner that your plan is not only good but profitable.

d) Having looked at the relevant characteristics of this land you may still find it difficult to pick the best land for development. A technique that enables you to compare the distributions of a number of characteristics is the use of overlays. On a sheet of acetate or tracing paper rate the various soil areas for urban development. A soil type could be rated as high, medium, or low. Low would be areas that should not be developed. High would be areas that could be urbanized at minimum cost to the environment. Similarly, on a second sheet of acetate or tracing paper map the potential for urban development of the different types of vegetation. Place one sheet over the other. If you have used the same color legend, the areas of darkest color should be the lowest in urban potential. These lands should not be developed. On the basis of the pattern resulting from the overlaying of these two maps, evaluate the proposed plan and suggest, if you think it is necessary, an alternative ecoplan.

e) Your plan should include any changes, such as zoning bylaws or servicing improvements, that are necessary for its success.

f) As a last step, consider what other elements of the site's environment might have been evaluated before determining a final plan for the area.

7.17 GREEN SPACE: GREENBELTS, GREEN WEDGES OR WHAT?

All plans for city growth now designate certain quantities of land as permanent green space. These lands can be used for parks or playgrounds, kept as woodlots or meadows, or used for agriculture. They cannot be built upon or paved over. How much green space is necessary, the location of that green space, and the shape that it should take are questions about which planners generally disagree. Should green space be used to shape and restrain growth or should it be chosen on the basis of its aesthetic or recreational value? How permanent can green space be if its only justification is a geometric pattern such as a belt or wedge? Do the belts or wedges suggested in many urban plans save too much green space? Will future urban growth create so much pressure on these green spaces that eventually planners will be tempted to develop them? The answers to these questions are not easy. Planners have been debating these issues for years. The answers that they come up with will affect the quality of your life within the urban environment. You should be able to evaluate their plans. To do so it is necessary to examine your relationship with the green spaces around you. The following exercise will help you make this examination. You will evaluate the three basic planning concepts related to green space preservation.

Fig. 7-9
Ways of allocating green space an urban community.

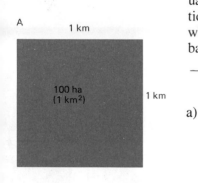

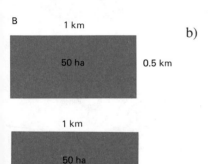

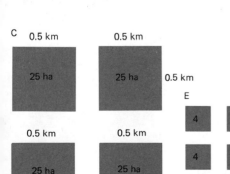

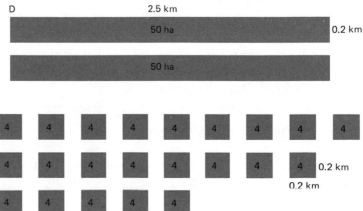

Procedure

a) Which green spaces in your community do you use the most? Are they located near or far from your home? Are they big or small? Do you prefer natural green spaces like woodlots and meadows or man-made green spaces like golf courses and flower gardens? How do you generally make use of green spaces around you? Do you recreate in them or look at them?

b) Considering the kinds of green space you prefer, how would you allocate 1 km² of green space in your neighborhood? Figure 7-9 illustrates the size possibilities you have. Explain the reasoning behind your decision. You might wish to consider the following questions as you allocate the green space: How does the perimeter of green space differ in each case? Is there any value in maximizing the perimeter of green space? Of what importance is the number of pieces of green space? How small can green spaces get before they become too small to be of recreational value?

Green Space: Greenbelts, Green Wedges or What?   191

c)   Figure 7-10 gives three plans for a community. Evaluate the quality of green space provided in each. Which plan is the most feasible as far as you are concerned? See Section 6.4 for further information about each of these planning concepts and for references.

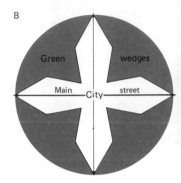

7.18   WATER TREATMENT

This section gives a list of questions that could form the basis for a visit to your municipal water treatment plant.

Questions

a)   Where does your community get its drinking water?

b)   Will the available water supply be sufficient to handle the demand in 10 years? in 20 years? If not, what plans are being made to increase the water supply or to conserve existing supplies?

c)   Does your municipality have a water shortage at any time of the year? When? What action is taken?

d)   What pollutants are present in the untreated water? Where do these pollutants originate?

e)   What steps are involved in water treatment?

f)   What chemicals remain in the water *after* treatment?

g)   Compare the hardness, odor, iron and manganese content, and bacterial levels of the original water with those of the treated water.

h)   Is any attempt made to recycle water; that is, is any used water treated at the plant?

i)   Water treatment is often referred to as "water purification". Is this an accurate term? Why or why not?

j)   Draw a flow chart of the steps involved in water treatment, using arrows to indicate the direction of flow.

k)   What effects would increased pollution of available water supplies (by industry or sewage) have on your community's water treatment program?

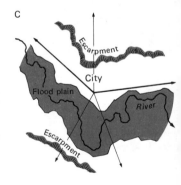

Fig. 7-10
Green space options for an urban community: A) greenbelt; B) green wedges; or C) ecoplanned green spaces.

7.19   SEWAGE TREATMENT

Sewage treatment is a process that remains largely invisible to the general public. A visit to a treatment plant can, therefore, provide much new information on such aspects as the type of wastes the city produces, its potential for water pollution, and the costs of this service to the city.

The following questions should help you gather useful information on your field trip.

Questions

a)   What percentage of the raw sewage comes from industry and what percentage comes from households?

b)   Are storm sewers and sanitary sewers in a combined system? Does this present contamination problems during a large storm?

c)   What *primary* treatment procedure is used?

d)   Which potential water pollutants are removed by primary treatment? Which are not removed?

e)   What *secondary* treatment procedures, if any, are used?

f)   Which potential water pollutants are removed by secondary treatment? Which are not removed?

g)   Is any *tertiary* treatment applied to the sewage? Why or why not?

h)   How is the *sludge* (solid residue) treated and disposed of?

i)   What is the most expensive part of the treatment process? What is the total cost to the consumer?

j)   Are any plans being made for improvement of treatment methods or facilities?

k)   Construct a flow chart of the steps involved in sewage treatment, showing the direction of flow by means of arrows.

Notes

If you wish to test the effluent from the plant to check on the answers received to questions d) and f), consult the book in this series titled *Environmental Pollution,* Section 6.26, pp. 193-196. Before you do so, check the safety of your methods with the plant manager. If the results of your tests indicate that your municipality is seriously polluting the surrounding water, you may wish to prepare a plan for improved sewage treatment. Consider carefully the factors of cost, time, industrial component of waste, sludge-disposal problems, and desired environmental quality. You may wish to submit this plan to your municipal sanitation or public works department.

7.20 SOLID-WASTE DISPOSAL

Garbage (solid-waste) disposal is generally considered an unsightly but essential service. Only when a lengthy strike or other inconvenience stops this service do we realize the importance to the city of a smoothly operating refuse-disposal program.

Materials

a) camera

b) tape measure

Procedure

There are three main ways to study solid-waste disposal. Your class may decide to do all three together, or divide them among smaller groups for later combination into a joint report.

A. *Interview*

a) Interview a municipal official in charge of solid-waste disposal. Obtain definitions of garbage, trash, litter, and refuse. Are they the same?

b) Ask for statistics on the composition of local refuse. What percentage is paper, tin cans, glass, iron, etc.?

c) Ask for statistics on the main sources of refuse—households, municipal containers, industry, stores, restaurants, etc.

d) Ask him to describe the disposal method or methods used.

e) Enquire about the cost per tonne of each method used.

f) Discuss with him future plans for solid-waste disposal. Do they include recycling, other new methods, stricter pollution controls, or changes in collection procedures?

B. *Site Visitation*

a) Visit several different types of disposal sites from among the following: sanitary landfill; incineration; automobile wrecking; composting; recycling or salvage depots.

b) Take pictures of each operation to record any health hazard or apparent pollution.

c) Rate each facility on a four-point basis (poor, fair, good, or excellent) for the following criteria (and any others you may wish to add): appearance; odor; cost to taxpayer; whether any attempt is made to recover revenue; amount of land used; pollution-control devices used; refuse tonnage that can be handled per day.

d)   (Optional) Tests may be performed at landfill sites to measure nearby water pollution and at incinerators to measure air pollution. Procedures and equipment needed are outlined in a companion volume to this book, *Environmental Pollution,* Units 6 and 7.

C. Street Survey

a)   Choose a sample street. Carry out a survey on garbage collection day to estimate the amount of solid waste produced per person per day in your community. A bathroom scale would be helpful.

b)   You may also wish to carry out an in-depth study of the amounts of each major type of refuse produced (paper, glass, etc.). Remember to ask permission and wear gloves.

c)   Measure a section of highway near or in your town or city. Count (or preferably collect and photograph) the litter found on both sides of this section. Estimate the proportion of the total amount formed by glass, cans, paper, etc. Calculate the density of each type per kilometre of highway.

Discussion

a)   Summarize your findings on the methods used, disposal cost per tonne for different methods, amount of litter found, and pollution (of air, water, nose, and eyes) caused by disposal facilities.

b)   If your municipality has a poor record in any of these aspects, suggest in a written report ways of improving the situation.

7.21   THE USE OF CENSUS-TRACT DATA

This exercise explains the use of census-tract data, derived from US and Canadian census bulletins. You should have examples of such data in front of you as you read this material.

Every ten years the governments of the United States and Canada conduct a major census. This is a collection of information about the citizens and businesses in the country. Why is it necessary for the government to collect such information? Samples from a major census will demonstrate to you the great variety of information that is collected.

Because of the size of large urban communities and the density of population within them, it is necessary to subdivide them into small units called *census tracts*. Only the largest cities in the country are divided into census tracts since the smaller centers are less complex and do not require subdivision. These units will be most important in our studies. Of the mass of data collected, our main concern will be with the population and housing characteristics within urban communities.

Census tracts are imaginary divisions of the urban landscape. They were drawn up to represent similar areas and populations. As a result, each tract is fairly uniform in population characteristics, economic status, and living conditions. These tracts were created so that comparisons may be made from census to census. Therefore, they rarely change in size.

What purposes do they serve? The data from census tracts are very useful for comparisons of economic and social factors within a large urban community. Such comparisons could not be conducted if only data for the community as a whole were available. The data are of value to planners, researchers, and businesses because they provide basic information about the living conditions in the area. Over a period of time the census information shows changes in population structure which helps city planners provide needed services.

Census tracts were originally conceived by Walter Laidlaw in New York City in 1906. They were created because of the need for data from uniform subdivisions within large cities. These subdivisions would then serve for studying neighborhoods smaller than political divisions. Since this time they have proved so useful that all major North American cities may now be studied using census-tract data.

In order to utilize the data effectively and correctly, it is necessary to realize just what is meant by each census term (or category). Within each census bulletin you will find an explanation of the terms used. Do not assume that you know what a term implies as this may lead to error. The census definition is explicit and there is often very little difference in meaning between terms.

It is also necessary to read the section on explanations because of the changing definitions used from one census to the next. The definition is changed, not to confuse the user, but to make it more explicit or to encompass a greater number of situations.

If these precautionary measures are taken, the census can provide a great deal of information that would otherwise have to be collected in very time-consuming interviews. A number of the following studies use census-tract data.

7.22 STUDIES OF A CULTURAL AREA

The study of a cultural (or ethnic) area can be of great benefit. Not only does it help us to understand the different life styles that exist but it also contributes to our comprehension of the great diversity found within short distances in the urban community.

Each cultural group brings with it traditions and customs that are often quite different from those of the majority of people living within the urban area. Such differences are reflected in the language spoken in the stores, the store signs, the use of the streets and parks for various activities, the color of paint used on houses, and the number of people living in each dwelling. These and other differences add greatly to the city's vitality, its attractiveness, and its diversity.

Materials

a) clipboard

b) sketching paper

c) lined paper

d) pencil, pen, ruler, eraser

e) bus fare

f) a camera and/or tape-recorder may also be useful

Procedure

A. Pre-field Trip Planning

a) Select one or more areas in the city inhabited by a large cultural group. If you are unfamiliar with such an area, a study of ethnic populations by census tract will prove useful.

b) Each individual or group may wish to choose one particular feature of the ethnic area to study, for instance, the types of food in shops, the types of churches, the clothes people wear (this often reflects the traditional dress of their place of origin), or the services offered in the area not found in other parts of the city.

c) In addition to these suggestions, can you think of any other characteristics that you would like to investigate?

d) Before going on the field trip it is important that you know what information you are basically interested in. With this in mind, write the questions down on a sheet of paper so that you can ask a merchant or other member of the community specific questions. The questions outlined below will also prove useful in organizing your thoughts and subsequent actions.

B. In the Field

a) The first thing is to become familiar with the area. Walk through it and make notes and diagrams of points of interest.

b) Now you are ready to investigate the topic or area of interest that was decided in the planning stage.

C. Things to Investigate

a) Delimit and investigate the area. The language used on store fronts is often a useful index for delimitation.

b) Describe the housing conditions. Compare the houses in this area with those in the area around your school.

c) Are there special types of recreational activities or facilities within the area?

d) What type of food do people eat in the area? Is the food labeled in the language of the people living in the area? Do you see foods unfamiliar to you? Write some of them down. Compare the prices of some common food items in this area with prices in the stores in the area where you live. Describe the selling techniques of the merchants.

e) Is there a local newspaper? If so, what are the major concerns of the community? If the paper is in a different language, perhaps a fellow student who speaks the language will be of assistance.

f) Ask about the social values. Do married children live with their parents? Do teen-agers have the same freedom or goals as your group?

g) Describe your overall impressions of the area (sight, sound, smells, and any other personal reaction).

Discussion

a) Using the census, determine the population density. Does it differ from non-ethnic areas of a similar income group? Discuss.

b) Compare and contrast the cultural area and its characteristics with your own area.

c) Describe the general location of the area in relation to the rest of the urban area. Why did it develop in this area? Give a brief history of the area.

d)   Describe the problems that you feel exist in the area.

e)   What are the best features of the area?

Note

This could be made into a laboratory exercise by using census-tract data.

7.23   SITE SELECTION BY A LOCAL BUSINESS

When you walk through your local community do you ever wonder why certain businesses are located where they are? There are reasons why a business will locate on one site and not on another. Each business sets certain criteria by which one location is chosen over another.

In this field exercise it will be necessary to speak to a local businessman and discover why he chose that particular location for his business.

Materials

pencil, paper, eraser

Procedure

A. Pre-field Preparation

a)   Select a local business that you will study.

b)   Phone or visit the business and obtain permission to visit and ask questions pertaining to the topic. Make arrangements to visit on a specific day at a given time.

c)   In addition to the questions listed below, create some questions of your own. These questions will vary depending upon the type of business studied.

d)   Draw a sketch map of the area in which the business is located and mark on the map the location of the business and other businesses in the immediate vicinity.

B. In the Field

a)   Draw a map of the business area in which the business is located.

b)   Stand in the vicinity of the store and observe the customers. Do they drive or walk to the business you are studying? In what directions do they come from? Are they mostly men or women? Do the customers go directly to the business or do they visit several businesses?

c) Visit the businessman and ask questions such as the following: When did you locate at this site? Why did you choose this particular location over others? Where do your customers come from? What attracts customers to your place of business? At what times of the day/week are you the busiest? Do the other businesses in the area hinder or help your business? In what ways?

C. *Follow-up*

a) Compare the answers that you received with those of your classmates. Make up a chart for this comparison and see if you can find a pattern of location for different types of businesses.

b) Draw some general conclusions on business location based on your field work.

7.24 POPULATION CHARACTERISTICS FROM CENSUS-TRACT DATA

What would be the easiest procedure to follow in order to determine the characteristics of people living in a particular area of an urban community? You could make a trip to the area and observe the people living there. Once you arrived in the area what characteristics might you look for? You might observe the age of the people, their income levels, the number of children in each family, or the language they speak. You might also speak to them to learn the number of people living in each household or their levels of education. The possibilities are enormous.

Such a procedure, however, would be very time consuming and the information might be difficult to obtain, depending upon the cooperation extended by the people with whom you talk. A much more efficient way of obtaining your information would be through the use of census-tract data. Population characteristics by census tract can provide you with a great deal of information about an area even though you have never been there. The knowledge gained about an area depends upon the categories in the census that are selected for study.

Materials

a) population and housing characteristics by census tract for your community or a large urban center

b) pencil, eraser, paper

c) a calculator, if available

Procedure

a) Your teacher will determine the census tracts that you will be observing.

b) On the map in the census bulletin, locate the tracts that you are observing.

c) Determine the following values for each census tract:
    1) the population density;
    2) the percentage of the population that is male;
    3) the percentage of the population that is female;
    4) the percentage of the population that is married;
    5) the percentage of males and females in the labor force that are employed;
    6) the percentage of males and females in managerial and professional positions;
    7) the average wage and salary incomes for males and females.

Discussion

a) Which area is the most densely populated and which is the least densely populated? What are some reasons for this variation?

b) In which areas of the city are there more married people than others? Give reasons for this variation.

c) What are the variations between census tracts in the percentage of males and females in the labor force who have a job? Account for these variations.

d) What is the relationship between the percentage of males in managerial and professional positions and the average wage and salary incomes for males? What does this relationship indicate about the area? Complete the same interpretation for females.

e) Are there areas that have greater male or female populations than other areas? If so, account for these differences.

f) This exercise demonstrates that by using census-tract data we are able to learn something about the characteristics of people who live in various parts of the city. However, the determination of certain characteristics about different areas of the city is of little value if it cannot be used constructively. How may such information be used?

7.25 COMPARISON OF POPULATION DENSITIES AND DISTRIBUTION IN DIFFERENT NEIGHBORHOODS

The density of population varies from place to place throughout an urban community. In some places we find large expensive homes on large lots and in other places there are a great many dwellings clustered tightly together. With the advent of high-rise apartment dwellings, large numbers of people are housed on a small amount of land. All these different types of housing contribute to varying population densities.

These are not the only considerations that must be taken into account, however, when considering population densities. For example, several apartment buildings may be the only form of residence in a census tract and the rest of the land is industrial. In a neighboring tract all the land may be used for residential purposes but the total population is equal to that of the tract with the apartment buildings. When these data are transformed into density figures both will appear to have the same densities. Thus the type of dwellings and the spatial distribution must also be considered when studying population densities. If this is not done, an erroneous picture of the population may result.

Materials

a)   population and housing characteristics by census tract

Procedure

a)   Locate three neighborhoods in the city that you consider to be occupied by low-income, middle-income, and high-income groups. Use census-tract boundaries to delimit these areas.

b)   Describe the types of housing and the housing conditions found in each area.

c)   On a land-use map, determine if the population is spread evenly throughout the census tract or whether it is clustered in certain areas.

d)   Using census data, determine the population densities for each area. What conclusions can you draw from this about population density and income levels?

e)   How close is the nearest industrial area to each income group? What conclusions can you draw from this information?

f)   Describe the physical landscape of each type of residential area (a topographic map will be useful). Suggest reasons for the differences that are noted, if any.

g) Select three more census tracts: one downtown, one midtown, and one in the suburbs. Determine the population densities. Where are the highest densities and where are the lowest? Explain the possible factors that caused the differences or similarities in density.

7.26 YELLOW PAGES EXERCISE: THE LOCATION OF VARIOUS ACTIVITIES IN THE URBAN COMMUNITY

Each type of activity or function carried out in an urban community locates in a certain area in order to take advantage of characteristics of that location. Some activities tend to locate in very specific areas of the city while others, requiring less specialized locations, are able to locate almost anywhere.

Whenever a company or businessman decides to locate within the urban area it is necessary to find a site that will make the business prosper. If the most advantageous location is not sought, there is a good possibility that the business will not survive.

By examining the locational patterns for several activities we should be able to determine some of the major advantages of one location over another. Thus we will be able to understand why some activities are found in one part of the city and not in another.

Materials

a) detailed road map of your community
b) an outline map of your community
c) Yellow Pages Directory
d) pencil, eraser

Procedure

a) Select an activity or function to be mapped. Examples are investment companies, department stores, apartment buildings, stock brokers, milk stores, law firms, automobile dealerships, hotels, motels, theaters, gas stations, supermarkets, laundries, cinemas, camera shops, and bookstores.

b) For each activity it will be necessary to map 30 or more locations. In some cases there will be less than 30 members of an activity listed in the Yellow Pages Directory. In such a case, map as many as are available. In other cases, however, there will be hundreds of members listed. In this case, a sampling procedure must be employed. Set the sampling interval at an arbitrary number. If, for example, you choose an interval of five, the mapping procedure is as follows:

1) plot the location of the first listed member;
2) move down the listing five members and plot its location;
3) move down another five members and plot its location, and so on, until at least 30 members have been mapped.

Discussion

a) What type of pattern is shown by the function that you mapped?

b) Describe the possible reasons for an individual or company locating where it did. Consider the type of activity you are looking at and the factors of location that will make the business prosper in that particular location.

c) Using map overlays, compare the different patterns shown by various functions. Do certain activities tend to locate near one another? If so, why? If not, why?

7.27 DEMONSTRATION OF CHRISTALLER'S CENTRAL-PLACE THEORY

This exercise is designed to simulate the settlement of a flat plain according to Christaller's Central-Place Theory. The final diagram of the exercise will represent the theoretical distribution of settlements according to this theory. In reconstructing the history of this prairie region we will describe the settlement pattern and the distribution of urban functions throughout the region.

Materials

a) colored pencils, ruler, eraser

b) copy paper

Procedure

a) During the nineteenth century the vast plains and prairies of central North America were settled. The pioneers made their way westward in wagons filled with all their worldly goods. Upon reaching the flat prairies of the interior many decided this was where they wanted to settle.

The dots shown in Figure 7-11 represent the small villages that were established by these early settlers. The

Fig. 7-11
Central-place theory.

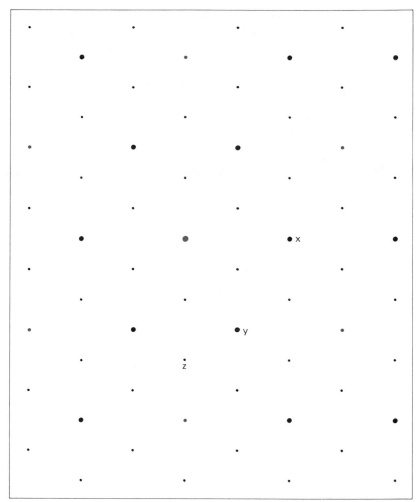

villages were spaced evenly over the flat landscape so that each village would have an equal share of the fertile farmland and farmers. As well as being equidistant from one another, the villages were located at such a distance that every farmer could travel in a small wagon from his farmstead to the village market and back again in one day. A farmer who lived exactly half way between two villages could go to either village market and return home in the same day.

b) During the early part of the twentieth century, settlers continued to arrive in the area. Some villages were more attractive than others and these grew into small towns. These are indicated on the map by large black and all red dots. As the population of the towns increased the number of functions that they offered increased. The towns are more widely spaced than the villages because farmers now have better methods of transportation and can travel further in a day. In addition, since the towns offer higher-order goods than the villages, they must have a larger threshold population.

c) The area that surrounds and is served by each town is called its *umland*. Although different goods and services have different ranges, the umland between two towns offering the same goods and services usually extends half way between the two.

We can show the umland that surrounds each town in the following manner. (To avoid marking up your text, copy the pattern of dots onto a sheet of copy paper.) Using straight lines join the villages that surround town X. Do the same for town Y. The result in each case is an umland in the shape of a hexagon (Fig. 7-12).

1) How many villages are served by town X?
2) How many villages are served by town Y?
3) What is the total number of villages served by both towns?
4) How many villages are served jointly by towns X and Y? Draw the umlands for all the other towns shown on the map. You should extend some of the lines off the map since they will be connected to villages beyond the area covered by the map. The result should be a map covered with equal-sized hexagons.

Fig. 7-12
A hexagon.

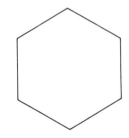

d) After World War II the region's population continued to grow. By the late 1950s several of the towns grew into cities. These are shown on the map in red.

Using the same procedure that was used for the towns, draw the umlands around each of these cities.

1) Why are the cities equidistant from one another?
2) Why are the cities located farther apart than the towns?

e) During the 1960s and early 1970s one city grew more than any other. It did so because its location was best suited to serve most of the region. Where is this urban center located on the map? We can call this very large city a *metropolitan center*. If we compare the urban centers according to their size and number of functions offered we get the following situation:

Village. This is the smallest urban center and may contain a gas station, a grocery store, a hardware store, and an elementary school.

Town. A town has all the functions that the village has plus drugstores, restaurants, a high school, and a weekly newspaper.

City. A city has all the functions that the village and town have and may also have a department store, a college, and an automobile dealership.

Metropolitan Center. This is the largest urban center and contains all the functions of the smaller settlements and more of them. In addition it will contain very high-order functions such as a university, modern hospitals, theaters, expensive jewelry shops, and daily newspapers.

f) Draw the umland around the metropolitan center.

g) Make up a scale for your map, for example, 1 cm = 10 km.

Discussion

a) If a person lived at village Z how far would he have to travel to find a gas station; a college; a drugstore; a theater?

b) Why are there many villages and towns, so few cities, and only one metropolitan center?

c) Why are theaters, a university, expensive jewelry shops, and modern hospitals found only in the largest urban center while gas stations are found in each village?

d) Look at the area served by the large metropolitan center. How many cities does the metropolitan center serve? How many total hexagons served by cities can be found within the hexagon of the metropolitan center? *Note:* Include partial hexagons in determining your answer.

7.28 TOWN PLANNING EXERCISE

The map in Figure 7-13 shows an area approximately 70 km from a large city. This area will form the site of a new town. The purpose of this new town is to decentralize the surplus population of the large city and to prevent urban sprawl. The new town should eventually support a population of 30 000 people and provide those people with the necessary goods, services, and employment so that they are not dependent upon the large city. As a result, the town should be relatively self-sufficient. Your task, as an urban planner, is to design a town that both fulfils this function and is suitable for the site.

To obtain some useful ideas about town design you may wish to refer to the concepts of Howard, Le Corbusier, Frank Lloyd Wright, Clarence Stein, and any other architect or planner who can offer suitable ideas. Select what you consider to be the most valuable ideas or create your own design concept. Above all, *plan for people*.

Materials

a)   colored pencils, ruler, eraser

b)   drawing paper

c)   Bristol board

Procedure

a)   Make several copies of the map shown in Figure 7-13. These will be your working copies on which to plan the town.

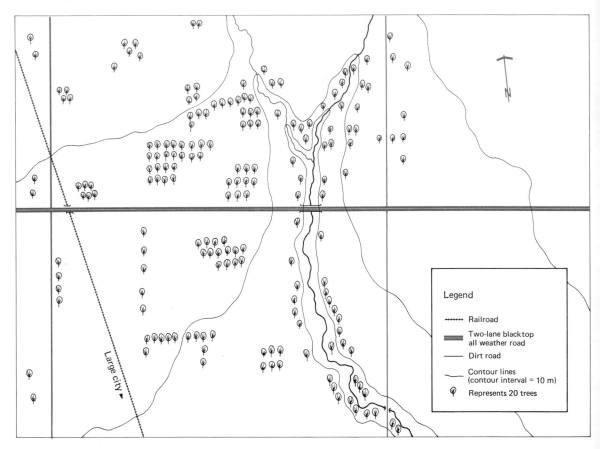

b)   *Planning Considerations.* In planning any town there are many things that have to be taken into consideration. Some of these include:

    1) Family Structures: The makeup of families in the town will be approximately as follows:
widowed and single (over 18 years old, does not include children living at home)   12%

Fig. 7-13
Site for the new town.

childless families	21%
families of 3-4 people	47%
families of 5-7 people	15%
families of more than 7 people	5%

As you can see, the majority of people living in the town will be family oriented. How many people will be included in each of the above categories?

2) Accommodation: The majority of people moving to this town would be young families seeking reasonably priced housing. Therefore, work toward a balance of housing types: detached houses, townhouses, duplexes, semidetached houses, high- and low-rise apartment buildings. This variety would suit the various income levels of the prospective residents. In addition, remember that the distribution of housing types may determine to a large extent the social structure of the community (that is, high-, middle-, and low-income areas).

   In order to determine the number of units of each housing type that will be required, you will have to determine the housing needs of the town's population. For example, how many people can be accommodated in each apartment building and therefore how many buildings will be required for the number of people you want housed in apartment buildings. Discuss the types of accommodation that you have used to house the town's population.

3) Services: The town must contain such essential services as police protection, fire protection, medical services, municipal services, places of worship, and educational facilities. In all cases the buildings housing these services must be placed with their maximum potential use in mind. Approximately how many elementary and secondary schools will be needed to accommodate the children of the town?

4) Street Pattern: Determine the type of street pattern that is most appropriate for each area and function. Consideration should also be given to the separation of pedestrian and vehicular traffic.

5) Town Center: The town should have a center which will fulfil administrative, business, and entertainment functions. It should be the focus of the town, a showplace that reflects the character of the community.

6) Commercial Land Uses: There must be sufficient commercial development to service the whole town. Each neighborhood should have easy access to shopping facilities.

7) Office Space: There should be some office buildings. Determine the type of activities that require office space in the town.

8) Industry: As this is to be a new town, a balance should be attempted so that most people who live in the town will be able to work in the community. To attract industry to the town, areas should be set aside and provided with industrial services, a transportation network, and room for expansion. Discuss the type of industry that you hope to attract to the town. Discuss the reasons for locating the industrial area where you have in the town.

9) Recreation: The town should be planned so that there is sufficient parkland to accommodate the community. Parks should be planned to be used by adults and children. You may landscape the area by bulldozing, building dams, etc., if you wish. You must, however, remember to keep the costs under control.

10) Prevailing Winds: Westerlies.

c) On the basis of your planning considerations draw the town design on a working copy of the map. Label all the functions and features that are shown. For example, mark the sewage treatment plant, police station, elementary and secondary schools.

d) If you feel that the rough outline on the working copy of the map meets your requirements, transfer the town plan to the large sheet of Bristol board. In constructing the map, the following colors should be used to distinguish the different functions:

1) residential: houses - red; apartments - pink
2) commercial: light blue
3) office: dark blue
4) industrial: light industry - grey; heavy industry - black
5) institutional (schools): light brown
6) recreational: orange
7) services: dark brown
8) open space: vacant - light green; park - dark green
9) streets and parking: regular HB pencil

Notes

a) It is not necessary to show individual houses. Color in the blocks of land that are designated as houses. However, show each apartment building.

b) Establish a scale for both the working map and the final town plan.

Discussion

Describe, in detail, the planning concepts that you have used and what you hope to achieve through the design of your town. In effect, you must justify everything that you have done in the creation of the town plan.

7.29   A SOCIAL SURVEY OF YOUR COMMUNITY

Even after observing your community and carrying out the many exercises in this book, questions will occur to you that cannot be answered by books, maps, or statistics. You may wish to know how the citizens of your community feel about some new development—an expressway, a high-rise apartment complex, a new park, or an urban-renewal project. You may wish to know why people move within the community the way they do, or where they go for recreation. You may wish to know where the workers of a factory or the students of your school live. You may wish to find out how people feel about air, water, or noise pollution. You may wish to know where people shop, when, and how they get there. Has a recent change in transportation affected the patterns of shopping behavior? Does age, sex, or socio-economic status affect consumer behavior or attitudes toward air pollution?

For the answers to questions like these you must ask people. No business would think of putting out a new product without first surveying the opinion of potential customers. There is a need to do the same thing when changing the urban environment. It is not enough that a project should be economically profitable or ecologically wise. A project must also be acceptable to the public. Conducting a social survey can provide answers as to what people do, how and when they do it, and what people think about almost anything. It can provide the kind of information that you cannot get anywhere else. To do a survey correctly is often difficult but it is a worthwhile field study in the urban community.

Materials

a)   depends on the study

Procedure

a)   Select the problem. What do you want to investigate? Does it justify the time and effort necessary, both yours and the people you ask? Is asking people the only way to get the information you want? How can the results be used? For example, a pedestrian shopping mall has been proposed for the downtown. Are the people in favor of it? Do they think it is worth the cost? The outcome of the survey could either give the plan the go-ahead or justify its rejection.

b) Whom does the problem concern? Does it concern the entire population of the community or only part of it? If only part of the population, which part—a specific age group (e.g. adults); a specific sex (e.g. women); a specific occupation group (e.g. retail-store owners); a specific employment group (e.g. housewives); a specific income group (e.g. low income); a specific race or ethnic group (e.g. Italians); tax-payers only; citizens only; a specific geographical area (e.g. flood plain area); a specific political area (e.g. a city ward)?

c) How will contact be made?
   1) Mail is cheap and fast. Addresses are easy to obtain. A large sample can be obtained. However, mail is impersonal, has a high rate of non-returns, does not allow follow-up questions, and questions must be simple and brief. Mail is suitable for a survey that requires a large number of responses to mainly factual questions.
   2) Phoning is cheap, quick, and more personal than mail. Phone numbers are easy to get. A large sample can be obtained and follow-up questions are possible. The disadvantages of the phone are high refusal rates, incomplete population coverage, and necessary brevity. Phone surveys are recommended mainly when large samples are necessary and the questions are short and factual.
   3) Interviewing is personal. Explanations and follow-up questions are possible to allow in-depth enquiries. However, person-to-person contacts can be expensive and time consuming. Fewer possible contacts make this type of surveying useful when in-depth answers to complicated questions are required and the number of responses is less important.

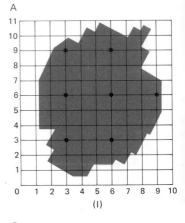

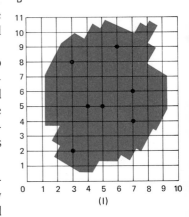

d) Determining who will be questioned. In step b) you determined whom the problem concerned. This may be a very large number of people, spread over a large area. You could ask everyone concerned but that would be time consuming and costly. Usually by taking a sample of the population, answers representing the opinions of the whole can be obtained. This method is based on the idea that you do not have to eat a whole pie to know if it is good. You can tell from one piece. Of course, a pie is usually the same throughout; people are not. Samples have to reflect the differences in people if they are going to reflect the opinions of the whole population. Below are some ways to select a sample.

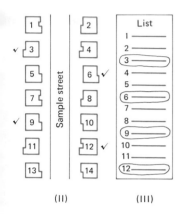

(II)   (III)

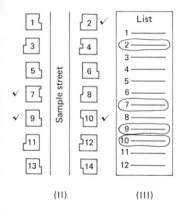

(II)   (III)

Fig. 7-14
Sample selection methods: (A) systematic and (B) random, using (i) map and grid, (ii) houses along a street, and (iii) lists, eg., phone book or polling lists.

1) Personal Selection. The surveyor uses his or her personal preferences in choosing who will be asked. This method is the least dependable, though the easiest. It can be biased if you choose to select only people with Anglo-Saxon names, or people with well-kept houses, or people living in certain parts of the city, or people who are home at a certain time of the day. If you ask only persons in the downtown area whether they are in favor of a new pedestrian mall, you are asking a biased sample.

2) Systematic Selection. In this method the surveyor determines whom he will ask before he sees them, their names, or their homes. It is predetermined that every third person, for example, will be surveyed. The surveyer must then stick to this method, avoiding personal preferences and biases that would alter his choice. Figure 7-14A shows how this method can be adapted to lists, maps, or houses along a street used in selecting the sample.

3) Random Selection. This method also removes personal bias by predetermining who will be selected. In this case a table of random numbers is used to select the potential candidates to be interviewed. As in the previous method the randomness of the sample depends on the surveyor adhering to the method. Figure 7-14B shows how this method works with maps, lists, and houses along a street.

4) Quotas and Representative Sampling. This technique can be added to systematic or random sampling to ensure that the sample is proportionate to some known composition of the whole population. For example, you may wish to reflect the 50:50 ratio of men to women. You choose your sample by the systematic or random method but select half women and half men. You can also obtain equal representation from different areas. For example, if your community has four census tracts of equal population, you could ensure geographic representation by selecting a quarter of your sample from each census tract. This quota method is used mostly when some specific characteristic of people is expected to be important to the opinions surveyed and there are available statistics for the total population concerning that characteristic.

e) Determining the size of the sample population to be surveyed. The larger a sample is, the greater is its chance of being reliable. There is no magic figure to ensure that the sample is large enough. The best rule here is to sample as large a population as time, money, and manpower will allow. Many statistical analysis techniques require at least 30 in the sample. Remember that depth of answers may be more valuable in some problems than the size of the sample.

f) Determining what to ask. This should be determined before you actually start interviewing. You may already know what you want to ask, but you have to word the questions so that you get answers in a form you can use. Also the question must be easily understood by the person interviewed. You have to decide what other information about the person interviewed might affect the answers he gives, for example, age, sex, occupation, income, family status. Questions concerning income may be refused if you are too specific. You probably do not need an exact amount. Thus you might ask the person what range of income he would place himself in. In the case of the proposed mall, the fact that someone works there or owns a store there may be important to his attitude.

Everyone must answer the same questions so results can be tabulated and analyzed. Thus a questionnaire is usually made up before interviewing starts. Figure 7-15A shows part of a typical questionnaire.

g) Tabulating the results. After interviewing, results have to be totaled. You may also want to break down the results according to sex or some other factor. Figure 7-15B shows how some of the data from Figure 7-15A were treated.

h) Interpreting the results. In order to interpret the results of the survey you may wish to do more than just count responses. Raw scores could be converted to percentages. Graphing and mapping can be done. Where appropriate, alternatives may be ranked. Remember, it may be more important to know how groups of people differ on some question than whether or not the majority are in favor of something. See Figure 7-15C for the interpretation of some of the results from Figures 7-15A and B.

i) Drawing conclusions. When you draw conclusions from your study, be careful to avoid letting your own opinion interfere.

Some Suggested Topics

1) Downtown urban-renewal opinion survey
2) Shopping behavior survey
3) Transportation preference survey
4) Noise, water, or air pollution attitude survey

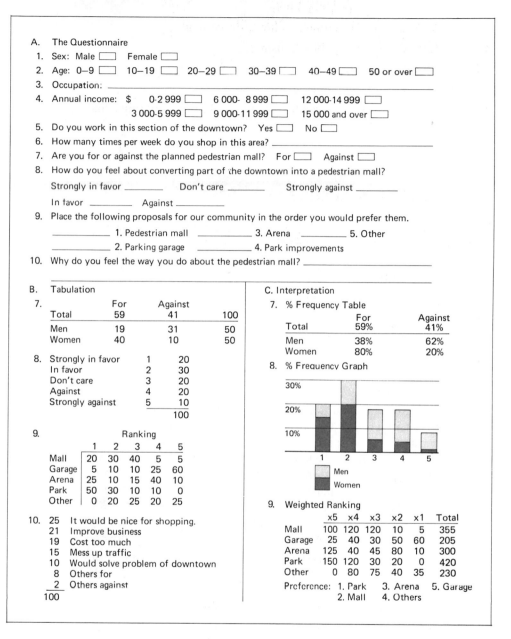

Fig. 7-15 A, B, C
Example of survey methods.

5) Urban recreational needs survey

6) Planning proposal survey

7) Housing preference survey

8) Attitudes concerning apartment living

9) Metropolitan (regional) government vs. neighborhood control

10) Attitudes toward crime and law enforcement

11) Attitudes toward public housing

12) Attitudes toward control of development

13) Attitudes toward littering

14) Attitudes toward speeding, snowmobiling, hunting, and other controversial topics

---

7.30 ZONE OF INFLUENCE OF A STORE

The purpose of this field trip is to determine how far people will come to a particular store and why they choose it.

Materials

a) a map of the city or neighborhood

b) clipboard, pencils, and data sheets

c) school identification

d) watches

Procedure

a) Prepare sufficient data sheets so that you can interview at least 50 people for a particular store. Your data sheets should include space for date and time; location of respondent's residence; means of transportation to the store; time taken to get to the store; frequency of visits; why they chose to come to this particular store (closeness, reputation or name of store, cost of goods, variety of goods, nearness to stores with the same goods, nearness to stores with different goods); alternate stores that are used for the same purpose.

b) Be sure to identify yourself and your purpose to the store manager and to each respondent as he or she enters the store. Offer the store manager a copy of the results. Do not impede the flow of people to and from the store.

c) Be consistent in your choice of people to interview. For example, you could interview every fifth person to enter the store.

Discussion

a) On a map locate the site of each respondent's home.

b) Is there a great concentration or a wide dispersion of home location?

c)   Is the frequency of visits related to location of residence?

d)   Is there any relationship between distance from store and method of transportation?

e)   Make a list of reasons for shopping at this store. Arrange the list in order of decreasing importance.

f)   Locate alternate stores chosen for the same purpose. What were the reasons for variations in patronage?

g)   Does a certain kind of store have a separate territory or does it share part of it with other stores selling the same goods?

h)   Would this store be servicing the neighborhood, the community, or the region?

i)   Can you forecast the zone of influence for a particular store best by type of goods and/or by alternate stores?

7.31   SHOPPING PATTERNS OF LOCAL RESIDENTS

How well do the retail and wholesale establishments fit the needs and priorities of local residents in your community? An understanding of the achievements and failures in providing for consumer demands might provide a tool for better community planning.

In this investigation you prepare and administer a consumer questionnaire and draw conclusions from the results. Afterwards you will look at several general models of consumer behavior which might show the complexities and variables involved in the location of business establishments.

Materials

a)   a street map of your community

b)   a random-dot sheet

c)   a consumer questionnaire, pencils, envelopes, and stamps

d)   a calculator

Procedure

A. Preparing the Consumer Questionnaire

Several basic facts are required from each respondent regarding his or her shopping patterns. Design a questionnaire to obtain the following information. Remember that a questionnaire that is neat and easy to complete is more likely to be filled out.

a)   Location:

1) location of residence and place of work or school;

2) length of residency;
3) type of dwelling.

b)   Personal statistics of respondents:
1) age and sex;
2) marital status;
3) cultural background.

c)   Household characteristics:
1) number of related members in each household or home;
2) age of other members of the household;
3) location of work or school for each member;
4) approximate income bracket of the total family income.

d)   Shopping patterns of the household:
Type of shopping activity
1) food shopping—major and minor purchases;
2) clothes shopping;
3) drugs and grooming aids;
4) household appliances;
5) cleaning establishments;
6) materials for home maintenance;
7) furniture shopping;
8) sports equipment, instruments, and hobby supplies.

e)   For each of the activities in d) you should record:
1) location of store;
2) distance from home or place of work;
3) time taken to get to the store;
4) method of transportation;
5) frequency of visit;
6) reasons for choice of store (closeness; reputation or name of store; cost of goods; variety of goods; nearness to stores with the same goods; nearness to stores with different goods);
7) satisfaction level: bad, poor, fair, good, excellent. Why?

B. Choice of Study Area and Conducting Interviews

a)   Delimit the study area on a street map. This area could be a wedge-shaped area from the most accessible corners in your city or CBD to the boundary. It could also be a retail business cluster or plaza with a graded radius of a 5 min walk, 10 min walk, 10 to 15 min car or public transportation ride, and greater than 30 min ride.

b)   Using a random-dot sheet and the street map, choose the nearest household to each dot. Choose about 150-200 sample households to ensure enough respondents.

c) Either conduct a personal interview or mail the question-naire with an explanatory note. If you choose to mail the interviews and introductory letter, a stamped return envelope should be included. A city directory, found in the public library, might give you the right addresses.

Discussion

a) What percentage of the total sample completed the questionnaire?

b) What are the personal characteristics of the sample population? Do these characteristics vary with the type of dwelling and location?

c) Discuss one relationship between a personal characteristic and household characteristics.

d) What kind of relationship exists between personal and household characteristics and each shopping activity?

e) What are the basic needs of different kinds of people and households?

f) Which kinds of stores should be located near each other?

g) How far are people willing to go for each type of shopping activity?

h) Are the population's shopping needs being met by the facilities provided?

i) What suggested needs will or will not be met in future plans for the community?

Notes

a) In order to answer the preceding questions (and others), totals and percentages of various parts of the interviews will have to be obtained. A calculator will be helpful. Determine whether certain shopping patterns are explained by different personal and/or household characteristics.

b) Read the appropriate *Recommended Readings* from Unit 5. How well do your findings agree with or disagree with the established models?

7.32   THE FUNCTIONING OF A LOCAL INDUSTRY

Local industry is to a community what a stomach is to the body. What is involved in the establishment, feeding, and output of an industry in your town? Are the benefits greater than the costs to the community? How does this industry interact with other businesses in the community? These are a few questions that will be investigated in this field study.

Materials

a)   notebooks and pencils

Procedure

a)   Choose a local industry for your study. Decide where it fits in the following classification:

A. Production

1) Primary: Harvesting commodities from nature (agriculture, forestry, fishing, mining);
2) Secondary: Increasing the value of commodities by changing their form (manufacturing);
3) Tertiary: Performing services (repair, banking, government, teaching, entertainment).

B. Exchange

1) Location: i) Increasing the value of commodities by changing their location (freight transportation);
ii) Satisfying the needs of people by changing their location (passenger transportation).
2) Ownership: Increasing the value of commodities by changing their ownership (wholesale and retail trade).

O. Consumption

This area includes the purchasing activities of the population and consumption of services.

b)   Plot the location of your chosen industry on a map of your community.

c)   Make a list of the factors that might affect the establishment of this activity in this region, this community, and this location. *why does this company locate here.*

d)   Make a list of the factors that might affect the kinds of internal activities, facilities, and labor required for performing these activities. *what does it do , (ex) cement*

150 9 1/1 3a   what does it need to run?

Home — Down Town
Intern — School.

e) Make a list of the factors that might affect the <u>interaction</u> of this activity with other national, regional, and local economic activities. *How does it relate to other companies*

f) Make a list of the factors that might affect the ability of this activity to continue and improve for the benefit of owners, workers, and community.

g) Arrange to go to the business you have chosen. If you mention what your objectives are, you are more likely to speak to the right person and to see parts of the operation.

h) Take your lists from c) to f) with you on your visit. Discuss your lists with your host. Record changes he mentions. Make sure your recording is acceptable to the business.

Discussion

Back in class you should attempt to analyze the information you have collected. Here are a few questions to help you get started.

a) Compare your first list of factors affecting this economic activity to your list after the field trip.

b) What other economic activities are associated with this business?

c) Where are these related businesses located with respect to this business?

d) How is site space used to ensure production efficiency and the best working conditions for all employees? *Is it a safe place to work.*

e) Who or what seems to benefit from the presence of this activity?

f) Who or what does *not* benefit from the presence of this activity?

g) Try to assign a dollar and cent value to the benefits and costs of this industry to all involved.

h) Are any of your classmates studying a business that deals with your industry? If so, how closely are their futures linked? For example, if mine A closes will grocery store B close?

Research Topics

8

This unit contains a number of topics that are of great importance to all of us. You should have no trouble selecting one topic that interests you. When you have done so, research it thoroughly by yourself or with a few other interested students.

A list of things that you might do has been included with each topic. This list will help you to get started on your project. It is *not* complete. Many other ideas will come to mind as you research the topic. Some references have been included. You should also consult encyclopedias and other books in your school and community libraries. Many government agencies, industries, conservation groups, and nature clubs supply free information on some of these topics. You need only ask for it. Letters, telephone calls, and visits are effective ways of obtaining information.

At the end of your study you should prepare a written report so that others in your class can benefit from your work. Your teacher will give you instructions about the nature of the report.

8.1   DESIGN OF NEIGHBORHOODS

The neighborhood plays a vital role in the individual's existence within the larger urban community. In Section 7.2 you have already dealt with the complexity of the neighborhood concept. Perhaps you discovered the relationship of neighborhood to man and the urban environment as a whole. Just as the individual's home provides him with needed shelter and privacy, the neighborhood fills other needs. The neighborhood is a place where the individual feels familiar. He knows this area of the city very well. He knows many of the people.

Maybe the people have backgrounds or incomes similar to his. The neighborhood has within it many of the services he requires frequently.

If you have examined a number of different neighborhoods you may have noticed that some neighborhoods do their job better than others. Some would be nicer to live in than others. Some encourage neighbors to meet each other by focusing residences around a meeting place—a school, park, shopping center, or church. Others hinder movement and contact by having poor traffic patterns and no focal point. Of course some people may prefer to live in an environment that minimizes contact between neighbors. Whether a neighborhood is good or bad may be a question of personal preferences. Your evaluation will depend on what *you* think a neighborhood should be. Should it have residents who are all of the same race, income group, or ethnic origin? Should it have residents who are at the same stage of the life cycle, for example, all with children? What urban functions should be within the neighborhood—schools, stores, industry, recreation? The questions you can ask yourself are almost unlimited. You may find that, to answer some of these questions, you need to know more about residential design. Why are the street patterns laid out the way they are? How might pedestrian movement be separated from automobile movement? How might you achieve more public open space without reducing the density of dwellings within a certain area? More questions will undoubtedly occur to you as you begin to read some of the *Recommended Readings* listed here.

For Thought and Research

The following are some aspects to investigate:

1   If you want a neighborhood to have a homogenous population (people who share common social status or life-cycle stage) how could the design or plan of the neighborhood be used to encourage this? If you want a mixed population what design changes would you make? Which type of neighborhood design do you find most often? Why? In your opinion, which is best?

2   How can design be used to make the neighborhood's environment more attractive to its residents? Does making the environment more attractive have to mean a greater cost for the resident? Can low-cost housing be attractive? What are some design tricks that cost little but enhance the appearance of the neighborhood?

3   What activities should be provided within the neighborhood? Should each neighborhood have an elementary school? a high school? a church? a hospital? a grocery store? a shoe store? a park? an arena? a factory? What do you think belongs in a neighborhood?

4   Most urban planners today are middle-class whites. What problems might they face in planning an urban-renewal neighborhood for the poor of a downtown ghetto? How might these problems be solved?

5   Are low densities necessary to your concept of a good neighborhood? What design tricks can be used to incorporate good-neighborhood concepts into a high-density development?

6 In Chicago a new concept of the neighborhood has been built. Marina City is a skyscraper with a difference. Within this building is supposed to be everything you need for everyday living—schools, recreation, stores, entertainment facilities, and even the offices where you work. How do you feel about this new type of neighborhood?

7 By this point you should have a fairly clear idea of what you think a neighborhood should be. Put it on paper by designing your ideal neighborhood. Remember that it will be ideal for only a certain part of the population. Therefore you must specify who you think will live there. Specify the population of your neighborhood and its density. If your concept is futuristic suggest when it may be possible to build. You should be able to justify every aspect of your design. Can the people for whom you are building afford the cost? Are the streets of adequate width? Are the intersections potential traffic hazards? Present your design to others. Discuss its qualities and their importance at length. You may wish to revise your plan after this discussion.

8 Discuss the role of neighborhoods in urban planning. What happens when an expressway is planned without considering neighborhoods?

Recommended Readings

1 *Man-Made America* by C. Tunnard and B. Pushkarev, Yale, 1963. Read "Visual Principles of Small House Groupings". A prize-winning book.
2 *Nature of Cities* by L. Hilderseimer, Theobald, 1955. Read "Planning Problems".
3 *Last Landscape* by W. Whyte, Doubleday, 1970. See particularly "Cluster Development" for a discussion of a new type of suburban home layout.
4 *New Approaches to Residential Land Development,* Urban Land Institute, 1961. Recent residential neighborhood designs.
5 *Planning the Neighborhood* by American Public Health Assoc., US Administration Service, 1960. Government standards for good neighborhood design.
6 *Urban Villagers* by H. Gans, Free Press, 1962. This book deals with the implications of designing for ethnic groups using Boston urban renewal as an example.
7 *Design with Nature* by I. McHarg, Doubleday, 1971.
8 *Town Planning Guidelines* by The Department of Public Works, Information Canada, 1973. Gives specifications for planning residential areas.

8.2 THE URBAN IMPACT ON AGRICULTURAL LAND

How is the growth of urban areas affecting agricultural land in North America? The answer depends on whether you look at the quantity, quality, or productivity of the agricultural land involved. This is partly why there is such a dispute over whether or not the spread of urban communities is detrimental to our ability to produce food. It is very easy to get emotional over an orchard bulldozed for a new residential subdivision. It is also easy to rationalize that, for every hectare of hilly land converted to urban use, a hectare of formerly unproductive land has been brought into production by man's technological know-how. Is there a crisis or not?

For Thought and Research

The following are some aspects to investigate:

1 How much land is being converted from agricultural to urban use annually in your country? How much agricultural land is there? How much new land is being brought into agricultural production annually?

2 Is there a danger that, in the near future, North America will be facing a shortage of agricultural land?

3 Why is the quality of agricultural land lost perhaps more important than the quantity lost? Are cities expanding onto the best agricultural lands or the poorest? Explain.

4 Can technology be counted on to make up the lost agricultural production?

Recommended Readings

1 ''The Nature and Economics of Urban Sprawl'' by R. Harvey and W. Clark, *Land Economics,* Vol. 41, 1965. Discusses the alleged loss of agricultural land.

2 *Metropolitan Growth and Conversion of Land to Non-Agricultural Uses* by D. Bogue, Scripps Foundation, 1956. Measures the loss of farmland in the US between 1950 and 1960.

3 ''Loss of Farmland in the Growth of Metropolitan Regions in Canada'' in *Resources for Tomorrow* by A. Crerar, Queen's Printer, 1962. A study of Canadian farmland losses.

4 ''The Disappearing Niagara Fruit Belt'' in *Regional and Resource Planning in Canada* by R. Krueger, Holt, Rinehart and Winston, 1963.

5 ''Urban Pressures on California Land'' by H. Gregor, *Land Economics,* Vol. 33, 1957.

6 *The Destruction of California* by R. Dassmann, Collier-Macmillan, 1965.

7 ''Megalopolitan Agriculture'' in *Megalopolis* edited by J. Gottman, Twentieth Century Fund, 1961.

8 *Dimensions of Metropolism,* Urban Land Institute, 1968. Gives the land requirements for the year 2000.

9 ''Exclusive Agricultural Zoning'' by J. Lessinger, *Land Economics,* Vol. 34, 1958. Appraisal of Gregor's solution.

10 *Urban Problems: A Canadian Reader* edited by R. Krueger, and R. C. Bryfogle, Holt, Rinehart and Winston, 1971.

8.3   A HISTORICAL LOOK AT URBAN GROWTH

You have probably wondered at least once in your life why one city near you grew while another, perhaps at one time larger than the first, fell behind in the growth race. It is interesting to compare two or more communities in an area that are or were similar in size.

The following are some aspects to investigate:

1 When did their growth rates change so that one grew faster than the others?

2 How can the different growth rates be explained? What was happening in each community at that point in time?

3 Were the communities similar in the products and services they provided? (Labor statistics show this.)

4 If the communities had different urban functions might this explain the different growth rates? Explain your answer.

5 Were there any changes in technology at the time which might explain the rapid growth of one of the communities? For example, was a railway line built through one community?

6 What was happening to the economy as a whole during the time of the change? Was it booming or depressed? How could this affect one community more than another?

Recommended Readings

This is a fascinating area for original research. Census data on growth, occupations, and industries are the most helpful sources of information. Once you determine the years that were vital to the growth differences of the cities you are comparing, historical works may aid in explaining what happened. Local papers can be a valuable source of information. Many newspapers are now kept on microfilm in major libraries.

Another approach to this type of research would be to pick a period of significant change or crisis. Examine what happened to urban places during that period. The Depression years is one interesting period which might be researched. The immediate post-World War II years of rapid economic growth is another.

These topics are relatively untouched by historians or geographers. They are important to the question of how the urban community grows. Your biggest problem will be in limiting the scope of your research to a topic that you can handle thoroughly.

8.4 URBAN GROWTH: TO CONCENTRATE OR SPREAD?

A major question facing the urban planner and the urban dweller today is how the community should grow in the future. You undoubtedly have an opinion on this matter; it probably reflects your views on the effects that high urban densities have on people. But there is wide disagreement, even amongst the experts. Which is best? What difference does it make? Almost every major city is now planning for the year 2000. You may be able to influence those planners' decisions now. It may be too late in the year 2000. However, the debater has to know the facts. The readings here present the various arguments for and against the major alternatives for urban growth. This topic would make an excellent class debate.

For Thought and Research

The following are some aspects to investigate:

1 What are the alternatives for future urban growth?

2 Are there examples of any of these types of cities in existence today? What is the quality of urban life like within these cities?
3 Is growth inevitable?
4 Can the environment accommodate ever-increasing concentrations of people?
5 Is there a natural capacity for the support of humans in one spot?
6 What projections have been made about your community's growth in the future, both in population and size? Is it feasible? Is it desirable?

Recommended Readings

1 *Cities and Space* edited by L. Wingo, John Hopkins, 1963. Compares the views of Melvin Webber, Stanley Tankel, and Catherine Wurster presented in their essays on the use of space in cities.
2 *When Democracy Builds* by F. L. Wright, University of Chicago Press, 1945. The thinking that started the suburban movement. Wright's Broadacre City is the prototype for low-density cities everywhere. The arguments for decentralization are presented in this book.
3 *The City of Tomorrow* by Le Corbusier, revised edition, Architectural Press, 1971, (original 1929). Origin of the skyscraper movement. New York City was not what he had in mind, however. Read the chapter on the "Contemporary City" to discover his vision of a high-density city.
4 *Accessible City* by W. Owens, Brookings Institute, 1972. Approaches the question from the point of view of transportation alternatives.

8.5   HOW YOUR TOWN OR CITY DEVELOPED

You probably know more about the history of Rome, Paris, or New York than you know about the history of your own town. We are all familiar with our community as it exists today, but we may not know the causes of its modern form. Urban history can be fascinating, explaining such things as why the old ornate houses on one street are so run down while similar houses on another street are fashionable and expensive.

When we study urbanization, we investigate common stages in urban development. These may be noticed in any town's growth, but are always made more interesting when they take on the unique character of one particular place. Each town's physical, economic, and social environment influences its characteristic shape and life style. Cities have even responded differently to the same external event, such as a world war or a disastrous flood.

Although people study local history to provide examples of general principles, perhaps the main reason for local research is personal interest. Time and its effects have fascinated men for centuries. After all, knowledge of past trends often helps us to predict the future.

For Thought and Research

The following are some aspects to investigate:

1 The original economic base of the town. Was this function closely related to the town's site?
2 Have the basic functions of the town changed? If so, how and why?
3 The pattern of population growth during the town's history. A graph would illustrate this well.
4 Reconstruct maps of the city at 20-year intervals, or 50-year intervals if it has a very long history.
5 Make a chart to correspond to the maps in question 4. For each time period describe:
a) how the shape of the city evolved;
b) what major external forces influenced this growth (e.g. federal government policies);
c) what major internal forces influenced this growth (e.g. changes in shopping patterns).
6 Compare old and new pictures of the same location. How has urban life changed?
7 Estimate the age of a neighborhood. This can be done by architectural styles, by dates on cornerstones of buildings, by street names, by asking older residents, and by researching old city records. Use as many methods as possible.

Recommended Readings

Most of the material on this topic can be found in municipal records, books of local history such as county histories, and in local newspaper archives. In addition, some general information on factors and trends in urban development can be found in the following:

1 *The Rise of Urban America* by C. M. Green, Hutchinson, 1966.
2 *Urban Canada* by J. and R. Simmons, Copp Clark, 1974.
3 *Modern American Cities* edited by Ray Ginger, Quadrangle Books, 1969.

8.6 PUBLIC VERSUS PRIVATE TRANSPORTATION SYSTEMS

There has already been much discussion in previous sections of transportation problems. However, since this is a factor of great importance to the future of our cities, in-depth research into this question would be valuable.

Debates about the form of transportation that should be emphasized in the future are taking place in almost every major North American city. The outcome of such debates will surely affect the future urban landscape. Many people in the cities of today find getting around in the city increasingly difficult, in spite of an expanded network of roads. This makes one wonder whether planners are designing the urban environment for automobiles or for people. Can automobiles and expressways solve the transportation needs of the city without destroying it?

For Thought and Research

The following are some aspects to investigate:

1 What are the benefits and costs of public and private transportation systems respectively?

2 What alternative types of transportation systems are possible now and in the immediate future?

3 How do you get people to change their transportation patterns if this is needed? Do you remove their options for forms of transportation that are considered undesirable for the community as a whole? Or, do you make undesirable forms of transportation less convenient or more costly to the individual?

4 If public transportation is thought to be better for the community how do you overcome its present image of slowness, crowding, and inconvenience?

Recommended Readings

1 *The Death and Life of Great American Cities* by J. Jacobs, Johnathan Cape, 1961. See "Erosion of Cities or Attrition of Automobiles".

2 *Autokind vs Mankind* by K. Schneider, Norton, 1971.

3 *Sick Cities* by M. Gordon, Penguin, 1965. See particularly "Traffic Jam".

4 *City and Suburb* edited by B. Chinitz, Prentice-Hall, 1964. See Meyer's article, "Knocking Down the Straw Men" for the pro-automobile view point.

5 *The Bad Trip* by D. and W. Nowlan, Anansi, 1970. The arguments against the Spadina Expressway in Toronto by a citizens' group.

6 *The Shape of Towns* by K. Rowland, Ginn, 1966. A case study of the transportation question in Leicester, England is of particular value.

7 *Man-Made America* by C. Tunnard and B. Pushkarev, Yale, 1963. See "The Paved Ribbon" for insights into freeway design.

8 *Accessible City* by W. Owen, Brookings Institute, 1972. Owen is one of the foremost authorities on urban transportation problems.

9 *Quality of the Urban Environment* edited by H. Perloff, Resources of the Future, 1969. See "Transport: Key to the Future of Cities" by W. Owen.

10 *Urban Transportation in Canada, Commercial Letter,* Canadian Imperial Bank of Commerce, January 1969.

8.7   FUTURE URBAN TRANSPORTATION

In the future you may have transportation alternatives not in existence today. The car may be radically changed or may even disappear as a common means of transportation. Speculation as to the nature of future transportation systems for the city can be found in many books and articles.

The following are some aspects to investigate:

1 What are the benefits and costs of the proposed means of transportation as far as the individual is concerned? as far as the urban environment is concerned?

2 How are they likely to affect the growth of the urban community? Will they concentrate it? decentralize it?

Recommended Readings

1 *Britannica Book of the Year,* 1969. See "Urban Transportation Systems" by E. Davies.

2 *Britannica Book of the Year,* 1972. See "Automobiles of the Future" by J. Flint.

3 *Britannica Book of the Year,* 1968. See "Ecumenopolis—Tomorrow's City" by C. Doxiadis.

4 *Urban Transportation in Canada, Commercial Letter,* Canadian Imperial Bank of Commerce, January, 1969.

5 *New Movement in Cities* by B. Richards, Reinhold, 1966.

6 *The Year 2000: A Framework for Speculation on the next Thirty-Three Years* by H. Kahn and A. Wiener, Macmillan, 1967.

8.8 DESIGNING A PERFECT CITY

Almost as long as there have been cities there have been complaints about the quality of urban life. These complaints have led to much wishful thinking and even some concrete attempts at designing the perfect city. The vision of such a city, without congestion, crime, and pollution, has challenged many of the world's most brilliant minds. How would you like an opportunity to design *your* perfect city?

Exactly what is meant by a perfect city? There are two ways to view this problem. Many plans have been made of ideal cities which combine the best elements of existing urban form. Other experimental cities have been designed to test untried theories of urban design. Obviously the two types are often combined. In fact, most plans for perfect cities combine the best elements of today's cities with innovative ideas for the future.

The enormous economic and social cost involved in building a perfect city has meant that rarely, if ever, has a full-scale perfect city been constructed beyond the paper stage. Brasilia and the English Garden Cities are attempts at designing perfect cities. Clearly they are far from perfect. Why, then, is so much effort expended on perfect city designs? There are at least two reasons—one philosophical and one more practical.

Man has always been intrigued by perfection, by Utopias, which in our urbanized society has meant consideration of the ideal city form. More practically, while perfect city plans have not been adopted in whole, parts of them and ideas from them have been effectively used in the development and redevelopment of our cities.

When we design a perfect city what things must we consider? For example, what is the optimum size for a city? How should such a city be serviced? What type of housing is best? How will industry be accommodated and pollution avoided? You will have to consider these and many other questions.

For Thought and Research

The following are some aspects to investigate:

1 What are some of the social and economic costs of trying to build real-life perfect cities?

2 What urban form is best—a conventionally dispersed city? a high-density city? a superblock (the entire city in one building)?

3 How large should the city be: 20 000; 200 000; 1 000 000; 10 000 000?

4 What should be the attitude toward economic and/or ethnic segregation?

5 What are the physical requirements of the city (site and situation)? topography? soil? open space? environmental maintenance? weather control (domed city)?

6 What balance of housing types is best? How important is private ownership?

7 What is the best way of servicing the city? What should the energy sources be?

8 How should the city's people be employed? Does heavy industry have a place in the city?

9 What forms of transportation are best? What balance should there be between public and private transportation?

10 How can pollution be controlled?

Recommended Readings

1 *M.X.C.* by University of Minnesota Experimental City Project, 1969. A four-volume work on a new city with a population of 250 000. Volume four is a bibliography of more than 1 700 items.

2 *Future Shock* by Alvin Toffler, Random House, 1970. A general reading which suggests some of the problems and trends of the future that will face the inhabitants and the planners of the perfect city.

3 *The Living City* by Frank Lloyd Wright, Horizon Press, 1958.

4 *The Search for Environment. The Garden City: Before and After* by Walter L. Creese, Yale University Press, 1966.

5 *The Levittowners* by Herbert J. Gans, Pantheon Press, 1967.

6 "The City of the Future", *Ekistics,* Vol. 20, July 1965, pp. 4-52.

7 *The Future* by Theodore J. Gordon, St. Martin's Press, 1965.

8.9 MEGALOPOLIS: CITY OF THE FUTURE?

The ancient Greeks called a certain small town Megalopolis. They thought that Megalopolis (from *megas*—meaning great and *polis*—meaning city) would grow to be a large city. They were wrong but the name they coined is still used today to refer to any very large urban complex.

The term *megalopolis* was revived by a French geographer named Jean Gottman. He used the term to refer specifically to the large, mostly urbanized area of the United States Northeast. Many people study this area as the best example of the possible super-city of the future.

The *Bosnywash* (*BOS*ton-New York-*WASH*ington) megalopolis is 960 km long and from 50 to 120 km wide and is said to be *poly-nucleated*. While New York, with a metropolitan population of 12 million, dominates the area to some extent, Boston, Philadelphia, Baltimore, and Washington, each with over 2 million, tend to give the area many centers.

Will we all live in a Bosnywash of the future? Is this good or bad? Where are the Bosnywashes of the future developing? These and related questions deserve careful consideration.

For Thought and Research

The following are some aspects to investigate:
1 Origins of the Bosnywash megalopolis. What factors account for its present size and importance?
2 What relationships exist between Bosnywash and the rest of the United States? North America? the world?
3 Growth of the different parts of Bosnywash. Why did New York grow to dominate it while other cities such as Newport and Salem stagnated?
4 What problems face a megalopolis? Consider the problems of environmental quality; housing; governmental form; transportation; social disorder; loss of agricultural land; and shortage of recreational land.
5 Where are other potential megalopolises in the United States? Canada? Europe? the rest of the world?
6 Compare the advantages and disadvantages of living in a megalopolis to living in a smaller city, a town, or in the country.

Recommended Readings

While many of these readings are at the college level, most can be readily understood with careful reading. Remember also that newspapers and magazines very often contain articles which are useful in studying aspects of a megalopolis.
1 *The Challenge of Megalopolis* by Wolf Von Eckardt, Macmillan, 1964. Read this book first as it is readily available and easily understood. It is based on Gottman's original work on the subject.
2 *The Bosnywash Megalopolis* by L. A. Swatridge, McGraw-Hill, 1971. As well as an

examination of the region, it includes sections on each of the five major cities. It is also a source of many useful and up-to-date statistics.

3   *Megalopolis* by Jean Gottmann, Plimpton Press, 1967. The original massive (810 pages) work.

4   *Taming Megalopolis* edited by W. H. Eldredge, Doubleday, 1967.

5   *Problems in the Bosnywash Megalopolis* by L. A. Swatridge, McGraw-Hill, 1972.

6   *Downtown — Our Challenging Urban Problems* by Robert A. Liston, Dell Books, 1965.

7   *The World Cities* by Peter Hall, McGraw-Hill, 1966. Includes chapters on New York and other megalopolitan areas of the world.

8   *Metropolis on the Move: Geographers Look at Urban Sprawl* edited by Jean Gottmann and R. A. Harper, John Wiley, 1967.

8.10   GREAT CITIES OF THE PAST

Man has lived in cities for over 5 000 years. About 180 generations separate us from the first cities. Since then the size, function, and structure of cities have changed in detail. Yet the physical layout of cities often reflected adaptations to physical problems such as floods. Cities also gave expression to the ever-renewable religious, political, social, and economic ideas that revolutionized man's environment. Without an adequate understanding of the nature of past cities, their dominance and their decline, we cannot evaluate present urban life, its potentials, and its future.

Consider the problem of garbage. Garbage collection is a relatively recent addition to urban activities and is certainly not found throughout the entire urban world. In the past, the garbage dump was as close as your front door and adjacent street—at great expense to nose and foot. As the garbage reached new heights one simply added another step to the front stoop, then a higher door, and then a second floor. Soon one was living on a little hill. Why did the citizens tolerate this condition?

Today when a man escorts his favorite lady along a sidewalk, by tradition, he walks closest to the street. This custom originated in urban communities where sewage disposal was a quick heave out the second-floor window. Below, the lady would be spared the shower by walking under the second-floor overhang.

Syracuse in Sicily was reportedly the greatest of Greek cities, and possibly the most beautiful city that has ever been built. Today it is not even a ruin; it has utterly passed away under the neglect and energy of man, the endless days of sirocco, the centuries of summers, and the countless winters' rain.

Truly, the only slaves to history are those who are ignorant of it. It is enlightening, therefore, to look back at how the world's first cities began. You will gain many insights that will be helpful in understanding your own city environment.

For Thought and Research

The following are some aspects to investigate:

1 What are the similarities and differences between some of the famous urban communities of the Ancient World? Investigate such things as: location, raison d'être, building priorities, activities to house, segregation of people and activities, environmental adaptations, and cultural expressions.

2 Illustrate by sketches and discussion the structure and life of several different ancient cities, for example, caravan cities, an Indian city, Mecca, Rome, and Pompeii. How did these or other cities grow, decline, or change up to the present time?

3 *Communitas Christiana* or Christian Community is a phrase often applied to medieval cities. How appropriate is this description? What evidence supports or alters this concept?

4 What effect did the industrial, agricultural, and liberal revolutions have on European communities? Investigate such things as dominance, decline, internal activities, and structures.

5 Where are the revolutions of question 4 occurring today? How are the effects similar to or different from the European urban experience?

6 Trace the birth, growth, and possible death of a great city of the past. What were its strengths and problems? Did the problems change over time? How did ideas and inventions affect the nature of the community? In what form has this city survived today? Some suggested cities are Pompeii, Vienna, Rome, Athens, Jerusalem, Mecca, Angkor, and Timbuktu.

7 What is a primate city?

8 Has the urban environment reflected the state of the nation in the past? Is this true today?

9 In what ways are North American cities similar to urban environments of the past? How are our cities different from those of the past?

Recommended Readings

1 *Vanished Cities* by Hermann and Georg Schrieber, Alfred A. Knopf, 1962. An excellent and readable book that discusses the growth and decline of cities by power, the elements, and wealth.

2 *Out of the Past of Greece and Rome* by M. I. Rostoutzeff, Biblo and Tannen, 1963. A very readable book containing specific examples.

3 *Buried Cities* by Jennie Hall, Macmillan, 1964. A good book for junior grades. Interesting investigation of life in the shadow of Mount Vesuvius.

4 *How the World's First Cities Began* by Arthur S. Gregor, Dutton, 1967. Brief and easy to read. Good discussion on Mesopotamia's urban experience.

5 *Lost Cities of Asia* by W. Swaam, Elek Books, 1966. A well-illustrated book focused on India and the Far East. Shows the effects of strong government and different cultures.

6 *Lost Cities* by Leonard Cottrell, Robert Hale, 1957. Deals with the less well-known cities of the Hittites and Incas.

7 *The Twilight of Cities* by E. A. Gutkind, Macmillan, 1962. This very readable book gives many insights into cities from the earliest times to the present.

8 *The First Cities* by D. J. Hamblin, Time-Life Books, 1973. A well-illustrated, interesting, and easy-to-read account of early cities.

9 *Imperial Rome* by M. Hadas, Time-Life Books, 1973. A well-illustrated description of early Rome.

10 *Classical Greece* by C. M. Bowra, Time-Life Books, 1974. A well-illustrated and detailed account of the early Greek civilization.

8.11 CITIES IN DEVELOPING COUNTRIES

Throughout this book our study has centered on the North American city. The emphasis was placed on North American urban communities because these are the cities with which you are most familiar. However, cities around the world do not all conform to the same patterns. Cities in Europe are not identical to North American cities because of different historical factors affecting their growth. Although European cities do have similar patterns to those found in North American cities, they exhibit some different characteristics as well.

In this exercise we will look at cities in the world that have marked differences from those found where we live. These cities are found in the newly developing countries of Latin America, Africa, and Asia.

The models discussed in Unit 4, describing urban growth patterns, can also be applied to cities in the newly developing countries, but with some reservations. No one theory is sufficient by itself. Cities that did not develop in a similar pattern to those in Europe and North America will be referred to as ''non-Western'' cities.

In many cases newly developing countries were colonies of European powers. As a result, the urban growth patterns reflect the influences of the colonial power. Yet, there may also be present urban patterns that developed before Europeans arrived on the scene. For example, railroad and street patterns in some parts of the non-Western city may reflect European influences while, in other parts, the street patterns that existed before the arrival of the Europeans may remain intact. In Latin America, influenced by the Spanish, the central part of the city was established and has been maintained as a high-value, high-prestige area. As a result, squatters and newcomers were pushed toward the outskirts of the city. How does this differ from the general pattern found in North America?

In cases where the old city is the core of the present-day city, a general concentric pattern is found, particularly if defensive walls were built throughout its history. As the area within the wall became overcrowded, a new wall was built further out. Thus, several concentric rings of development may be observed. When the walls became obsolete a radial pattern of growth developed along major transportation routes. This pattern of development in non-Western cities is similar to the development of many European cities. It is interesting to note that many rapidly growing cities in newly developing countries have skipped certain stages that cities of Europe and North America have gone through. For example, the trolley car or streetcar stage with its implications to city growth and development may be completely lacking.

The older parts of cities in newly developing countries are characterized by high population densities, small lot sizes, and very narrow streets which are often very winding. Because of the small lot sizes there are many more shops per unit area than are found in the newer parts of these or modern Western cities. In addition, many commercial activities take place on the street itself. This is different from our cities where commercial activity is restricted to a specific piece of land. In some instances a vendor does not own a piece of land, but may move his business from place to place and set up shop at a convenient corner. This is often the case with barbers. Can you think of examples of this type of activity in our cities?

There are other characteristics that distinguish these cities from ours. A truck terminal may be a street curb and not an organized terminal on its own piece of land. One street may contain shops that all sell the same thing. A shopper will move from shop to shop looking for the best price—there is no fixed price for an item. The price is determined through bargaining.

Perhaps the most interesting feature of non-Western cities is the existence of squatter areas within the city. A piece of land may be vacant one day and occupied by several hundred squatters the next. The squatters plan their move in advance and, under cover of darkness, move onto the piece of desired land and set up shanties.

This brief discussion has demonstrated some of the similarities and differences that exist between cities in different parts of the world. There are, of course, many more which make such a study both fascinating and rewarding. The more we know about the way we and others live, the better able we will be to appreciate others' problems and to live together in harmony and understanding.

For Thought and Research

The following are some aspects to investigate:
1   The influence of colonial powers on development and structure of cities in newly developing countries.
2   Many developing countries have one city that has become the main focus of economic, political, and cultural activity. Such a city is known as a "primate city". Investigate the meaning of primate city and the advantages and disadvantages of such a situation.
3   In most Western cities there is a horizontal separation of land uses. In the non-West-

ern city, however, the pattern is often vertical sorting. What is meant by these terms? Give examples of each.

4   One of the most difficult problems facing developing countries is the provision of adequate shelter for urban residents. It is a highly complex problem which requires a great deal of attention. What are some of these problems and how might they be resolved? See *Recommended Reading* 6.

5   A problem facing many developing countries is that of over-urbanization. Investigate this term by defining what it means, its causes, and its consequences. See *Recommended Reading 1*.

6   Commercial activity is often quite different in the non-Western city. Describe these differences.

7   The problems of supplying services such as transportation, water, and sewage disposal to cities in developing countries.

8   The role of cities in the economic development of newly developing countries.

9   It is often a dramatic experience for individuals to migrate from the countryside to urban centers. The differences in life style between countryside and city are often great. Investigate the problems faced by such migrants particularly in terms of family life.

Recommended Readings

1   *Urbanization in Newly Developing Countries* by Gerald Breese, Prentice-Hall, 1966.

2   *The City in Newly Developing Countries* edited by Gerald Breese, Prentice-Hall, 1969. This book contains many articles that are worth reading.

3   *The Southeast Asian City* by T. G. McGee, Praeger, 1967.

4   *The Pre-Industrial City* by Gideon Sjoberg. The Free Press, 1960.

5   *Urbanism in World Perspective* edited by Sylvia F. Fava, Thomas Y. Crowell, 1968. See Part One and Part Two.

6   *Man's Struggle for Shelter in an Urbanizing World* by Charles Abrams, M.I.T. Press, 1964.

7   *The Growth of Latin American Cities* by Walter D. Harris, Jr., Ohio University Press, 1971.

8   *The Study of Urbanization* edited by P. Hauser and L. F. Schnore, Wiley, 1965. See ''On the Spatial Structure of Cities in the Two Americas'' by L. F. Schnore.

9   *Urbanization in Nigeria* by A. L. Mabogunje, University of London Press, 1968.

10   *The City of Ibadan* edited by P. C. Lloyd, A. L. Mabogunje, and B. Arve, Cambridge University Press, 1967.

8.12   DESIGNING A MOBILE COMMUNITY FOR THE ARCTIC

To see how well you understand the principles of the urban ecosystem, you are asked here to research the nature of the Arctic environment and design an urban community for it. This community must be specially adapted to the Arctic environment to ensure that it can operate successfully without damaging the sensitive natural setting.

Some Specifications

1   The function of the community is Arctic oil exploration and drilling.

2   The community is needed at a certain site for just a year or two. Hence the company should be able to move the community easily.

3   It should accommodate 200 persons, including the families of workers.

4   It must be a self-sufficient community providing all necessary services for its citizens. Assume that there is no other community nearby.

5   Complying with the government's native employment policy it should accommodate native as well as southern workers and their families.

For Thought and Research

Before you start designing consider these questions:

1   In what parts of the Arctic will this oil exploration be likely to take place? What are the principle characteristics of this environment? How will these characteristics affect construction techniques?

2   How can mobility of a community best be achieved? Why would mobility of the community make minimal environmental damage vital? How can this be achieved?

3   What facilities must be provided for 200 persons, including families, in this isolated situation?

4   Will the inclusion of Eskimos in the community require any special accommodation design or facilities to meet their cultural needs? Can the different cultures be accommodated without segregation or ghettoization?

5   Can you provide running water and sewage disposal in a sub-zero climate? How would you dispose of solid wastes?

Recommended Readings

1   *Britannica Book of the Year,* 1971. See the article ''Arctic Dilemma'' by T. Brown. You may find other relevant articles in encyclopedias and the yearbooks accompanying them.

2   *National Geographic,* October, 1971. See ''North Slope: Will Alaska's Oil and Tundra Mix'' by W. Ellis and E. Kristof. *National Geographic* is another resource in which you may find other relevant articles.

3   *National Geographic,* March, 1972. See ''A Look at Alaska's Tundra''.

4   *Canada's Changing North* by W. Wonders, McClelland and Stewart, 1971. Excellent and easy to read.

5   *The Arctic Basin* by J. Sater, Arctic Institute of North America, 1969. More advanced reading; useful for looking up specific information.

6   *The Arctic Townsmen* by J. and D. Honigmann, Saint Paul University, Ottawa, 1970. A sociological study of Eskimo communities.

7   *The Northland* by John Wolforth, McClelland and Stewart, 1970.

8   *Communities in Canada* by L. Marsh, McClelland and Stewart, 1970. See the sections on "Frontiers" and "Resource Towns".
9   *The Arctic Imperative* by R. Rohmer, McClelland and Stewart, 1973. Discusses many of the problems associated with oil exploration in tundra environments.
10   Don't overlook materials available to you in the many geography texts on Canada and the United States.

8.13   COLONIZING THE MOON

Our world is getting closer to the world of science fiction every year. Astronauts are sent on advanced moon explorations. Satellite space stations and interplanetary communications are a reality. With these changes, we can finally give serious consideration to setting up colonies on the moon.

The problem of setting up a colony on the moon is an enormous one. The natural environment and its potential problems must be thoroughly investigated. Planners must consider what technology to use, what people to send, what sort of culture to encourage, and what effects settlement will have on the moon environment. Most science-fiction writers have assumed that a moon civilization would consist of cities, usually domed and featuring high-rise dwellings. We must look critically at these assumptions and at our own urban planet before we make the important decision of how to colonize the moon.

For Thought and Research

The following are some aspects to investigate:
1   Consider the environmental conditions for life on the moon—soil (for building and farming), topography, climate, atmospheric composition, available minerals and fuels. Can life exist on the moon without artificial surroundings?
2   Can the moon be called an ecosystem?
3   Ideas for moon colonies in science-fiction novels—are they possible or worth using in reality?
4   A plan for a moon colony. Here you might try constructing a model or using diagrams to illustrate your written plan.
5   Problems involved in maintaining a moon city would involve communications with earth, supplying food, water, and industrial raw materials, emotional problems of isolation, disposing of wastes.
6   Environmental effects of a moon city. Can pollution be avoided? Does it matter if the moon is polluted?

Recommended Readings

There are few completely up-to-date books on the moon, since scientific information is multiplying rapidly with each moon flight. The periodicals *National Geographic, Space*

World, Science Digest, and *Science* have published many articles on various aspects of the moon in the past few years and keep up with new data. Established facts about the moon's surface, atmosphere, and possibilities for life can also be found in the following:

1 *Planets* by C. Sagan, J. Leonard, and the editors of Life, Time-Life Books, 1966.
2 *Exploring the Moon and the Solar System* by T. Dickinson, Copp Clark, 1971.
3 *Pictorial Guide to the Moon* by D. Alter, Thomas Y. Crowell, 1973.
4 *Earth, Moon and Planets* by F. L. Whipple, Harvard University Press, 1968.
5 *Survival on the Moon* by L. Maisak, Macmillan, 1966. An easy-to-read description of how man would live if he colonized the moon.
6 You may also want to consult selected science-fiction novels for theories about moon colonies.

8.14 INDUSTRY: BLIGHT OR BLESSING?

What does industry mean for a community? It can mean such things as jobs, security, tax base, prosperity, gross national product, and inventions. It can also mean such things as air pollution, water pollution, noise pollution, congestion, blighted areas, urban sprawl, land speculation, and parking lots. It is not without mixed feelings that one views industrial developments.

Industry reportedly dumps three times as much organic pollution into the waters of the United States as do the 120 million people serviced by sewers. One may counter this remark by asking what happens when the 100 million people without sewers are included in the picture. In 1969 Harden applied the ordinary cost-accounting procedures of business to an enterprise that creates oil damages, and air and water pollution. He concluded that the economy as a whole would be better off if the enterprise had never been undertaken. Yet business can argue that the biggest polluters of the Great Lakes are the little cottage communities. Large firms have also invested enormous sums of money into pollution research, pollution control, and product research.

Industry, blight or blessing? The questions keep recycling! Where does the fault for urban pollution lie? Does it lie with the producer, the automobile owner, the law, technology that has got out of hand, attitudes, or apathy? Is blight balanced by blessing in our industrial sectors? Where are we heading—to one gigantic garbage apocalypse? Perhaps clearing away some of our mental debris on the problem would be a good place to start.

For Thought and Research

The following are some aspects to investigate:
1 Industry in New York City and Los Angeles should have different pollution restric-

tions from other North American cities. Why?

2 Is your neighborhood ready for suburban manufacturing?

3 Why have pollution-free automobiles not been marketed?

4 Who is to blame for smog—the automobile owner, the producer, or the law?

5 What laws control industrial pollution? Can they be enforced?

6 Should pollution be a criminal offence? Does your government lay charges against public enterprises?

7 What pollution problems do some of the major industrial sectors in your area have to solve?

8 How have various industrial sectors helped the fight against environmental pollution?

9 What are the social costs of industrial pollution? How do they vary from city to city, and from area to area within a city? How can you assign a dollar and cents value to these social costs?

10 Do trends seem to indicate a greater environmental pollution problem from industrial (private) pollution or from public (sewage) pollution?

Recommended Readings

1 *Technology: The God that Failed* by D. Slusser and G. Slusser, The Westminster Press, 1971. This very readable book looks at the roots of our relationship with our environment. Industry, public attitudes, and change are given thoughtful inquiry.

2 *Issues for the Seventies: Environmental Quality* by N. Sheffe, McGraw-Hill, 1971. This book is an attack on industry and its pollution-control program.

3 *The Environment* by the editors of *Fortune,* Harper and Row, 1970. This little book delves into the big clean-up by industry, what industry thinks about its environment, the shared responsibilities for pollution control, and suggestions for covering the costs.

4 *Pollution, Profits and Progress* by H. A. Schroeder, The Stephen Greene Press, 1971. Attitudes, laws, public pressure, profit from pollution products, and more are part of this investigation.

5 *Environment and Good Sense—Environmental Damage and Control in Canada* by M. J. Dunbar, McGill-Queen's University Press, 1971. The changing responsibilities of private industry are discussed. What are externals and who pays? Industrial awareness of environmental pollution problems.

6 *Crisis in Our Cities* by L. Herber, Prentice-Hall, 1965. This book contains a description of air and water pollution created by the growth of urbanization in the United States. The specific problems of some of America's greatest cities are vividly described.

7 *Environmental Side Effects of Rising Industrial Output* by A. J. Van Tassel, Heath Lexington Books, 1970. Articles included deal with the general urban crisis, the demands on water resources, water pollution, and a discussion of various industrial sectors.

8 *Ecology and Economics: Controlling Pollution in the 70's* by M. I. Goldman, Prentice-Hall, 1972. Discusses social costs of pollution and economic factors in an interesting and readable fashion.

9 *The Economics of Environmental Protection* by D. N. Thompson, Winthrop, 1973. Similar to reference 8 but at a higher level.

10 *Environmental Economics* by J. J. Seneca and M. K. Taussig, Prentice-Hall, 1974. An advanced but readable text that considers all the costs of environmental pollution.

8.15 THE CITY AS A GAME

It has long been considered a virtue to be able to laugh at oneself. By seeing things from an unusual or funny viewpoint, we are often able to get to the root of a problem more quickly. We take this viewpoint when we play games.

Games are many things. A game is a pattern of behavior, involving players, rules, and a goal. Most of our urban activities can be seen in these terms. When we go shopping, for example, we follow a certain route, buy only certain products, and attempt to achieve such goals as saving money or time or maximizing our pleasure with our purchases. Each type of businessman, sportsman, civil servant, and the like follows an understood, though not necessarily formalized, code of behavior.

Games are a part of our lives from the time we are very young children. Do we unconsciously pattern our lives after games we have known? One of the most popular games in North America, for instance, is Monopoly. Has it made us into a money- and property-conscious society, unconsciously longing to own hotels on the Boardwalk? Sociologists often talk of our society as a complicated fabric of poses, attitudes, and habits which they call the games people play.

The structure of a game may or may not be a model of a real-life pattern (of streets, stores, and houses). However there must always be elements of competition and of role-playing. Many people have already translated their views of city life into games, but they have captured only a small part of the total picture. What more can you add?

For Thought and Research

The following are some aspects to investigate:
1   The theory of games in general. What is a game? What is a good game?
2   Existing games of city life like Ghetto and Monopoly. To what extent do they fit reality? Are there any similarities among them?
3   Can a game be interesting and playable but true-to-life at the same time? Should it be true-to-life?
4   Steps in designing a game.
5   Aspects of city life that might make good games and why.
6   Design your own game. Draw up rules and construct all necessary equipment.
7   Explain what elements of city life you are intending to show and the problems you encountered in designing your game.

Recommended Readings

Your own imagination and experience with games is probably your best source of ideas. However, you may wish to consult one or more of the following for samples of other games.

1 *Games in Geography* by R. Walford, Longmans, 1969. This paperback contains a number of games as well as an excellent outline of how to design your own games.
2 *The Study of Games* by E. Avedon and B. Sutton-Smith, John Wiley, 1971. This complete study of games and the people who play them includes chapters on the history of games, uses of games, and games in education.
3 There are several urban land-use games already available. Most are simulation games, such as the "Portsville" activity of the *High School Geography Project* which involves reconstruction of the growth of Portsville. This is available from Macmillan. "Metropolis" is a role-playing game, outlined in *Gaming Simulation in Urban Research* by Richard Duke, Michigan State University, 1964. A different approach, based on such popular games as Monopoly, is taken in the "Community Land Use Game", described in an article by Allan Feldt in the January 1966 issue of the *Journal of the American Institute of Planners,* Vol. XXXII, pp. 17-23.
4 *Simulation Games in Geography* by R. Dalton et al., Macmillan or St. Martin's Press, 1972.

8.16 URBAN GOVERNMENT

In our urbanized society, the governments of large cities become more and more important. New York City alone has a budget larger than that of some countries. Mayors such as John Lindsay, Jean Drapeau, Richard Daley, and Sam Yorty have been better-known than most federal politicians. Decisions made by city councillors and administrators can change not only the physical shape of the city but also the way of life of each citizen living there. Such environmental concerns as parks, sewage and garbage disposal, expressways, water quality, and population density are almost entirely under the control of our local governing body.

Few people are aware of the true workings of their urban government. The real power may lie, not with elected officials, but with professional civil servants such as the town clerk and chief planner. The bigger the city, the more involved and self-perpetuating is its bureaucracy.

Certain classifications have been made to help simplify urban political studies. Whether a city has a weak or strong mayor, a powerful planning body, or whether it is run by party machines will have a profound effect on the future of that community. A more thorough understanding of the structure and problems of urban government, aided by these classifications, may be the first step toward practical and workable urban reform.

For Thought and Research

The following are some aspects to investigate:

General
1 The major types of urban government and how each type influences the urban ecosystem.

2   Are party politics a good thing in municipal government?

3   The advantages and disadvantages of citizen participation in local decisions.

4   Is a highly centralized administration more efficient than one in which each neighborhood has its own government?

Specific

5   Classify your local government according to the categories in question 1.

6   How are issues handled concerning the environment, expressways, high-rise developments, urban renewal, parks, and so on?

7   Is the town council on the side of the average citizen or the rich developer?

8   Local planning. What plans exist and are they being followed? If not, why not?

9   Financing urban government. What are the major problems and the major sources of revenue?

Recommended Readings

For general information on urban governments, the following books may be of assistance:

1   *29 Ways to Govern a City* by I. O. Hessler, Rockwood Press, 1966. The author classifies 29 US cities according to five major forms of city government. Excellent introduction.

2   *Urban Canada and its Government, A Study of Municipal Organization* by T. J. Plunkett, Macmillan, 1968. This academic book describes various forms and problems of city government in Canada.

3   *Your Local Government* by D. C. Rowat, Macmillan, 1955. An easy-to-read introduction to Canadian local government systems.

4   *The Regional City* by H. Kaplan, Canadian Broadcasting Corporation, 1965. A short book discussing and criticizing political responses to rapid urban change in North America.

5   *City Politics* by E. Banfield and J. Wilson, Harvard University Press, 1967. The authors take a political approach to classifying and studying city governments in the United States.

6   *Government of the Metropolis* by J. Zimmerman, Holt, Rinehart and Winston, 1968. This is an advanced collection of readings about large-city government, problems, and possible reforms.

7   To study the local scene, attend council meetings, visit the public information office of the municipal buildings, follow newspaper articles and editorials, and read past volumes of Minutes of Council Meetings. Your local newspaper probably has a regular city hall reporter who can give you some insights as well.

8.17 THE EFFECTS OF URBAN DENSITIES ON PEOPLE

People have speculated since first living in urban communities that the densities of population there are unnatural and probably in some way harmful. Animal studies in psychology have been used to demonstrate that crowding leads to antisocial behavior and even sudden death. Yet other people suggest that, with proper design, high-density areas need not be harmful. Since projections into the future imply increasing densities, all of us should be studying this possible problem.

For Thought and Research

The following are some aspects to investigate:

1 Is man so different from experimental animals such as rats and deer that we cannot apply the findings of animal research to human behavior?

2 Is there evidence that the same kinds of antisocial behavior and nervous disorders are on the increase in large urban areas?

3 Can increases in crime rates, divorce rates, and mental illness rates be attributed to urban living only?

4 Why can Orientals live in much higher densities than Westerners without many of the problems we attribute to urban living?

5 How do the experts define crowded conditions as far as dwellings are concerned?

6 Can design of residences be used to achieve high-density living without the pressures of crowding? How?

7 Is low-density suburban living the solution to avoiding the stress of urban living?

Recommended Readings

1 *The Hidden Dimension* by E. T. Hall, Doubleday, 1966. A fascinating and easy-to-read book.

2 *The Last Landscape, A Case for Crowding* by W. Whyte, Doubleday, 1968. A controversial point of view.

3 *Personal Space* by R. Sommer, Prentice-Hall, 1969. Explores the effects of architecture on human behavior.

4 *On Aggression* by K. Lorenz, Methuen, 1963. Deals with animal behavior, particularly conflict between members of the same species. Difficult but worthwhile reading.

8.18   GHETTOS: CAUSES AND EFFECTS

Of the one hundred largest urban areas in the United States, not one is without a ghetto. A ghetto can be described as a segregated area, either forced or voluntary, occupied by a minority group.

In the nineteenth and early twentieth centuries newly arrived immigrants from Europe congregated in the slum ghettos of Boston, New York, and Philadelphia. As their incomes rose and their knowledge of English increased they moved out of these slums. Today, the influx of Puerto Ricans, Japanese, Mexican-Americans, and blacks to the large cities has created similar conditions. However, it is often much more difficult, if not impossible in some cases, for these groups to move out of the ghettos and into the mainstream of American Life. Through various social and economic pressures these groups are literally forced to reside in specific areas. At the present time the most residentially segregated minority group is the blacks. The remaining discussion will therefore concentrate on the black ghetto.

The ghetto is an area characterized by deteriorated dwellings, overcrowded housing space, and by the poverty and high unemployment rate of its residents. Often public services such as garbage collection are neglected and there is a general absence of playgrounds, modern schools, and new buildings. In such a situation it is understandable that juvenile delinquency and crime are very high. The differences between the haves and the have-nots in the city are very apparent to a ghetto dweller.

One factor that contributes to the formation and continuation of ghettos is the poverty of the urban black. This poverty forces him to reside in low-cost housing located in areas of the urban community away from high-cost housing. However, poverty is not the main reason for the perpetuation of the ghetto. The primary reason is forced segregation, whereby pressure is exerted on the ghetto resident to remain there. Thus, even economically well-off blacks rarely live in white areas and, conversely, poor whites rarely live in black residential areas.

The ghetto is also maintained by several other forces in the urban community. The prejudice against blacks is the obvious point. Less obvious is the more subtle discrimination by the real estate agencies and by financial institutions. To prevent blacks from moving into a white area, real estate agents may inflate the prices of houses beyond their reach. In addition, blacks may find it hard to obtain loans in order to buy houses. Or, they may fear the hostility that could result if they moved into another area of the city. Yet some blacks may prefer to remain in the ghetto because they enjoy the association with others of their group. This preference results in voluntary segregation. For these and other reasons the ghetto system is maintained.

As the number of people within the ghetto increases, the need for it to expand also increases. Along the edge of the ghetto there is usually an area of old and often deteriorating houses occupied by whites. Although the people in this area may have considered moving because of deteriorating housing and services, this desire to move is often reinforced by the encroaching ghetto. Owners living near the ghetto may be anxious to sell. The ghetto thus expands block by block in a series of invasion and succession.

The problem of ghettos in the urban communities of North America is a serious one which requires immediate attention if human needs are to be adequately served.

For Thought and Research

The following are aspects to investigate:
1 Historical trends in residential segregation.
2 Voluntary and involuntary segregation.
3 Segregation of the black community.
4 Residential segregation of other racial and ethnic groups.
5 The process of ghetto expansion.
6 The centralization of blacks within cities.

7 The location of ghettos within the city.
8 The patterns of interaction of ghetto dwellers.
9 The nature of resistance to ghetto expansion.
10 The influence of the housing market, real estate agents, and financial institutions.
11 Alternatives to the ghetto.
12 The ghetto as seen through popular music.

Recommended Readings

1 *Cultural Geography* edited by F. Dohrs and L. Sommers, Thomas Y. Crowell, 1967. See Chapter 19, "The Negro Ghetto: Problems and Alternatives" by Richard M. Morrill.
2 *Cities and City Life* edited by H. M. Hughes, Allyn and Bacon, 1970. See "Segregation: Where Whites and Blacks Live" by K. E. Taeuber and "The Negro Family Moves to the City" by E. F. Frazier.
3 *Cities in Trouble* edited by N. Glaser, Quadrangle Books, 1970. See "A Way Out of the Exploding Ghetto" by B. Rustin.
4 *Downtown: Our Challenging Urban Problems* by R. A. Liston, Delacorte Press, 1968. See Chapter 4, "The Urban Ghetto".
5 *The Social Consequences of Residential Segregation of the Urban American Negro* by S. P. Berger, Metropolitan Applied Research Center, 1970.
6 *Urban Problems and Prospects* by A. Downs, Markham, 1970.

8.19 URBAN RENEWAL

Urban renewal, or city redevelopment, is not a new concept. It has existed since man began building urban communities. Almost all cities have undergone redevelopment at some time. This redevelopment is a result of the changing needs and desires of man, and the changing technology which makes city structures inadequate. For example, the Greeks rebuilt Troy nine times before the time of Christ, and in the mid-1850s medieval Paris was redeveloped into a baroque city. In North America, the squat skyline of the last century has given way to the modern skyline of today. All this came about through urban redevelopment, or, as it is known today, urban renewal.

Perhaps the main reason for urban renewal today is the need to replace the blighted areas of the city. By blighted areas we mean those parts suffering from decay and deterioration either of the physical structures, the houses and buildings, or of the service systems, water, sewage, and roadways. Such areas are often slums or consist of old buildings that are no longer economical to maintain. So much urban renewal has involved the removal of slums that it is often seen as a polite expression for slum clearance.

Another reason for urban renewal, particularly in the Central Business District, is for the rejuvenation of the city core. In the past decade there has been a great deal of movement of offices and commercial outlets out of the core and into the suburbs. Through urban renewal new office towers are erected, streets are widened, and more open space is provided. This is an attempt to attract commercial establishments and office functions and to make the center of the city the heart of the urban community once again.

If you have ever had the opportunity to hear a debate among city politicians and citizen groups on the topic of urban renewal, you will probably be well aware of the many opinions that exist. Basically these views can be expressed in terms of two divergent opinions: urban renewal is good, or urban renewal is bad for the urban community and its inhabitants.

First of all, let's examine some of the benefits derived from urban renewal. The clearance of slums and deteriorated areas gives the city a face lift by making it more attractive to the eye and more functional and economical in terms of land use. The resulting higher density of land use provides more money to the city in the form of tax assessment. With the building of modern office buildings, apartments, and shopping complexes, the streets can be widened to reduce congestion, and parks and walkways may be added. This may make the area attractive to people so that they want to come to the area for shopping and for recreation purposes. This, in turn, results in increased activity in the area and an increase in civic pride and citizen involvement.

As the slums are removed, the people living in them can be rehoused in modern low-rent housing projects. Thus, these people are moved from deteriorated, unhealthy settings to attractive, healthy living quarters.

On the other hand, there have been many criticisms directed at urban-renewal projects. Many critics see such schemes as being more concerned with physical appearance than with people's welfare. Urban-renewal projects are being directed at people who are least able to help themselves and their neighborhoods. This includes small businessmen, the elderly, recent immigrants, and low-income families. Most low-rent housing which has resulted from urban-renewal projects in downtown areas has been a dismal failure. These new housing units have become slums in a short time. Urban renewal complicates rather than alleviates the problems faced by such groups.

Other critics have attacked urban renewal because it replaces the diversity and charm of certain neighborhoods with modern, sterile, unimaginative high-rise developments. In this sense, the unique character of the city is ruined because of the newly created sterile environment.

As you can see, these opinions show completely opposite points of view. They do reflect, however, some of the basic problems presently facing many urban centers, both large and small. The future structure and environment of urban communities depends on how present-day technology and philosophy are used in urban renewal.

For Thought and Research

The following are some aspects to investigate:

1   What is the present philosophy toward urban renewal in your community?
2   What are the advantages and disadvantages of urban-renewal projects?
3   What factors contribute to the movement of offices and commercial functions from the CBD to the suburbs?
4   There are many proposed solutions for slum clearance. What would you suggest?
5   How do people living in slums feel about their neighborhood? What reactions are they likely to have on being told that they may have to move?
6   What are the problems accompanying high population densities?
7   If there have been any recent urban-renewal projects in your community, what effects have they had on the community as a whole?
8   How much control should the federal and provincial or state governments have over local affairs in regard to urban renewal?
9   Is the removal of blight automatic once the dilapidated structures are removed?
10   Should urban-renewal projects be more concerned with the removal of physical blight or with individuals' welfare? In other words, what is more important, renewal of part of the city for the benefit of all, or the welfare of those living in the area marked for renewal?
11   Is urban vitality a reflection of the physical structure of the city?
12   Should urban-renewal programs include public involvement or should they be completely in the hands of professional planners?
13   Urban-renewal programs are constantly in the news. Take one program and make a brief study of it.

Recommended Readings

1   *Downtown: Our Challenging Urban Problems* by R. Liston, Delacorte Press, 1968. See Chapter 6, ''Urban Renewal'' and Chapter 7 ''Rebuilding Our Cities''.
2   *People and Plans: Essays on Urban Problems and Solutions* by H. Gans, Basic Books, 1968.
3   *Urban Renewal: The Record and the Controversy* edited by J. Wilson, M.I.T. Press, 1966.
4   *Cities in Action* by E. Van Cleef, Pergamon Press, 1970.
5   *Urban Problems: A Canadian Reader* edited by R. R. Krueger and R. Charles Bryfogle, Holt, Rinehart and Winston, 1971. See Chapter 7, ''Urban Renewal''.
6   *Metropolis: Values in Conflict* edited by C. E. Elias, Jr., J. Gillies and S. Riemer, Wadsworth, 1964. See the following articles: ''National Planning for Urban Renewal'' by J. Dyckman; ''Instead of Urban Renewal'' by B. Alger; ''Class, Race, and Urban Renewal'' by R. Weaver.
7   *The Death and Life of Great American Cities* by J. Jacobs, Random House, 1961.
8   *Neighborhood Groups and Urban Renewal* by J. C. Davies, Columbia University Press, 1966.
9   *The Urban Complex: Human Values in Urban Life* by R. C. Weaver, Doubleday, 1964.

8.20   RIOTS: CAUSES AND EFFECTS

No urban community is immune from violence on a large scale. Every one of us has probably seen or read about riots and their devastating results. Riots are not merely a product of twentieth-century urban life, but occur whenever there is a period of social change on a dramatic scale. What are the causes of such violent behavior on the part of normally law-abiding citizens?

Riots may occur wherever there are large numbers of angry and/or frustrated individuals. Riots have recently occurred at rock concerts, on many university campuses, in industrial areas as a result of labor disputes, and in many black ghettos. Any unjust denial of man's basic needs, rights, or aspirations and desires can lead to a feeling of frustration, bitterness, and desperation. Whether or not this denial is real or imagined by the individuals involved, the mere fact that people believe it to be so is often sufficient to make them resort to violence. When socially accepted means of achieving desired ends are found to be unsatisfactory, the result may be violence in order to vent discontent. Riots may also be partly due to a permissive society in which the emphasis is on rights with little reference to responsibilities. It is often said that rioters may not know where they are going, but they dislike where they have been.

Two of the primary causes of urban violence in the form of riots are poverty and hostility toward established institutions. This hostility may be due to frustrating social conditions or it may stem from political philosophies. The most numerous and widespread riots of the past decade have occurred in the black ghettos of the large American cities, particularly in the north. Of all the minority groups affected by social alienation, why has it been the blacks who have protested most violently?

The factors that have helped trigger these race riots are racial discrimination, economic deprivation, involuntary residential segregation, consumer exploitation, and the general feeling of alienation from the mainstream of life. During many long hot summers in the 1960s, non-violent protest gave way to violent protest. The results, of course, were catastrophic losses of property and, in many cases, human lives.

During these riots, which were confined to the ghettos, looting and destruction were often widespread. Stores that were regarded as having exploited their customers were special targets. However, churches and schools usually suffered little damage.

The scars of past riots are still etched on the physical landscapes of many urban communities. Rebuilding has not yet taken place. If such riots are to be prevented in the future, action must be taken now to attack the underlying causes that have led to the frustration manifested in violence.

For Thought and Research

The following are some aspects to investigate:
1   What are the basic causes of riots?
2   Why are urban riots occurring now? Why did they occur in the past?
3   What can be done to prevent riots?
4   Why do riots occur in some cities and not in others?
5   Some people see rioters as hoodlums who are not willing to conform to the laws of society. To others, the rioters' lack of respect for the law is seen as reflection of their loss of confidence in the social order which has not accorded them their full human dignity. Who took part in the riots? Investigate their level of education, age, origins, employment, and their roots in the community.
6   What effect do the mass media have on riots?
7   What are the geographic location of riots and the pattern of violence and damage within cities?
8   What are the conditions of life like in the ghettos?
9   To what extent, if any, is there planning and organization in riots?
10   Have riots helped improve the lot of the people involved?

Recommended Readings

1   *Violence As Protest: A Study of Riots and Ghettos* by R. M. Fogelson, Doubleday, 1971.
2   *Violence and Riots in Urban America* edited by R. F. Allen and C. H. Adair, C. A. Jones, 1969.
3   *Alternatives to Violence: Alienated Youth and Riots, Race, and Poverty* by S. Bernstein, Associated Press, 1967.
4   *Black Rioters* by B. D. Singer, R. Osborn and J. Geschwender, D. C. Heath, 1970.
5   *Ghetto Revolts: The Politics of Violence In American Cities* by J. R. Feagin and H. Hahn, Macmillan, 1973.
6   *The City in Crisis* by I. Iseberg, H. W. Wilson, 1968.
7   *Report of the National Advisory Commission on Civil Disorders: New York Times Edition*, Dutton, 1968.

8.21   SLUMS

Every city throughout history has had some wealthy sections and some poor sections. Even today, with the high level of affluence in North America, there are millions of poor people who live in urban slums. Slums are not just poor areas within a city. Many poor areas meet the basic necessities for life. The slums, on the other hand, are areas of extreme poverty, contain a large percentage of buildings that are beyond rehabilitation, are rat-infested, without decent heat, light, or plumbing, and whose social structure is probably unstable. Despite this general description of a slum area it is difficult to find agreement on what is and what is not a slum. For example, what may be a rat-infested tenement to one person may be perfectly acceptable to another. In fact, various studies have indicated that residents of slum areas have a deep affection for the area because it is their home and because this is where their friends live. Thus, despite the physical decay, the area may be vibrantly alive socially.

Why do slums continue to exist despite all our efforts to overcome them? Obviously the answer to this question is not simple. If it were we might have solved the problem already. Perhaps the root of the problem lies in the fact that poor people must be housed cheaply. This can be achieved by offering low rents in run-down tenements. But why must conditions be so bad?

Most slum areas are found just beyond the Central Business District. In Burgess's Concentric-Zone Theory this area was referred to as the Zone of Transition. This is the area into which the CBD moves when it expands horizontally. Real estate investors buy properties adjacent to the CBD in anticipation of rising land values as the CBD moves. During the waiting period the developer is not anxious to invest much money in the property because he anticipates that it will soon be torn down when redevelopment takes place. In addition, he is able to obtain a better return on his capital by buying more property rather than by improving the ones he already owns.

If redevelopment does occur as the CBD grows in one direction, the slum dwellers are evicted and forced to move to another slum area. This other slum area may be in the zone of discard, the area from which the CBD is slowly moving. In this area the developers will not make improvements to the property because they are hoping the CBD will eventually expand back into the area. Thus, as evicted slum dwellers seek new homes in the discard area, population density increases, unhealthy living conditions persist, and the slum is perpetuated.

Slums cost the city a great deal of money every year. The slum dwellers are poor and thus not able to pay very high taxes. Usually a great deal of money is pumped into the slum in the form of welfare payments and other municipal services. In addition, the growth of slum areas has helped increase the exodus of middle- and upper-income residents from the city to the suburbs. This further lessens the city's economic base. What is to be done?

For Thought and Research

The following are some aspects to investigate:

1   Where do slum areas develop in cities? Do a historical study of the development of slums in several cities.

2   What types of people live in slums? Why do slums usually have a high population density?

3   What role have developers played in the development and perpetuation of slum areas?

4 Is slum clearance the solution?

5 What happens to slum dwellers when something is done to correct a slum situation?

6 Why do some slum dwellers want to continue to live in the slum?

7 What role should slum dwellers play in urban-renewal programs?

8 The politics of slums. Describe a political decision regarding slums. Give both sides of the argument.

Recommended Readings

1 *The Making of a Slum* by M. Dorman, Delacorte Press, 1972.

2 *The Social Order of the Slum* by G. D. Suttles, University of Chicago Press, 1968.

3 *A Geography of Urban Places* edited by R. G. Putman, F. J. Taylor, and P. G. Kettle, Methuen, 1970. See Chapter 37, ''A Theory of Slums'' by Charles J. Stokes.

4 *Metropolis: Values in Conflict* edited by C. E. Elias, Jr., J. Gillies, and S. Riemer, Wadsworth, 1964. See ''The Slum and Its People'' by Svend Piemer and ''Slum Schools'' by J. B. Conant.

5 *Modern American Cities* edited by R. Ginger, Quadrangle Books, 1969. See ''An Antibiotic for the Slum'' by M. Roche.

6 *Human Behavior and the Environment: Interactions Between Man and His Physical World* edited by J. H. Sims and D. B. Baumann, Maaroufa Press, 1974. See Chapter 4, ''Attitudes Toward Slums and Public Housing in Puerto Rico'' by A. B. Hollingshead and L. H. Rogler and Chapter 13, ''Some Sources of Residential Satisfaction in an Urban Slum'' by M. Fried and P. Gleicher.

7 *Sick Cities* by M. Gordon, Penguin, 1965. See Chapter 14, ''Urban Blight and Civic Foresight''.

8 *Cities and City Life* edited by H. M. Hughes, Allyn and Bacon, 1970. See Chapter 16, ''The Slum: Who Has to Live There and Who Chooses to Live There?'' by J. R. Seeley and Chapter 17, ''The Slum as Home'' by M. Fried and P. Gleicher.

8.22 CRIME

Crime is perhaps the greatest problem now facing North American cities. It is found in all strata of society, from the rich businessman who commits fraud to the drug addict who steals in order to maintain his habit. Indeed, many ordinary citizens commit a crime every year when they fill out their income-tax forms. In many areas of the city it is unsafe to venture onto the streets or to walk through a park even in daylight. The newspapers offer daily accounts of murder, rape, burglary, theft, and robbery. The result has been a fear of becoming involved, an increase in the number of door locks and guns bought, and an increasing number of people moving into guarded buildings. The downtown cores of many cities are deserted soon after the sun sets. Is this any way to live?

Crime is not a simple phenomenon and it is, therefore, very difficult to solve. In fact we do not even know how much crime is committed each year. Although agencies in both the United States and Canada collect statistics each year, these only represent the tip of the iceberg. The successful crime is not often discovered. Many crimes are not reported because people do not want to become involved or because they are afraid. In addition, our techniques of measuring and recording crime are not perfect.

What induces a person to commit a criminal act? Some of the reasons may include the poverty and frustration that is bred in the slums and ghettos; a moment of violent anger; the need for money to buy drugs; disrespect for the law; or in the case of white-collar crime, the desire for advancement, power, or money. Regardless of the motive, the results of crime are the same: fear, anger, and distrust.

Crime is not just an urban problem. Most crimes are committed in urban areas because much of our population lives in cities. Within cities themselves crimes are not evenly distributed. Crime usually occurs where the opportunities are greatest. For example, most crimes are committed in and around the CBD because this is where we find the highest density of offices, commercial establishments, and daytime population. On the other hand, residential burglaries are most frequently committed in middle- and upper-income residential areas. The highest rates of auto theft occur in areas with a high density of automobiles. Thus a frequency of a specific type of crime is related to the number of opportunities available.

A large number of academic disciplines examine crime from various points of view: psychological, sociological, historical, geographical, and, of course, legal. All have contributed to our knowledge of the phenomenon but none have been able to offer successful solutions how to solve it or how fully to understand it.

For Thought and Research

The following are some aspects to investigate:
1 Make a study of crime in your area.
2 What is the relationship between poverty and crime?
3 What are the high crime areas in the city?
4 White-collar crime.
5 Compare the spatial pattern of crimes against property to the spatial pattern of crimes against people.
6 Make a survey of newspapers as an indicator of crime patterns.
7 What are the regional variations in crime in the country as a whole?
8 Urban crime versus rural crime.
9 Inter-metropolitan crime patterns.
10 Intra-urban crime patterns.
11 Variations in the law across the country.
12 Crime and its treatment.
13 Juvenile delinquency.
14 Make a study of police procedures in an urban area.

15 How does crime relate to population and cultural factors?
16 Organized crime.
17 Crime prevention through urban design.

Recommended Readings

1 *The Geography of Crime and Justice* by K. D. Harries, McGraw-Hill, 1974.
2 *Urban Geography: A Social Perspective* by D. Herbert, Praeger, 1973. See the section on "Delinquency, Crime and Social Geography".
3 *Cities and City Life* edited by H. M. Hughes, Allyn and Bacon, 1970. See Chapter 13, "Crime in the City, Town and Country" by M. B. Clinard and Chapter 18, "Delinquency Areas" by H. D. McKay.
4 *Crime in the City* by D. Glaser, Harper and Row, 1970.
5 *Downtown: Our Challenging Urban Problems* by R. A. Liston, Dellacorte Press, 1965. See Chapter 9, "Crime and Criminals".
6 *Crime and Its Prevention* edited by S. Lewin, H. W. Wilson, 1968.
7 *The Crime Problem,* fifth edition, by W. C. Reckless, Meredith, 1973.
8 *The Sociology of Deviant Behavior,* fourth edition, by M. B. Clinard, Holt, Rinehart and Winston, 1974.
9 *Defensible Space: Crime Prevention Through Urban Design* by O. Neuman, Macmillan, 1972.

8.23 PARKS AND RECREATION

The importance of recreational activities in the lives of urban inhabitants is far too often ignored in the development of North American cities. This lack of awareness is demonstrated by the lack of park space. Nature has almost been erased from the city landscape. The many open spaces now found in our cities consist primarily of parking lots, scrap yards, abandoned industrial sites, and vacant land. The most potentially attractive land in many of our cities, the waterfront, is frequently isolated by freeways and railway tracks or is inaccessible because of industrial development.

In recent years there has been a growing awareness among social scientists and urban planners that park facilities are necessary for the emotional and physical well-being of urban residents. The tensions, strains, and ordered nature of urban life create a need for some form of escape or alternative activity. Recreation within the confines of a park is one approach to this problem.

The term recreation is not confined to strenuous activities such as baseball, football, or hockey. It includes any activity engaged in during a period of leisure. As such, walking or riding a bicycle through a park, sitting under a tree looking at people, or even dozing off in a park may be considered valid recreational activities. The activity itself is not necessarily the most important thing. We must also consider the emotional and physical release or rebuilding that takes place.

Urban parks should be designed to fulfil the many needs of the users. Different parks should have different uses to cater to the different moods, ages, and backgrounds of the users. Parks located in the downtown core need only be small as long as they provide a breathing space away from the pressures of business and shopping. Larger parks outside the core may provide an entire block of grass, flowers, and a canopy of leaves. On a larger scale, parks that use the features of the landscape, such as a ravine, waterfront, or island, can cater to different types of recreational pursuits. Finally, in more rugged settings surrounding the city, large parks situated along rivers, by reservoirs, or around lakes may serve more varied recreational needs of urban residents. However, parks should be easily accessible to their users regardless of their design or size.

For Thought and Research

The following are some aspects to investigate:
1   What is leisure?
2   More parks! Is the cost justified?
3   Describe the development and use of parks in your city or in a city close by.
4   The value of land and water resources when used for recreation.
5   The effects of various types of pollution on recreation.
6   Current thoughts of planners on parks and recreation.
7   The future demand for recreational areas and facilities.
8   The use of parks by teen-agers (or by any age group).
9   The role of outdoor recreation in our lives.
10 How many facilities do parks require?
11 The overuse of parks.
12 Construct a questionnaire to be given to:
    a) people who use the parks in your area;
    b) people who do not use the parks in your area.

Recommended Readings

1   *Economics of Outdoor Recreation* by M. Clawson and J. Knetsch, Johns Hopkins Press, 1966.
2   *Recreation in Modern Society* by M. H. Hormachea and C. R. Hormachea, Holbrook Press, 1972.
3   *Modern American Cities* edited by R. Ginger, Quadrangle Books, 1969. See ''Think Big About Small Parks'' by T. P. Hoving.
4   *Sick Cities* by M. Gordon, Penguin, 1965. See Chapter 5, ''No Place For Fun''.
5   *Taming Megalopolis,* Vol. 1, edited by H. W. Eldridge, Doubleday, 1967. See Chapter 12, ''Recreation, Leisure and the Higher Culture''.
6   *Planning for Parks and Recreation Needs in Urban Areas* by E. C. Guggheimer, Twayne, 1969.
7   *Land and Leisure: Concepts and Methods in Outdoor Recreation* by D. W. Fischer, J. E. Lewis, and G. B. Priddle, Maaroufa Press, 1974.

8.24 THE ECOLOGICAL ROLE OF OPEN SPACE

Open space is an important aspect of urban and regional planning and one that is directly related to the problem of environmental quality. Most of us are aware of the great emotional appeal of open space, but the physical, economic, and social aspects of this land use are poorly understood. Not only are the roles of open space poorly understood, but there are as many definitions of open space as there are people.

One thing we do know about open space is that, once lost, it is almost always impossible to restore that site. Further, open space is almost defenceless in the face of many types of development. If the time should come when we feel our community should leave certain areas as open space we need to be prepared to defend our views. Perhaps we should make a start now.

For Thought and Research

The following are some aspects to investigate:
1   What are the various definitions of open space?
2   "It is felt that an initial indication of a society's perception of space can be gained from an analysis of land-use problems and habitat forms." Discuss.
3   What is an adequate distribution of open space for the following: urban recreational activities; housing density; wildlife areas; aquifer recharge areas.
4   What role can open space play in maintaining and developing a wildlife community in the city?
5   What is the relationship between open space and urban climatic variation?
6   Does land subdivision and development include open-space planning in theory and/or practice? Where?
7   Variations in soil types may be one valid argument for or against using land for open space. Discuss.
8   Can valleys and ravines in urban areas provide open space for a community and accommodate more intense land-use functions? Support your argument with theories and examples.

Recommended Readings

1   "Bird Populations in Delaware's Urban Woodlots" by J. T. Lineham in *Audubon Field Notes,* Vol. 21, December 1967.
2   *The Plan for the Valleys* by I. McHarg, Wallace-McHarg Associates, 1964.
3   *Future Environments of North America* edited by F. Darling and J. Milton, Natural History, 1966. See "Ecological Determinism" and "An Hypothesis for the Adequate Distribution of Open Space" by A. L. Strong.
4   "Man and His Thermal Environment" by W. Viessman in *Interaction of Man and His Environment* edited by B. Jennings and J. Murphy, Plenum, 1966.
5   *Open Space Communities in the Market Place* by C. Narcross, Technical Report No. 58, Urban Land Institute, December 1966.

6 "Fit Suburbia to its Soils" by C. Kellogg in *Soils, Water and Suburbia* edited by U.S.D.A. and H.U.D., Government Printing Office, 1967.

7 "Wildlife Habitat in Urban and Suburban Environments" by F. Stearns in *Transactions of the 32nd North American Wildlife and Natural Resources Conference,* Wildlife Management Institute, 1967.

8 *Where Not to Build—A Guide to Open Space Planning,* United States Government Printing Office, Washington, 1968.

9 "Environmental Quality: A Review" by I. Burton in *Geographical Review,* Vol. 58, July 1968.

10 "Factors Influencing Local Distribution of Shrews" by L. Getz in *American Midland Naturalist,* Vol. 65-55, No. 5, 1966.

11 "Land Subdivision" by P. Green in *Principles and Practices of Urban Planning* edited by W. Goodman, International City Managers' Assoc., Washington, 1968.

8.25   SITE OF THE CITY

What is the land beneath the buildings of your town like? Have the physical features on which your town is built, the *site,* been a help or a hindrance in the town's development? Was the best possible location for your town chosen? All these questions can be answered by a careful consideration of the site.

When the first settlers moved into an area they were not likely to realize that they might be establishing a future metropolis. They may not have even been aware that they were beginning a town or village. Each settler was looking for certain things: a potential mill owner for a rapidly flowing stream; a military commander for an easily defended hill; a storekeeper for a plain, easily accessible from surrounding farms. When more than one land use must be accommodated, second-best solutions must often be accepted since a potential townsite will rarely be best for everyone.

In the years following a town's formation many things can happen that put added strain on the original site and sometimes cause serious problems for the town's continued growth. What about your town? Why was it built where it was? Has the choice proven successful?

For Thought and Research

The following are some aspects to investigate:

1   What was the land in the area of your town like when the first settlers arrived?

2   What role did site characteristics play in the choice of the location of your town?

3   a) How has the site of your town been modified?
   b) Why were these modifications necessary?
   c) For what land uses is site modification most commonly needed?

4   a) Where has the site not been modfied? Be very careful in deciding if modification is necessary.

b) For what land uses is site modification generally not necessary?
5 a) Explain what is meant by a town outgrowing its site and site characteristics.
   b) Has your town or city outgrown, either in size or function, its original site?
   c) Could a better site for your town be found in the area in which you live?
6 a) Onto what type of land do most towns and cities expand?
   b) In what ways is this a natural result of the economic and government framework within which urban expansion occurs?
   c) Is expansion onto this type of land generally desirable or not?
7 When a new town is being established today are site requirements as demanding as they might have been in the eighteenth or nineteenth centuries?

Recommended Readings

1 Consult the *Recommended Readings* of Section 2.1 for general information on the site of a city.
2 Consult old maps and historical records in your muncipal hall, library, or museum for information on your town or city.

Case Studies

9

These case studies are derived from information collected by scientific means. They are included here to give you a chance to find out if you can apply the knowledge that you have gained from this book.

9.1 LAND-USE STRUCTURE AND CHANGE WITHIN THE CBD

In order to understand the ongoing changes that are taking place within the urban community, we will examine here some of the changes that take place within the CBD. As one area of the city changes other areas must also change since they are all interrelated.

TABLE 11

Category of land use	Percentage of the total area in the CBD (excluding roads)				Percentage change 1961-1976
	1961	1966	1971	1976	
Residential	6	6	5	4	− 2
Retailing	22	21	14	10	− 12
Office	17	20	26	22	+ 5
Industry/warehousing	14	11	9	8	− 6
Institutional	19	16	20	22	+ 3
Parking	14	18	20	24	+ 10

A study of the land use within the CBD is often a good indicator of the vitality of the city, particularly the downtown areas of the city. A healthy city will have a core that is dynamic and expanding to meet new situations and requirements.

Examine Table 11 and answer the questions.

Questions

1   Which categories have increased in the amount of land they occupy? Which have decreased in the amount of land they occupy?

2   Account for the various changes in the amount of area occupied by various functions within the CBD.

3   What is a major drawback of only looking at the area occupied by a function?

4   What does the increase in the area used for parking indicate about changes taking place in the CBD?

5   How would you describe the vitality of this urban core, based solely upon the data in this table?

6   Why is the residential function becoming less important in the CBD?

9.2   CHANGES IN THE OFFICE FUNCTION IN THE CBD

One of the most important functions found in the CBD is the office function. The very high office towers attest to its importance. In Part A of the exercise we will observe the amount of land occupied by office functions. In Part B we will look at the availability of office space within the CBD. In both cases the data from the CBD will be compared with the entire city so that we may determine the changes that are taking place over a period of time.

A. OFFICE FUNCTION: LAND-USE CHANGE OVER A FIVE-YEAR PERIOD

TABLE 12

Category	CBD	Entire urban area (ha)
Time period 1 (1971)		
a) land used for offices (in hectares)	100	200
b) land used in the CBD as a percentage of land used for offices in the entire urban area	50%	—
Time period 2 (1976)		
a) land used for offices (in hectares)	88	220
b) land used in the CBD as a percentage of land used for offices in the entire urban area	40%	—
Percentage Change	−10%	

1   What occurred during this five-year period?
2   Explain the factors that might have caused this situation.
3   What difficulties are encountered in using these land-use figures? What do they not tell you?

B. AVAILABILITY OF OFFICE SPACE

TABLE 13

Year	Number of office buildings in the CBD	Number of office buildings in the entire city	Total office space available in the CBD (in m²)	Office space in the CBD as a percentage of office space available in the entire city
1970	125	410	0.74 million	41%
1974	95	340	0.93 million	40%
1975	90	355	1.11 million	39%
1976	92	370	1.13 million	37%

Questions
1   Account for the decrease in the number of office buildings in the CBD and in the entire urban area over the six-year period.
2   a) Account for the increase in the amount of available office space in the CBD despite the reduction in the number of office buildings.
    b) What does this indicate about the intensity of land use in the CBD?
3   Describe the situation that exists between the amount of office space available in the CBD and the rest of the urban community. Suggest reasons for this situation.

9.3   RETAIL FUNCTION: COMPARISON BETWEEN THE CBD AND THE REST OF THE CITY

As the use of the automobile increased and the urban population moved more and more into the suburbs, changes took place in the retailing structure of major North American cities. In this study we will examine some of the changes as they apply to the CBD and the rest of the urban area.

Examine Table 14 and answer the questions.

TABLE 14

Time period	Retail category	In the CBD	The situation in the CBD as a percentage of the entire urban community
1961	a) Number of stores	880	8%
	b) Sales ($1 000s)	340 000	28%
1971	a) Number of stores	690	5%
	b) Sales ($1 000s)	350 000	16%
1976	a) Number of stores	560	4%
	b) Sales ($1 000s)	385 000	13%

Questions

1   In terms of the number of stores found in the CBD, what has been the trend in the period 1961-1976?
2   What has the trend been in the CBD, as a percentage of all stores in the urban area?
3   What are the factors that have affected the decline in the number of stores in the CBD in comparison to the total urban area?
4   What has been the trend of the percentage of sales in the CBD compared to the total urban area?
5   What has brought about this change in the position of the CBD?
6   What is the trend in terms of the volume of sales?
7   What explanations can you give for the contradiction that is seen in your answers to questions 4 and 6?

9.4   BENEFIT-COST ANALYSIS: AN EXAMPLE

There is a need for a major transportation route from the suburbs to the city core. Two alternatives seem possible—an expressway or a subway. Which is the better solution? Benefit-cost analysis may be used to help answer this question. Some of the benefits and costs thought to result from the decision to build either an expressway or a subway are listed in Table 15. Use these facts to weigh the alternatives and make a decision. In doing this you may want to consider the answers to these questions:

1   Are all the benefits and all the costs of equal importance? If not, rank them in order of decreasing importance to you.

2   Can you put a dollar value on items such as air pollution or the annoyance caused by the crowding or inconvenience of

public transit? If you can how would you do it? If you do not think you can, how does this affect the outcome of your benefit-cost analysis?

3   From the costs and benefits listed in Table 15, which solution seems best? Explain your reasoning.

4   Are there any benefits or costs that you think should be added to those listed here? Would this change your decision?

5   Why should you be suspicious in the future of any proposed project for your community that estimates only construction costs?

6   Is the most profitable solution necessarily the best solution?

TABLE 15

Benefits	Costs
Expressway	
accessibility 7 000 people/h	construction costs $143 000 000 ($12 000 000/km)
time saved 10 minutes per trip (excluding trip to expressway)	lost assessment 700 residences; 44 businesses; 1 factory
convenience and flexibility of automobile use	displacement of owners, workers, and users of those lost buildings
increased land values near transportation artery	loss of a city park (2 ha)
spread of suburbs further from city due to decreased travel time by car	noise pollution
	air pollution
	provision of more downtown parking space
Subway	
accessibility 40 000 people/h	construction costs $104 000 000 ($10 000 000/km)
time saved 20 minutes per trip (excluding trip to subway)	lost assessment 100 residences; 5 businesses
increased land values near subway route	inconvenience, lack of privacy, and crowding
high-density development along subway route	
quiet and non-polluting	
parking not needed downtown	

9.5   WHERE IS URBAN GROWTH TAKING PLACE?

We have noted that an increasing proportion of the population in North America is moving to urban areas. In order to project where the growth problems are most likely to occur it would be valuable to know which communities seem to be growing the fastest and which communities are losing population. The statistics given in Table 16 suggest some of the answers. The data are for the United States.

TABLE 16

RURAL/URBAN POPULATION BALANCE AND PERCENTAGE POPULATION CHANGES

	Rural/Urban Population Balance			Total Population Change	
	1950	1960	1970	1950-60	1960-70
United States	100%	100%	100%	18.5%	13.3%
Urban	64.0	69.9	73.5	29.3	19.2
250 000 +	23.0	22.0	20.8	13.0	7.2
50 000-250 000	12.3	14.2	15.2	36.6	21.7
25 000-50 000	5.8	8.3	8.8	69.2	19.4
5 000-25 000	13.3	15.3	16.9	36.3	25.6
under 5 000	4.7	4.6	4.3	16.4	6.0
Other urban territories	4.9	5.5	7.5	34.1	54.2
Rural	36.0	30.1	26.5	−0.8	−0.3
1 000-2 500	4.3	3.6	3.3	−0.3	−2.5
under 1 000	2.5	2.2	1.9	−3.5	−1.1
Other	29.2	24.3	21.3	−0.6	−0.7

Questions

1   What percentage of the total US population lived in urban places in 1950, 1960, and 1970?

2   Compare the change in urban population with the change in total US population during the period from 1950 to 1960. Make the same comparison for the period 1960 to 1970. Which is growing at a faster rate, urban or total population? Is the rate of growth in urban and total population increasing or decreasing?

3   What are some of the possible sources of the increased urban population in the US?

4   What category of urban place has had the greatest single percentage of urban population in 1950, 1960, and 1970? Explain this.

5   What size of urban place grew at the fastest rate between 1950 and 1960 and between 1960 and 1970? Explain this.

6 What is meant by the term "other urban territories"?

7 Project the population of "other urban territories" for 1980. This can be done graphically by plotting the percentages in this category for 1950, 1960, and 1970. By spacing the years equally, the position of 1980 can be located. Join the percentages for each year by a straight line. Extend that line at the same slope to the year 1980 and you can see what percentage might be predicted.

8 Calculate the number of people that will be living in "other urban territories" by 1980, based on your projected percentage from question 7 and the projected population of the US in 1980 (226 million).

9 According to census figures for 1970, people lived in a density of 13.0/ha in incorporated urban communities and 6.25/ha in other urban territories. Calculate how much land will be urbanized by 1980 by people living in other urban territories. Compare that figure to the land that would be used if those people had lived at the densities of incorporated urban communities.

10 Use the calculations from question 9 to discuss the significance of the increasing trend to living in "other urban territories".

11 What other problems may result from this magnitude of growth outside of incorporated communities?

12 Where are the greatest rural losses of population taking place? Explain.

13 Examine the growth of your community. Compare its growth rate to the growth rate of communities of its size category in your country.

9.6 PROJECTED GROWTH IN THE NEW YORK REGION TO 2000 A.D.

In the past our cities have always been surrounded by non-urban land. People could readily get out of the urban community and into the surrounding countryside. However, as our cities became ever larger, spreading out into the countryside in all directions, they also grew nearer to neighboring communities. Villages on the outskirts of cities were swallowed by urban growth. Cities merged with other cities. This means that, not only is it more difficult for the urbanite to get into the countryside, but, in some cases, the countryside has disappeared as a buffer zone between urban communities. This process of filling in the spaces has been most apparent between the large cities of the Eastern Seaboard of the United States—Boston, New York, Philadelphia, Baltimore, and Washington. In fact two terms for the new agglomeration have already been coined— "Megalopolis" and "Bosnywash".

To get an appreciation of the size of the growth expected within this region, the New York region's past and future growth in population and area are examined in this case study. A comparison with Toronto is also made because, although it is smaller, an agglomeration of urban communities is projected there too.

TABLE 17 HISTORICAL TREND OF DENSITY IN THE NEW YORK METROPOLITAN REGION

Year	Density (people/km²)
1860	25 000
1940	7 800
1954	5 300
1970	3 000

TABLE 18 PROJECTED GROWTH FOR THE NEW YORK- NEW JERSEY-CONNECTICUT METROPOLITAN AREA

Year	Population	New land required (km²)
1970	17.2 million	—
2000	24.8 million	7 200

TABLE 19 TORONTO REGION TRENDS IN GROWTH

Year	Population	New Land required (ha)
1951	1.7 million	—
1964	2.8 million	—
1980	4.0 million	—
2000	6.4 million	133 200 to 165 200*

* depending on density of development projected

Questions

1 a) What trend in density is evident in Table 17? Try to explain this surprising trend.

b) Put the density figures in terms of ha instead of km² to get a better idea of the housing required to achieve such densities.

c) If you assume that the average family size is four and that each family occupies a dwelling, how many dwellings per hectare are there at each density? What type of housing could achieve these densities?

2 a) From Table 18 calculate the increase in population projected from 1970 to 2000 A.D.

b) Use the new land projection to calculate the density of development in persons per square kilometre and in persons per hectare.

c) Compare this density with the density of New York in 1970. What significance do you attach to the difference?

3 Using topographic maps or detailed road maps of the New York region from Connecticut to New Jersey try to determine where this growth will take place. Will it cement these communities together or will there still be open spaces between?

4 If you were in charge of the planning for the New York region what would you do when faced with these projections? (The answers to this question could form the basis for a good classroom discussion.)

5 Toronto planners did not simply project density trends into the future to obtain land requirements for the year 2000. Density of development was a choice that people had to make. They took what they considered to be two possible densities, one high and one low, to show the difference the choice would make on Toronto's future growth needs. Calculate the densities they assumed from the figures given in Table 19. How much greater did the density have to be to reduce land requirements by almost 40 000 ha?

9.7   DISEASE IN THE CITY

In the Middle Ages, cities were places of filth. Diseases such as cholera and typhoid fever were not linked to polluted drinking water until the late nineteenth century. We now pride ourselves on our high standards of sanitation in North America, but evidence shows that we are again making our cities unhealthy places to live. Although this fact is not yet a matter of public concern, statistics are becoming alarming. Recent medical studies have compared urban and rural areas in various parts of North America. Some of the findings are shown in Table 20.

TABLE 20

Subject of survey	Results of survey
all types of cancer	38% more incidence in urban areas
heart disease (among males under 35)	25% more incidence in urban areas
heart disease (among males 35-55)	100% more incidence in urban areas
heart disease (among males over 55)	300% more incidence in urban areas
death rate for lung cancer among smokers	20% more incidence in urban areas
death rate for lung cancer among non-smokers	900% more incidence in urban areas
asthma	incidence 100-200% higher under conditions of high air pollution

Questions

1 a) What elements of urban life could be responsible for the significant increase in heart disease in the cities?

b) Why does the urban-rural difference in heart disease increase so markedly with age.

2 Medical science has not yet been able to pinpoint all causes of cancer. If all types of cancer are more common in cities, what new lines of investigation could you suggest?

3 Is the crusade against smoking and cigarette advertising justified in the light of these statistics?

4 Many urban theorists predict that we will all eventually live in super-cities of many millions such as the Eastern Seaboard megalopolis. If the North American population became 100% urbanized, what would the probable percentage increase be in the following:

a) heart disease;
b) lung cancer;
c) general physical fitness

9.8   URBAN GOVERNMENT FINANCING

Many people complain of high property taxes and the generally high cost of living in urban areas. It is often unclear why taxes are high and what our money is being used for. The statistics in Tables 21 and 22 were included in the recent financial reports of a Canadian town of around 15 000 population, and a Canadian city of around 420 000 population.

TABLE 21 TOWN FINANCES

Revenue		Expenditures	
Taxation		General municipal activities	
residential	$1 079 149	*general government*	$187 978
commercial and		*protection to persons and*	
industrial	449 717	*property*	243 703
business	201 858	*public works*	353 070
special charges	8 147	*sanitation*	213 626
Total	$1 738 871	*health*	14 078
Other governments'		*social and family*	
contribution	388 220	*services*	40 765
		recreation and libraries	104 085
		planning and	
		development	13 331
Other revenue		*financial expenses*	32 475
(licences, rents, fines,			
penalties, income from		Total	1 203 111
investments)	196 770	Education	965 469
		Share of county	
		expenditure	155 281
Total Revenue	$2 323 861	Total Expenditure	$2 323 861

Taxation per capita $115.92

TABLE 22   CITY FINANCES

Revenue		Expenditures	
Taxation		General municipal activities	
residential	$58 447 221	*general government*	$1 708 173
commercial and		*protection to*	
industrial	22 723 249	*persons and*	
business	10 231 659	*property*	4 882 233
special charges	2 177 523	*public works*	9 740 694
Total	$93 579 652	*sanitation*	4 918 531
		health	2 429 464
Other governments'		*recreation*	5 667 895
contribution	13 026 336	*planning and*	
		development	644 757
		financial	243 441
Other revenue	4 982 643	*other*	2 378 180
		Total	$32 613 368
		Share of metropolitan	
		area's expenditure	24 444 721
		Education	53 794 438
Total Revenue	$111 588 631	Total Expenditure	$110 852 527

Taxation per capita $222.81

Questions

1 For each municipality, examine the percentage of the revenue that comes from a) residences and b) other governments' contributions. Why is the tax per capita so much higher in the large city?

2 Many complaints are made about the cost of running the big government bureaucracy in large cities. Are these complaints justified in terms of the relative costs of general municipal activities in the two communities?

3 List the top five government activities in each place and compare the two lists. What differences do the lists suggest between the problems of living in big cities and in small towns?

4 What is the cost of education per person in each community? Account for the difference.

9.9   A SECOND AIRPORT FOR TORONTO?

The following arguments and statistics were presented during the debates over the need for a second international airport in one major Canadian city, Toronto. Whether the airport is built or not will probably not be of great interest to many people reading this book.

They are not directly affected by the decision. However, all of us are likely to be affected by similar situations at some time in our lives. Analyzing this particular situation should prepare you to cope logically with other issues as they arise.

SUPPORTING THE AIRPORT

1. The average annual growth rate in all passenger traffic at the present airport is 13.7% (including an annual growth rate in charter flights of 39.3%).
2. Work trends indicate a continued increase in paid vacations, four- and three-day work weeks, and earlier retirement, which leaves more time for travel.
3. Forecasts of growth rates until the year 2000 are shown in Table 23.

TABLE 23

Time period	Percentage annual growth	Annual passenger load in millions (by the end of time period)
1971-75	10.5	9.2
1976-80	9.3	15.9
1981-85	8.0	23.2
1986-90	7.1	32.5
1991-95	6.7	44.8
1996-2000	6.4	61.9

4. The capacity of the present airport is 12 000 000 people per year.
5. At the present airport location, 69 000 people live within noise areas and any expansion of the airport could affect up to 200 000 people in nearby new residential areas.
6. STOL (short takeoff and landing) aircraft will not eliminate the need for a new airport since they are used primarily for short-distance travel (less than 800 km). Short-distance travel now accounts for 50% of trips, but will only represent 30% of trips by the year 2000.
7. A new airport will stimulate growth in industry, hotels and related services, and transportation on the outskirts of the city.

OPPOSING THE NEW AIRPORT

1. The projected number of passengers per year (62 million) is unrealistic for a country that will have, at most, 34 million people in the year 2000.

2   Even at the rate of 50 million passengers per year, planes would land or take off every 45 seconds from 7 am till midnight (based on an average of 200 passengers per plane while currently the average is about 100 passengers per plane).

3   In 1968 an expansion of the existing airport was planned that would have been capable of handling projected traffic until 1985 at least. This expansion, which would have occupied 7.5 km² of land, was rejected in favor of the new airport which will occupy 75 km² of prime farmland and destroy established 140-year-old communities.

4   Estimates of total cost for the new airport range from \$1.5 billion to over \$3 billion.

5   Escalating costs and shortages of fuel in the future have not been considered.

6   STOL aircraft, which are much quieter, should be commercially available by the early 1980s. They will be capable of carrying 100 to 200 passengers at about 800 km/h.

Questions

1   a) Construct two line graphs to compare the annual percentage growth of air travel with the growth in actual number of passengers between 1970 and 2000. Which graph shows the trend more strikingly?

    b) Why does the percentage increase get smaller in each time period?

2   Explain why fuel costs and availability are an important factor to be considered.

3   a) How will the development of STOL aircraft affect the need for a new airport?

    b) Where are STOL airfields most likely to be located? What would they look like?

4   The proposed airport site has excellent farmland—fairly flat, with well drained and fertile soils. Explain why this is important to both sides of the controversy.

5   One anti-airport group has called itself "People or Planes". Explain the meaning of this slogan, supporting your answer with some of the statistics given in Table 23.

6   In your opinion, which side of the dispute has the strongest case and why?

7   Investigate the outcome of the dispute to date.

9.10 CHANGING PATTERNS OF ACCESSIBILITY IN THE CITY

Transportation patterns in a city change as the city grows and land uses change. When an individual changes his route to work or when an apartment complex is built, a change, small or large, is made in the city's transportation pattern.

One of the most important aspects of transportation in the city is *accessibility*. It can be viewed in two ways. First, it can be thought of as the ease with which any point in the city can be reached by all those in the city. This is the way we shall view accessibility. It can also be considered as the ease with which a person at one point in the city can reach all other parts of the city.

Figure 9-1 is a map representing a hypothetical city in the year 1900. It is assumed that the entire population is centered in seven locations, A to G. The relative population of each location is shown, together with the average travel time between adjacent centers. In 1900 the main methods of transportation were electric streetcar and foot. The wealthier people had carriages, or horse-drawn taxis. Table 24 is a summary of total travel time to each center, weighted by the population. For example, the first numeral in the third column (14.00) was obtained by taking 40% of 35. The value 14.55 (the total for the first column) represents the time required to travel to point A from all points of the city.

TABLE 24

ACCESSIBILITY VALUES IN 1900

From Center	To Center						
	A	**B**	**C**	**D**	**E**	**F**	**G**
A	—	6.00	14.00	16.00	24.00	8.00	8.00
B	4.50	—	15.00	7.50	13.50	10.50	10.50
C	2.45	3.50	—	4.20	6.65	3.85	3.85
D	0.40	0.25	0.60	—	0.55	0.06	0.06
E	4.20	3.15	6.65	3.85	—	3.15	4.55
F	1.00	1.75	2.75	3.00	2.25	—	1.00
G	2.00	3.50	5.50	6.00	4.50	2.00	—
Total	14.55	18.15	44.50	40.55	51.45	27.56	27.96

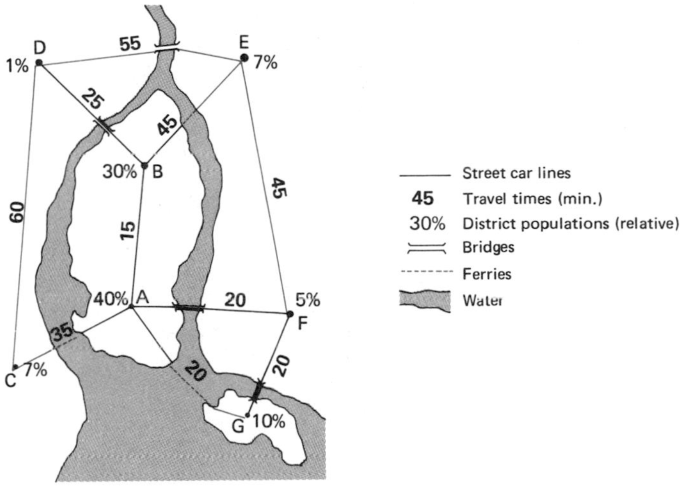

Fig. 9-1
Transportation patterns in 1900.

Figure 9-2 and Table 25 represent the same town in the mid-1970s. The population pattern and also the accessibility pattern have altered. From these two views of the transportation pattern of an imaginary city it is possible to make some useful generalizations about the transportation characteristics of North American cities.

TABLE 25   ACCESSIBILITY VALUES IN MID-1970s

From Center	To Center						
	A	**B**	**C**	**D**	**E**	**F**	**G**
A	—	1.00	1.00	2.00	2.00	1.25	1.50
B	3.00	—	6.00	3.75	4.50	6.75	7.50
C	2.00	4.00	—	2.00	3.50	4.50	5.00
D	9.00	5.00	4.00	—	3.00	6.00	11.00
E	10.00	7.50	8.75	3.75	—	3.75	10.00
F	5.00	9.00	9.00	6.00	3.00	—	5.00
G	1.50	2.50	2.50	2.75	2.00	1.25	—
Total	30.50	29.00	31.25	20.25	18.00	23.50	40.00

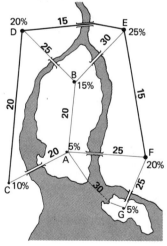

Fig. 9-2
Transportation pattern in mid-1970s.

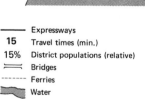

——— Expressways
15 Travel times (min.)
15% District populations (relative)
⹀ Bridges
------ Ferries
▨ Water

Questions

1 a) Describe the population pattern in 1900.

b) In view of the transportation available why did this population pattern develop?

2 Explain the relationship between the existence of bridges, streetcar lines, and travel times in 1900.

3 a) What point in the city was most accessible to the entire city in 1900?

b) What types of business, government, and commercial activities would tend to locate here? Why?

c) What do we call this part of the city?

4 Where could transportation improvements usefully be made in 1900?

5 What changes had been made in the transportation system by the 1970s?

6 What would be the predominant form of transportation?

7 Describe the changes in the population pattern between 1900 and the 1970s.

8 How is this typical of what has happened to North American cities?

9 Why are trips to the center of the city relatively slow in the 1970s compared to trips around the perimeter of the city?

10 Why are trips to the center of the city in the 1970s not significantly faster than in 1900?

11 Is the most accessible point the same as in 1900?

12 a) Is one part of the city much more accessible than other parts?

b) Explain how this could result in a polycentric city.

13 What change in the shopping pattern of this city has probably occurred as a result of the transportation changes?

14 a) Where would transportation problems be likely to occur?

b) What transportation improvements could be suggested for this city?

15 Apply the approach of this case study to your town or city. Identify population centers, travel time and patterns, and transportation trouble spots.

9.11 SNOW AND THE CITY

To many people a 15 cm snowfall brings pleasant visions of skiing, sledding, and tranquil winter scenes. To the road departments of the urban centers of the northern United States and Canada, the same 15 cm of snow means traffic jams, extra hours of work, and large expenditures of money for snow removal. Few things can paralyze a city more completely than even a moderate snowfall. Communication is disrupted as telephone lines are torn down. Schools and airports are closed. Stores experience a decline in sales.

In this case study we will attempt to discover what aspects of snowstorms cause them to be such disruptive elements in the urban environment.

TABLE 26 CRITERIA FOR CLASSIFYING DISRUPTIONS

Activity	Type of Disruption				
	Paralyzing (1)	Crippling (2)	Inconvenient (3)	Nuisance (4)	Minimal (5)
Internal transpor- tation	Few vehicles moving on street; police department providing emergency transportation	Accidents at least 200% above normal; stalled vehicles	Accidents at least 100% above average; traffic slowed	Traffic slowed	No effect
Retail trade	Many stores and busi- nesses closed	Major drop in shoppers in CBD; mention of lower sales	Minor impact	No effect	No effect
Postpone- ments	Most civic, cultural, and athletic events cancelled	Major and minor events	Minor events	Occasional	No effect
Manufac- turing	Factory shut- downs	Moderate worker absen- teeism	Any worker absenteeism above normal	No effect	No effect
Power supply and com- munica- tions	Wires down; major diffi- culties	Moderate difficulties	Minor difficulties	Any difficul- ties	No effect
Schools	Closure of city and rural schools	Closure of rural schools; major atten- dance drops in city schools	Minor atten- dance drops in city schools	No effect	No effect
Inter-city highways	Official closure; vehicles stalled	Extreme driving conditions; warning issued	Hazardous driving warn- ing issued	Minor warn- ing given— "slippery in spots"	No effect
Airports	Closure	Commercial flights cancelled	Light plane cancellations; commercial delays	Any difficul- ties	No effect

TABLE 27 DISRUPTIONS IN RELATION TO PHYSICAL VARIABLES

Sites	Physical variables (average)	Paralyzing	Crippling	Inconvenient	Nuisance	Minimal
Muskegon	Depth (cm)	35.6	14.5	9.4	5.1	3.3
	Wind (km/h)	24.5	19.5	18.0	18.9	22.2
	Number per year	2.5	5.3	4.7	5.7	1.7
Rapid City	Depth (cm)	22.4	5.8	5.3	3.8	3.6
	Wind (km/h)	39.9	24.9	18.8	21.4	25.4
	Number per year	0.7	3.3	3.5	2.2	1.1
Milwawkee	Depth (cm)	30.5	10.7	6.7	4.1	3.6
	Wind (km/h)	37.8	26.7	21.4	23.0	12.1
	Number per year	1.1	2.6	3.4	2.9	0.4
Green Bay	Depth (cm)	17.5	7.4	6.7	4.6	3.6
	Wind (km/h)	26.9	24.3	18.4	15.8	13.4
	Number per year	1.1	1.4	3.3	4.2	0.4
Casper	Depth (cm)	19.6	10.7	7.9	7.9	4.3
	Wind (km/h)	25.6	19.5	19.0	20.8	19.6
	Number per year	0.5	2.7	2.9	5.7	6.9
Cheyenne	Depth (cm)	22.4	12.7	8.9	5.1	3.8
	Wind (km/h)	41.2	25.1	23.0	22.1	21.9
	Number per year	1.0	1.6	3.3	3.6	2.7

Questions

1 a) Which city in the U.S.A. receives the most snow (Fig. 9-3)? Why does it receive two to three times as much snow as any one of its neighbors?

b) Identify and explain two factors that can affect the amount of snowfall a town receives.

2 How much snow does your town receive? Check the records of your local weather station, newspaper, radio or television station. Best of all, check your school weather station, if it has one.

3 a) Use Table 26 to classify the snowfall over the course of a winter in your area. After each snow day (any day with snow) classify the event in one of the five categories. Newspapers, radio, and television reports will be helpful in deciding classifications.

b) Collect information on the physical variables of the snowfall such as snow depth and average wind speed during the storm.

4 Explain the role that each of the following plays in increasing the disruption of a city following a snowfall: depth of snow; rapidity of snowfall; wind speed; air temperature; water content of the snow; population of the city; prior experience with snowstorms; and time of day of the storm.

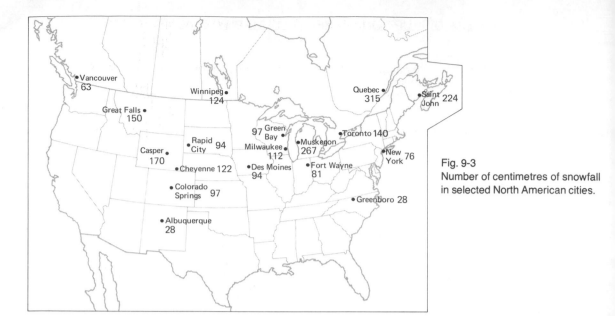

Fig. 9-3
Number of centimetres of snowfall in selected North American cities.

5 Compare the results of your study (question 3) to the data for other cities presented in Table 27 by answering these questions:

a) Is wind speed or snow depth more significant in causing serious disruptions in the cities listed? In your city?

b) Which city or cities are most severely affected by a moderate amount of snow and wind? Why?

c) In comparison to the other cities, does your town seem easily disrupted by snow-storms? Why?

6 Common methods for dealing with snow on the roads include plowing the snow to the side of the road; plowing and removing the snow from the roads; melting the snow with special machines; spreading salt or urea on the snow to melt it; and spreading sand on the roads to aid traction.

a) Describe the advantages of each method listed above.

b) Describe any economic, environmental, or social disadvantages that you see in any of the methods.

7 Municipal governments in the United States spent $44 million on salt alone during one recent winter. Total expenditures are hundreds of millions of dollars, yet snow-control programs are rarely of acceptable standards.

a) What is the snow-control program in your town?

b) How could it be improved?

c) What do you feel can be done to reduce the disruption caused by a snowstorm in your town or city?

9.12   INTRA-CITY POPULATION CHANGES

At first glance the city may appear to be a stable creation. However, it is anything but stable. It is constantly changing, although these changes may occur very slowly. The urban area may be expanding outward, the core of the city may be decaying, or it might be growing outward and upward. The possibilities are endless.

In this study we will examine statistics from a North American city in order to observe the changes that are taking place in terms of the population distribution and density. In Part A we will be concerned with the absolute changes and in Part B the relative, or percentage changes.

The data shown in Table 28 were arrived at in the following manner: A transect was drawn from the CBD (tract 1) to the outer edge of the urbanized area (tract 14). The population in each census tract that the transect passed through is shown for the years 1966 and 1976. In addition, the size of each census tract and its location relative to the CBD are given.

A. ABSOLUTE CHANGE (Total Gains or Losses)

Calculate the following:

a) The population change between 1966 and 1976 for each tract (fill in column 6).

b) The population density for 1966 (column 7).

c) The population density for 1976 (column 8).

d) The change in population density between 1966 and 1976 (column 9).

TABLE 28

					Part A						Part B	
1	2	3	4	5	6	7	8	9	10	11	12	13
Census tract	Distance from the CBD (in km)	Population in 1966	Population in 1976	Area of census tract (in ha)	Population change between 1966-1976 (+ or −)	Population density in 1966 (1966 pop. ÷ area)	Population density in 1976 (1976 pop. ÷ area)	Change in population density between 1966-1976 (+ or −)	Population change between 1966-1976 as a % (+ or −)	1966 pop. as a % of total pop. in 1966 (total pop. = 38 455)	1976 pop. as a % of total pop. in 1976 (total pop. = 72 088)	Difference between %'s in columns 11 and 12 (This is an Index Number) (+ or −)
1	0	120	138	28	+18	4.29	4.93	+0.64	+15%	0.3%	0.2%	−0.1
2		3 000	1 600	64								
3		4 000	1 700	88								
4		8 000	8 500	60								
5		4 200	4 500	68								
6		5 600	8 200	61								
7		5 500	6 600	56								
8		3 600	3 900	100								
9	5	55	4 270	208								
10		2 000	9 360	344								
11		1 000	11 600	336								
12		1 090	4 150	372								
13		160	4 900	290								
14	10	130	2 670	928								
Total		38 455	72 088									

Questions

1 Why do the census tracts get larger as distance from the CBD increases?

2 Why does census tract 1 have such a low population in relation to most of the other tracts (column 1)?

3 a) In what part of the city did the greatest population changes take place (columns 6 and 2)?

   b) Why did the greatest changes take place there?

4 Speculate why there was a decrease in population in tracts 2 and 3 (column 6).

5 Give some possible reasons for the fluctuation in population changes along the transect (column 6).

6 a) Describe the pattern of population density along the transect in each year (columns 7 and 8).

   b) What are the possible reasons for the pattern?

7 Why are the population densities so low in tracts 1 and 12-14 (columns 7 and 8)?

8 a) Which tracts show the greatest change in population density? Consider both positive and negative changes (column 9).

   b) Account for such changes. Consider the changes taking place in North American cities in general.

9 Despite the large increases in population in some suburban census tracts, why is the increase in population density relatively small (column 9)?

10 What appear to be the overall trends in terms of population growth and density for this urban community and, by extension, for North American cities in general?

B. RELATIVE POPULATION CHANGE (Percentage Change)

Calculate the following:

a)   The percentage population change between 1966 and 1976 for each tract (column 10).

b)   The 1966 population as a percentage of the 1966 total population (column 11).

c)   The 1976 population as a percentage of the 1976 total population (column 12).

d)   The difference between the percentages in columns 11 and 12. (*Note*: These numbers are index numbers and not percentages. They show a gain or loss in population relative to the other census tracts.)

Questions

1 a) Which census tracts experienced the greatest percentage change (column 10)?

   b) Describe the pattern along the transect (column 10).

2 What does this pattern tell us about the population realignment?

3 Compare the absolute changes (column 6) and the relative changes (column 10) for tracts 9 to 14.

   a) What does each column tell us?

   b) Explain the advantages and disadvantages of using each method.

4 What do the index numbers in column 13 mean?
5 a) What census tracts gained absolutely (column 6) but lost relatively (column 13)?
  b) Explain why this situation occurs.

Discussion

1 Compare the uses of both absolute and relative methods of observing population changes.
2 Describe the factors that must be considered in determining the reasons for population changes when the transect method is used.
3 What are the advantages and disadvantages of using the urban transect method for studying population change?

9.13 THE CORE-FRAME CONCEPT

The following table demonstrates the differences between the core and the frame in terms of the amount of ground floor space occupied by a selected number of activities.

TABLE 29

A	B	C
Function	Area of land occupied in the core as a percentage of the core's total area	Area of land occupied in the frame as a percentage of the frame's total area
1 Residential	4	23
2 Offices	22	6
3 Parking	23	7
4 Retail	10	9
5 Government/ institutional	11	6
6 Hotel	4	1
7 Warehousing/ manufacturing	9	22
Total		

Questions

1 Add the percentages in columns B and C. Explain the results.
2 Total functions 2-6 for columns B and C. Why would you expect the resulting totals to be as they are?
3 Total the functions 2-7 for columns B and C. Compare these totals with those found in question 2. Explain the new results.

4 Compare the percentage of land each function occupies in both the core and the frame. Explain, in detail, the significance of the two figures for each function.

5 a) Which component of the CBD has the largest area, the core or the frame? Explain why.

b) Explain the mathematical significance of this fact in interpreting the percentage figures shown in the chart.

9.14 THE EFFECT OF THE URBAN LANDSCAPE ON THE URBAN CLIMATE

The following climatic data were collected in a city park in the early spring. The purpose of the field study was to note and explain the effect of an open park area and the surrounding residential district on the urban climate.

Ten recording stations were established and located as shown on Figure 9-4. The sky was completely cloud covered (nimbostratus) and the ground was covered with snow. Data were recorded at 15 30, 16 00, and 16 30. The air temperature, the relative humidity, and the direction and velocity of the wind were recorded at each station (Table 30).

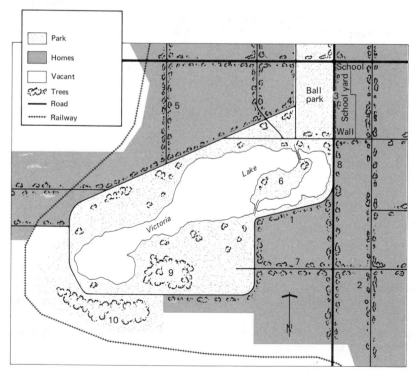

Fig. 9-4
Study sites in and around a park.

TABLE 30

	15 30	16 00	16 30
Station #1			
Air temp. (°C)	0.5	−1.0	−1.5
RH (%)	83	89	89
Wind direction and speed (km/h)	6.0 E	8.0 NE	10.2 E
Station #2			
Air temp. (°C)	1.0	0.5	0.0
RH (%)	74	83	90
Wind direction and speed (km/h)	3.0 S	3.0 NW	3.0 NW
Station #3			
Air temp. (°C)	0.5	0.0	−0.75
RH (%)	75	85	90
Wind direction and speed (km/h)	4.2 E	8.0 E	8.0 E
Station #4			
Air temp. (°C)	0.5	−0.5	−1.0
RH (%)	90	100	98
Wind direction and speed (km/h)	6-8 NNE	7-11 SSE	4-9 SSE
Station #5			
Air temp. (°C)	1.25	0.5	0.0
RH (%)	76	85	92
Wind direction and speed (km/h)	3.5 NE	3.5 NE	4.0 NE
Station #6			
Air temp. (°C)	0.0	−1.0	−2.0
RH (%)	83	90	91
Wind direction and speed (km/h)	12.0 E	9.0 E	10.0 E
Station #7			
Air temp. (°C)	1.25	0.0	0.75
RH (%)	78	83	91
Wind direction and speed (km/h)	5.3 E	5.0 E	5.0 E
Station #8			
Air temp. (°C)	0.25	−0.5	−1.0
RH (%)	85	89	92
Wind direction and speed (km/h)	14.0 NE	12.0 NE	10.0 NE
Station #9			
Air temp. (°C)	0.5	−0.25	−0.5
RH (%)	90	95	96
Wind direction and speed (km/h)	6.0 SE	7.0 SE	6.0 SE
Station #10			
Air temp. (°C)	0.0	−0.5	−1.0
RH (%)	88	100	98
Wind direction and speed (km/h)	8.0 SE	9.0 SE	10.0 SE

Questions

To assist in analysis, the data for each station during each time period might be plotted on a map similar to Figure 9.4.

1   Locate the two coldest stations for the 15 30 readings.

2   Where were the two warmest stations for the 15 30 readings?

3   Identify and explain any pattern you may find in questions 1 and 2.

4   Compare the rate of temperature decrease between the residential stations (5, 7, and 2) and open-space stations (6, 8, and 10). Explain this situation.

5   Identify and explain the temperature situations at stations 1, 3, and 4.

6   Account for the difference between temperature readings at park station 9 and the other park stations (6, 8, and 10).

7   Describe the effects of open space and buildings on the temperature of the urban environment.

8   Where were the two highest winds to be found at 15 30?

9   Where were the two lowest winds to be found at 15 30?

10   Identify and explain any pattern you may find in questions 8 and 9.

11   Account for the relationship between wind speed and temperature patterns for the stations you identified in questions 1, 2, 8, and 9.

12   Compare the wind-speed pattern between residential stations (5 and 7) and those at 1, 3, and 4. Explain this situation.

13   Identify and explain the wind-direction pattern of the study area as a whole.

14   What is the relationship between buildings, open space, and wind patterns in this environment?

15   What is relative humidity (RH)?

16   What, if any, stations might have had some form of precipitation?

17   What factors could account for the apparent inaccuracies at station 6, both in RH and temperature, at 16 30?

18   In general, as temperature decreases the RH increases in this study. Explain why this occurs.

19   Briefly list and describe the relationships between man's use of the urban environment and the urban climate as shown in this study.

20   Predict the outcome of a similar study undertaken on a hot summer day with isolated thundershowers forecast.

21   Predict the effects of the following changes in this urban landscape:
   a) a reduction in the size of the park;
   b) a high-rise apartment complex east and south of the park;
   c) removal of trees in the park and along the streets;
   d) reforestation of most of the park;
   e) a ground-level expressway through stations 1, 5, and 10.

9.15   HIERARCHY OF SERVICE CENTERS

Each business has a minimum number of customers necessary before that business can establish itself. It must also maintain this minimum number of customers to stay in business. This number of customers is called the business's *threshold population*. Studies have been conducted to tell businessmen how many people or families (the normal purchasing unit) are necessary in an area before they can expect the number of customers they need. For example, if statistics show that one in five families requires a unit of service of a camera shop every month and the camera shop owner needs at least 2 460 units of service to break even, then the threshold population of the camera shop is 12 300 families (2 460 × 5). Of course, every business will have its own particular threshold population. Table 31 gives the threshold sizes for different businesses. As such figures change frequently, the ones given here could be out of date. However, they still give an idea of the relative thresholds needed. Use these data to answer the following questions.

TABLE 31

Type of store	Threshold population	Type of store	Threshold population
Grocery store	250	Dry cleaning shop	1 300
Restaurant	300	Shoe store	1 900
Gas station	500	Bakery	2 400
Beauty and barber shop	600	Men's store	2 500
Drugstore	800	Women's accessories	4 600
Appliance store	1 000	Sporting goods	5 400
Hardware store	1 100	Infant's and children's store	5 500
Women's dress shop	1 200	Camera shop	12 300
Furniture store	1 300	Bookstore	12 800

Questions

1   Why do some businesses have larger threshold populations than others? Support your answer by referring to Table 31.

2   Which businesses are most likely to locate nearest to you? Explain.

3   Determine from the figures given what businesses and how many of each would locate in A - a community of 1 200 people; B - a community of 5 000 people; C - a community of 20 000 people. Assume an average of four people in a family. You may wish to present your answers in the form of a table.

4   Assume that you live 2 km from community A, 10 km from community B, and 40 km from community C. To which community would you be likely to go for each of the following: furniture; weekly groceries; men's shoes; car repairs; photographic film; a movie projector; a toaster. Explain your decision in each case.

5   Are there any services that you may not be able to obtain within these three communities? What might you do to obtain these services?

6   Question 4 is an example of a hierarchy of service centers. Explain what is meant by this hierarchy and why it develops.

7   County X contains 13 communities. Their respective populations are listed in Table 32 in order of decreasing size. Determine the services that you would find in each, as you did in question 4. Summarize your findings in a table similar to Table 32.

TABLE 32

Population	Services	Order
25 343		
10 210		
8 878		
6 575		
2 109		
1 952		
1 825		
1 765		
1 499		
1 346		
1 198		
1 078		
965		

8   a) What communities offer similar functions?

b) Communities that offer similar levels of services are said to belong to the same *order*. A community that offers a higher level of services is part of a *higher order*. How many orders of communities exist in County X?

c) The highest order is order 1; the next highest is order 2; and so on. Indicate the order of each community in your chart.

d) Explain why there are more communities in each successively lower order of the hierarchy of communities.

9.16   THE RURAL-URBAN FRINGE AREA

The purposes of this exercise are to identify the land uses of the rural-urban fringe, and to study the process of change from rural to urban land use.

Questions

1   a) What is a rural-urban fringe area?

b) According to Figure 9-5, what major land uses are characteristic of the rural-urban fringe area?

2   Which non-farm land uses depend upon a nearby urban population but *originally* would have located outside an old city boundary to the south of this area? Explain your choice.

3   Identify a particular area on the map that is undergoing the greatest pressure to change from farming to urban land uses. Explain your choice.

4   Explain why city land uses sometimes leap-frog into the countryside rather than first filling in all the land at the city's edge. Where has this occurred in Figure 9-5?

5 Predict the land-use characteristics in five years for the area on the map. Explain your predictions.

6 Assume that this area is the best farmland in the immediate vicinity and that it is the only place where water can seep through the ground and recharge the water table. Do you think there is any chance of preserving this area as open space or farmland? Account for your answer.

7 a) What rural-urban fringe businesses do you use?

b) Explain how these activities might be accommodated in areas other than the rural-urban fringe zone.

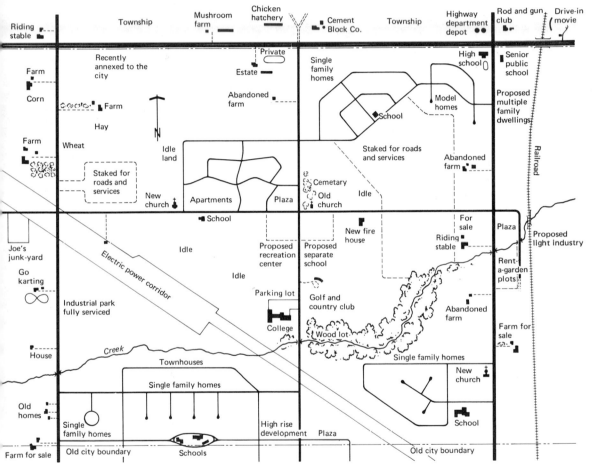

Fig. 9-5
The rural-urban fringe area.

INDEX

Numbers in **boldface** represent pages with illustrations.

Travel generators, 106
Travel patterns, 103-109, **104, 105, 107,** 128, 142
    individual's orbit, 185-187
Toronto, growth to 2 000 A.D., 266-268

U

Ullman, Edward, *see* Multiple nuclei theory
Umland, 206
Urban decline, *see* Blight
Urban field measurement, 172-173
Urban growth, 151-157
    historical approach to, 225-226
    to concentrate or spread, 226-227
Urbanization, **2-3, 12,** 13, 34, 138, 227

Urbanization (cont.)
    great cities of history, 233-235
Urban renewal, 75, 112, 211, 214, 221, 244, 247-249, 253
Urban sprawl, 124, 139, 151, **154,** 207, 224-225, 240
Urban transect, 169-171, **170**

V

Vertical city, **124**
Village, 2, 206

W

Water pollution, *see* Pollution: water
Water shortage, 134
Water supply, 44, 114, 115, 116, 118-**119,** 132, 135, 154, 192
    gravity system, 119

Water supply (cont.)
    pressure system, 119
    reservoir system, **119**
Welfare programs, 43, 44, 132
Wind direction, 92, 210
Wright, Frank Lloyd, **124,** 207
    See also Broadacre City

Y

Yellow pages exercise: the location of activities in the urban community, 203-204
"Yes, but not here" syndrome, 117

Z

Zipf, George K., *see* Rank-size rule
Zoning, 57, 70, 71, 75, 116, 127, 154, 155, 171, 181, 189, 190